D1209770

7
Steps
to
Emotional
Intelligence

**Patrick E. Merlevede, M.Sc.,
Denis Bridoux
& Rudy Vandamme**

Crown House Publishing Limited
www.crownhouse.co.uk

Published in the UK by

Crown House Publishing Ltd
Crown Buildings, Bancyfelin, Carmarthen, Wales, SA33 5ND, UK
www.crownhouse.co.uk

and

Crown House Publishing Ltd
P.O. Box 2223, Williston, VT 05495-2223, USA
www.CHPUS.com

© 1997, 1999, 2001 2003 Patrick E. Merlevede,
Denis Bridoux & Rudy Vandamme.

First published in Belgium in 1999, under the title
7 Lessen in Emotionele Intelligentie by Garant Uitgevers,
by Patrick Merlevede and Rudy Vandamme.
The first English edition in 2001 by
Crown House Publishing is a reworked and expanded version
by Patrick Merlevede and Denis Bridoux,
adding new material and new exercises.

Reprinted 2001 (twice), 2002, 2003.

All rights reserved. Except as permitted under current legislation no
part of this work may be photocopied, stored in a retrieval system,
published, performed in public, adapted, broadcast, transmitted,
recorded or reproduced in any form or by any means, without the prior
permission of the copyright owners. Enquiries should be addressed to
Crown House Publishing Limited.

British Library Cataloguing-in-Publication Data
A catalogue entry for this book is available
from the British Library.

ISBN 1899836500

LCCN 2002117314

Printed and bound in the UK by
Biddles Ltd, Guildford and King's Lynn

To Evelynn, who taught me much about Emotional Intelligence, and to my son Denis, who challenges it every day.

PM

To all the people, dead or alive, who stimulated me to study Emotional Intelligence and to wonder at the abilities of the human mind; and all my colleagues and friends in the neuro-linguistic community, among others, Richard Bandler, L. Michael Hall, and Philip Nolan.

DB

I would like to thank all my direct colleagues that made me discover the enormous amount of energy that is generated if you collaborate in an inspired way.

RV

PATRICK E. MERLEVEDE, M.SC. is the CEO of the *Integral Perspectives Group*, an international network of NLP-inspired companies. He has been combining work and study since 1990, and continues to do so. He graduated in 1990 as Commercial Engineer, majoring in Computer Science (a five-year university program combining Engineering and Economics). In 1992 he obtained his Master of Science in Artificial Intelligence, Cognitive Science Option at the University of Leuven (Belgium). During this multidisciplinary training, he learned about developments in Linguistics, Psychology, Medicine, and Engineering. He is currently working towards his Ph.D., in which he applies the NLP modeling strategies to, among other things, treat whiplash. He is also active writing articles in the fields of Computer Science, Neurolinguistics and Human Resources Management (HRM).

Since 1992 Patrick has been involved in the field of Neuro-Linguistic Programming. Some of his highlights in this area include the NLP Trainer Training at NLP University in 1996, and the development since 1994 of the "Merl's World on NLP" website, one of first websites dealing with NLP. He is also involved in running *PNL-REPERE*, one of the leading NLP institutes in France.

In 1997 he founded *Acknowledge*, his own consulting company, which is now one of the members of the *Integral Perspectives Group*. *Acknowledge* specializes in applying the principles of neurolinguistics in the domain of human resources (recruitment, training and coaching) and knowledge management. With this in mind, *Acknowledge* has developed a series of standard course materials aimed at helping participants to increase their emotional intelligence. Some of this material is now integrated in this book. The consulting and training experience of *Acknowledge*, used in combination with the accelerated pace of change in this "wired" world, led to the development of jobEQ.com, a company aimed at improving HR domains such as recruitment, coaching and training in an internet age.

Earlier in his career, Patrick's main business achievements were in the field of Knowledge Management. He worked as a consultant on projects for the Social Security sector, insurance companies, banks and a number of industrial companies. Entailing both a process/HRM aspect and a computer implementation aspect, these projects required him to apply both his engineering and neurolinguistic skills to work on tasks ranging from technical issues through analytical project steps to project coordination and negotiation.

Patrick's own main interests include finding better ways to recruit people, as shown by jobEQ.com, and emotional intelligence in general.

DENIS BRIDOUX has been based in the UK since 1980, where he operates as a therapist, coach and NLP trainer. Born in France, where he studied Linguistics at university, Denis also studied Education in the UK in the '80s. Before practicing NLP, Denis was a teacher and a health promotion and sexual health specialist in the British National Health Service.

Eclectic at heart, and trained by, among others, Tad James and Robert Dilts, Denis did his Trainer's Training with Richard Bandler and John LaValle in 1995. He has been assisting on many of Richard Bandler's courses and is one of the few trainers world-wide to have received permission from Richard to run Design Human Engineering® training courses. He trains in London and Yorkshire and has recently been exporting some of his courses to France.

Since 1997, Denis has been working in depth with L. Michael Hall, the developer of both the Meta-States model and the field of Neuro-Semantics® which integrates NLP and General Semantics at the highest level. Early in 2000 Denis was made Honorary Fellow of the Institute of Neuro-Semantics® for his significant contributions to the field. Most recently, he has been revising the Mind-Lines model (which Michael Hall and Bobby Bodenhamer developed to present and work on "sleight-of-mouth" patterns); identifying new patterns enabled him to, paradoxically, simplify the model further. His contributions are included in the book on this subject, *Mind-Lines: Lines for Changing Minds* from the fourth edition (2001) onwards.

Denis's breadth of cultural literacy means that he finds it easy to build bridges between very diverse disciplines and, as a result, enrich NLP even more. The NLP Master Practitioner training he offers is unique in Europe and was recently labelled "undeniably the most interesting currently available in the UK."

Marrying humor, intellectual rigor and flexibility to enable his participants to learn easily and effortlessly, Denis's enthusiasm for the subjects he presents is contagious.

Denis recently contributed chapters to Volumes II and III of Open University Press's *Pink Therapy* series. He is currently working on books on a complete revision and updating of the Meta/Milton Models, on the Mathematics of Psychology, and on a new Mind-Body Model.

RUDY VANDAMME has been a professional trainer and coach since 1987 and he was certified as an NLP trainer by the International NLP Trainer Association in 1996, the same year in which he became director of his own institute, *The School for NLP*. He has had many years of experience in training and coaching in large companies and corporations such as Nestlé, Capco, P & V, and Duracell. He is currently working for his Ph.D. at the University of Leuven (Belgium), where he is studying the application of psychotherapeutical techniques to coaching activities.

Rudy's university degrees are in Psychology (1980), Philosophy (1984) and Anthropology (1996). One of his fascinations is the structure of simple questions.

Table of Contents

Acknowledgments i
Foreword..iii

A walk through this book—How to use this manual 1

Introduction 5
What is Intelligence? 6
The Presuppositions Used in This Book 12

Emotions 101: Understanding the Power of Emotions 21
Managing Your Emotional Budget 21
Emotions, Health and Well-being 25

Lesson 1: Managing Your Emotions..31
Introduction: A Plea for Self-management 32
The Intertwining of Emotions and Experience 35
Association/Dissociation 46
Cases 58
Exercises for this Lesson..68

Lesson 2: Levels in Experience and Communication 75
Introduction: The Levels of Your Functioning 76
Basic Model of the Neurological Levels of Experience 77
The Meaning of Emotions 89
The Power of Emotional Beliefs 99
Applying Logical Levels to Enhance your Emotional Intelligence ...101
Appendix to Lesson 2: The Theory Behind The Model....................107
Exercises for this Lesson 110

Lesson 3: Planning for Success 117
Introduction: Models for Effectiveness..118
The TOTE Model: The Structure of Flexible Plans. 120
Conclusion: Some Tips for Emotional Development 142
Application 1: Sharing Goals with Others....................................143
Application 2: Expectations and the Structure of Happiness............146
Exercises for this Lesson..152

Lesson 4: Learn How You Perceive the World and Be in Charge of What Makes You Tick 157
Introduction 158
Representation Systems:
    How Do People Construct Their Internal World? 159
Submodalities: How You Format Your Own Reality 171
EQ and the Application of the Structure of Subjective Experience ...177
Conclusion: Realizing the Structure of Your Subjective Experience..183
Meta-Programs: The Filters in Your Thoughts.................................184
Conclusion: Patterns in Your Emotions...211
Exercises for this Lesson..214

Lesson 5: Emotional Intelligence in Company.....................................223
Perceptual Positions: Empathy for Yourself and for Others..............224
Projection: What Irritation Can Teach You about Yourself.................234
A Model for a Qualitative Co-operation...236
Look at Your Relationship from a Different Perspective....................241
Interacting Socially:
    How Do You Bring Emotion into Your Communication? 245
Exercises for this Lesson..250

Lesson 6: Asking the Right Questions 255
A Counter-example: What NOT to Do..256
Introduction 257
The Basic Model: Three Traffic Rules for "Good Questions" 262
The Meta-Model: Questions for Dealing with Emotions 270
Exercises for this Lesson..288

Lesson 7: Successfully Interact with Yourself and Others..............299
Introduction: Mastery in Building and Maintaining Relationships ..300
The Art of Calibration:
    What You Can Learn from Body Language....................................303
Achieve Rapport with Yourself 311
Getting into Rapport with Someone's Thoughts and Experience. 313
Rapport with Others: How to Achieve It...313
How Do You Know You've Got Rapport? 318
Levels of Rapport...322
Applications...326
Conclusion:
    Observation Skills as Key Elements for Emotional Intelligence..333
Exercises for this Lesson..336

Conclusions: Making Connections,
Gaining in Emotional Wisdom 341
New Emotional Abilities 341
Making a Full Model of Competence..................................344
Some Final Exercises 350

Recapitulation 353
Moving beyond Emotional Intelligence.............................353
Conclusion: From Emotional Intelligence to Emotional Wisdom......356

14 day program: A *"to do"* list for the next fortnight........................359

Bibliography and Further Reading......................................361
Overview of the Neurolinguistic literature 361
Other References for This Workbook 366
The Internet 368

Solutions to the exercises in this book...............................369

Appendix 1: Neuro-Linguistic Programming 371
Appendix 2: Meta-Programs in Recruiting and Management 377
Appendix 3: *Integral Perspectives Group* 383

Glossary 385

Index 391

Acknowledgments

"Writing books is the closest men ever come to childbearing."
Norman Mailer

An often-quoted saying is that a man should build a house, make a child and write a book. Some people add "plant a tree" to this "to do list," perhaps to ensure that there will be enough material from which to produce the next series of books. However, this book is a part of our mission and our contribution to mankind.

Learning about Emotional Intelligence is another task on the "to do" list of a great many people on this planet, ourselves included. This second version of our book is the result of all that we have learned from our teachers and colleagues, as well as what we have learned from interacting with our students and customers—especially those we had the chance to work with over the last few years—applying the material we teach in this book. We have learned from these interactions that a huge demand remains for a clear explanation of the principles of Emotional Intelligence, as well as how to practice them. Without this systemic interaction between practice and theory, this book would never have seen the light of day.

Given the number of students and teachers we have had, both formally and informally, we are sure that many would be forgotten if we tried to list them. So, rather than naming them all, we hope they will recognize themselves in this general acknowledgment. This also reminds us of Duggan's Law of Scholarly Research:[1] "The most valuable quotation is the one for which you can't identify a source."

We would like to thank all the people who have crossed our path in the last few years and to express our eternal gratitude for their Emotional Intelligence.

PM, DB and RV

---

[1]   We know where this quotation comes from, however: *Murphy's Law Book Two* by Arthur Bloch, Magnum Books, 1980.

i

Foreword

A basic tenet of this book is that there are many types of intelligence, and that it is wise to learn how to harness and harmonize with those somatic-emotional languages that pervade any meaningful human communication. Without such cognitive-emotional integration, things can go seriously awry. For example, several years ago I was visiting Japan on the occasion of the translation of one of my books. My translator and I were interviewed for a large daily newspaper, and the interviewer brought up a story that had shocked the country. A young boy had taken a family sword, gone over to the house of a slightly retarded classmate, and beheaded the boy. He then placed the decapitated head on the school steps, where it was found the next morning by horrified teachers. The boy was apprehended and police found in his home extensive diaries he had written. One repeated entry in the diaries described "this invisible presence within me that is filled with rage." He continued to write of his struggle with the "inner rage" that nobody saw, all the way up to the day that he murdered his classmate.

The reporter described how when these diary entries were included in the newspaper accounts, he was stunned that hundreds of readers immediately wrote in saying that there was an "invisible presence" filled with rage within them, too. They were not, of course, condoning the murder; they were resonating with the boy's description of some unnoticed emotional part of their core spirit.

The question, of course, must be raised: Is there an "invisible presence" that lives within each of us? Not just filled with rage, but also with creative intelligence, with curiosity, with both fierceness and tenderness, with intuitive knowing? Is there an other-than-intellectual intelligence that lives within each person?

I am happy to see how the authors answer this question in the affirmative. How they insist that we pay attention to the different languages of human knowing and being. And how they suggest explicit ways to cultivate emotional intelligence. For the stakes are very high: Simply stated, if you do not skillfully connect with your emotional intelligence, you will be less creative, less happy, and less productive. The disembodied intellect at war with emotional intelligence, or ignorant of its importance, is a sorry sight indeed. While the example of the Japanese boy is an extreme one, there are many other regrettable and avoidable outcomes of opposing emotional process—discord at work, unhappiness in families, lost time and energy fighting rather than working with differences, a loss of intuitive wisdom, etc.

While the authors duly note these dangers, they wisely focus even more on the advantages to be gained from coordinating cognitive and emotional intelligences. Rather than being EITHER in cognitive control OR in Emotional Intelligence, the successful and happy person is BOTH at the same time. We can see this wherever we see excellence. A top athlete has a superior mind-body unity; a gifted singer exhibits both impeccable control and beautiful feeling; an effective parent is both loving and disciplined in relating to a child. Similarly, any professional activity that requires interaction with others—which is to say, every professional activity—requires an equal integration of intellectual clarity and emotional sensitivity.

This book can help you develop your skills in this area. It is practical, sound, and clear. Please make use of it to help yourself and others become happier, more effective human beings.

Stephen Gilligan, Ph.D.
Encinitas, CA.
2001

A walk through this book—
How to use this manual

We begin this book by defining Emotional Intelligence and explaining the underlying philosophy of the field of neurolinguistics, on which the rest of this book is based. We summarize this philosophy in a series of presuppositions, or operating assumptions, which we consider in relation to Emotional Intelligence.

Each lesson is a step closer to achieving a higher level of Emotional Intelligence (EQ). In fact, measuring the EQ of participants, before and after several series of classes run by one of our training organizations (Patrick Merlevede's *Acknowledge*) in the first half of 2000, showed a measurable average increase of Emotional Intelligence of participants in 10 to 15%.[1]

In the following seven lessons you will encounter elements linked both to Classic Intelligence (IQ) as well as to Emotional Intelligence. We'll cover how to define a problem, how to find a solution as well as how to implement this solution. In fact, we will consider how closely EQ and IQ are knitted together. For instance, a child who is tested for its IQ will score better if the test is taken in a context that stimulates a resourceful emotional state. Also, having a high EQ doesn't seem to matter unless your IQ is above 90.

The following table gives you an overview of the structure of this book and the skills we will help you to develop.

---

[1]　Measured on the participants of two series of classes organized by Patrick E. Merlevede, M.Sc., between February and July 2000. The students took the same test before and after the series of classes (24 course hours in total). This test scores people on 14 different scales related to their Emotional Intelligence. Most people who had scores indicating that they were emotionally vulnerable, or had to exercise caution on any one of these 14 indicators, increased their level of competence to *proficient* or *optimal*.

Chapter Title	Abilities and Topics Covered
Introduction:	• Definition of Emotional Intelligence and its relationship to "classic" intelligence • Presuppositions help to develop one's Emotional Intelligence
Emotions 101: Understanding the Power of Emotions	• Managing one's emotional energy • Importance of taking emotions into account
1: Managing Your Emotions	• Recognizing and regulating your emotions, so that your emotions help you to achieve results • Associating with and dissociating from emotions • Using emotional states as resources to reach your goals • Using emotional states for a more complete creativity
2: Levels in Experience and Communication	• Knowing your mission and values in life and how to align what you do with these • Understanding the meaning of emotions • The power of emotionally driven beliefs
3: Planning for Success	• Having a precise outcome and knowing how to obtain it • Overcoming obstacles in the way of your goals • Making expectations and reality match

Chapter Title	Abilities and Topics Covered
4: Learn How You Perceive the World and Be in Charge of What Makes You Tick	• Being able to differentiate between emotions • Knowing how to regulate your states • Realizing how you and your conversation partners structure their experiences • Reducing misunderstandings and communication problems to the difference in communication which caused them
5: Emotional Intelligence in Company	• Examining an experience from different perceptual positions • Developing a higher degree of flexibility to handle conflicts • Bringing emotion into communication and de-mining conflicts
6: Asking the Right Questions	• Moving from unspecific communication to a precise understanding • Asking questions to better understand your own and others' experiences • Knowing the difference between fact and opinions • Identifying limitations and getting to a breakthrough
7: Successfully Interact with Yourself and Others	• Observation skills as a key element for more Emotional Intelligence • Knowing the synchronization categories as tools for calibration and rapport • Pacing and leading
Conclusions: Making Connections, Gaining in Emotional Wisdom	• Developing new emotional abilities • Using examples as a source for more Emotional Intelligence

Each subject will be treated in a similar fashion, beginning by presenting the goals we have in mind for you and why the topic is relevant. Then we explain our model and round it off by giving an example or an application. At the end of the topic you'll find a series of exercises to help you master the skill presented.

We designed our chapters as independent units, so that you can read them separately in whatever order you like. For instance, you could go straight to the third lesson and begin by making a well-formed plan for what you want to get from this book. Of course, this book can also be treated in a linear fashion, as you would probably do with any other book. From the feedback given to us by a few hundred readers of preliminary versions of this book, we'd like to recommend you study one chapter a week, so that you have time to do the exercises and find ways to integrate the model in your own life.

Have fun!

Patrick, Denis and Rudy

Introduction

"Love is too young to know what conscience is."
William Shakespeare

It was Daniel Goleman's bestseller and the press coverage around it which introduced the term *Emotional Intelligence* to the general public. I (Patrick) remember being thrilled by the prospect that this subject would now gain general acceptance. But soon afterwards, I faced some disappointment. Goleman's book identified a whole series of problems and suggested only a few solutions for immediate use. This left me with an empty feeling. From my experience I felt that there were solutions for what Goleman was writing about. That's why I wrote this book together with Rudy and Denis: I want to bring a more positive message to you, the reader. If we consider the various models of neurolinguistics, it becomes clear that this study domain provides most of the answers to the issues raised by Goleman. The irony is that in 1979 Goleman himself wrote an article about neurolinguistics, when the field was still in its early stages.[1]

Whether you are 12 or 65 years old, the solutions one can derive from neurolinguistics will help you to enhance your Emotional Intelligence. This shouldn't come as a surprise, since the field of neurolinguistics has been studying success for nearly 25 years to identify its structure. Indeed, geniuses such as Leonardo da Vinci, Albert Einstein, John F. Kennedy or Walt Disney were analyzed and indexed according to these very neurolinguistic models. Since 1974, millions of people have undergone training in this discipline, including employees of companies such as Hewlett-Packard, IBM and Boeing. Other companies, such as British Telecom in the United Kingdom, Volkswagen in Mexico, FIAT in Italy or Levi Strauss in the United States, came into contact with neurolinguistics through consultants using this approach.

Sales of Goleman's book *Emotional Intelligence*, as well as those of a number of other works which have appeared on this subject since 1995, indicate that EQ has become a concept which is hard to ignore. Unfortunately, it would appear that most of the authors

---

1   Daniel Goleman: "People who read People," *Psychology Today,* July 1979.

content themselves with teaching their readers only a few tricks interspersed with some anecdotes. Since we wouldn't qualify a dog that has learnt some smart tricks as "intelligent," we personally find this approach rather unsatisfactory. The purpose of this book is therefore to teach you a series of *models* which will enable you to develop your own tricks! We hope the effect it has will make you feel good about this.

This work is conceived like a manual, complete with exercises. In total you will find about fifty of these, placed at the end of the development of a subject. Although we recommend you do some of the exercises in pairs or in a small group, this book is mainly designed for self-improvement. Along with many concrete examples and demonstrations of some applications, the book also provides you with the theoretical models which underlie each lesson, as well as tips for further development of the model we suggest. The book has been especially designed to be used equally for a course in Emotional Intelligence or for a course in neurolinguistics. Although we use some of the neurolinguistic terminology, ignoring this terminology will in no way affect your understanding of the presented material, as we have endeavored to explain the models in plain terms. Finally, this book can also be an excellent step towards other books or courses dealing with this area of study.

What is Intelligence?

The least you should expect from this work is a clear definition of *Emotional Intelligence*. This term was coined when people began to observe that human beings with a high Intelligence Quotient (IQ) were not free from failing in everyday concrete situations, whereas others with an average IQ succeeded. The caricature of the absent-minded professor, used in certain comic strips, serves as an excellent example. Whether you call Professor Calculus a success or not depends on your definition of success. However, you may have difficulty in qualifying his life as "socially integrated." We therefore recommend, at least for the sake of a definition, that we distinguish between *"traditional"* intelligence and *"emotional"* intelligence.

Some authors conclude, following the observation of the above caricature, that traditional intelligence contributes only 20% of the success a person can achieve. This type of assertion immediately invites questions such as: *"How do they measure success?"* and *"How do they know that IQ determines only 20% of success?"* Based on this type of question, we can contest the validity of the pseudo-scientific approach which underpins most books on EQ. Thus we stumble upon the major problem of defining psychology as a science, namely: it is extremely difficult to prove whatever point you are trying to make! This is one of the reasons for which psychologists use statistics, but as Benjamin Disraeli said: *"There are three kinds of lies: lies, damned lies and statistics."*

"Classic Intelligence" can be defined as what is measured by the IQ tests. On further investigation, you'll find that these tests are about logical reasoning abilities, spatial orientation, analytical skills, language skills, etc. In short it's a series of skills which you require to rationally analyze and solve a problem (in the largest sense of the word).

However, solving problems requires more than just some cognitive skills. We distinguish three phases in a problem-solving strategy:

1. *Problem description*: to gather the facts together in a comprehensive overview of a problem (basically what we learn to do at primary school);

2. *Problem solving*: to propose a (theoretical) solution which takes into account all the elements identified in the problem description;

3. *Implementing the solution*: to find a way of applying the chosen solution.

The first two parts of the problem-solving process belong to the domain of "classic intelligence." They are the result of applying "logical thinking." However, the third, practical, part requires more Emotional Intelligence. This leads us to the definition of Emotional Intelligence we will be using throughout this book.

"Emotional Intelligence": the complex whole of behaviors, capabilities (or competencies), beliefs and values which enables someone to successfully realize their vision and mission, given the context of this choice. One can further distinguish[2] between:

a. *Intrapersonal Intelligence*: determining moods, feelings and other mental states in oneself and the way they affect our behavior, altering (or managing) these states, self-motivation, etc.
b. *Interpersonal or Social Intelligence*: recognizing emotions in others, using this information as a guide for behavior, and for building and maintaining relationships.

Classic Intelligence

Intelligence has been a mystery for centuries. Let us begin by mentioning some of the questions people have been asking (without claiming we can give you "the" answer for each):

- *Can you measure intelligence?* Given the number of books which have appeared on this subject, we can conclude that many authors really believe it can be measured objectively. The IQ test[3] suggests a relationship between a person's "real" age and the age which matches the intelligence the person has. How controversial conclusions based on this test can be is shown by reactions to *The Bell Curve*. This book about IQ and its distribution throughout American society appeared in 1994 and has caused controversy ever since.

- *Is intelligence genetically determined?* Is it transmitted from the mother? A gene was recently isolated that may be linked to intelligence.[4]

---

[2]   These distinctions can be found in the theory of Multiple Intelligences of Howard Gardner (Harvard University) and in the definition of Peter Salovey (Yale University).

[3]   William Stern coined the term Intelligence Quotient (IQ), and therefore presents the concept as a ratio: "If a child has an intelligence that is average for his age, its IQ will be 100. An IQ of more than 100 indicates the child is better developed, an IQ of less than 100 indicates a child is less developed than average."

[4]   Roger Plomin, a researcher at the Psychiatric Institute in London, found that the gene IGF2R appeared more often in 300 super-intelligent kids.

● *How does environment influence one's intelligence?* Elements that seem to play a role are parents, education, friends, etc. But who can tell? There is no objective way to conclude anything in this area.

At any rate, scientists seem to converge to a point of view where both genetic elements and environmental (socio-cultural) factors have their role to play in explaining one's IQ. The discussion is currently focused on explaining which elements have the *biggest* influence, as all sides brandish statistical "evidence" as well as strategies to pinpoint that the opponents' theories don't have much scientific basis (and moreover, that their IQ measuring tools include serious scientific mistakes). It is probable that a genetic link exists between the intelligence of the parents and their children, but it is not sufficient to inherit these genes to be intelligent. Basing theories on genetic data alone is far from sufficient for explaining a relationship between parents' intelligence and that of their children.

And then here is some good news for the "average" person: it seems that the average IQ has increased remarkably since World War II.[5] So, taken as a whole, we are becoming smarter! We can probably find explanations for this in environmental factors, such as the democratization of education and the increased length of schooling. On the other hand, we clearly need this additional intelligence, as some other studies show that the number of jobs requiring a higher level of intelligence has risen dramatically over the same period.[6]

Given the increasing divergence in opinions on this topic, the only thing we can state with certainty is that we can expect a rise in the amount of paper that is used up on the subject! Researchers have counted over 200 articles published between 1994 and 1996 in reaction to the book *The Bell Curve*.[7] Instead of continuing this

---

5 The rise in IQ since World War II is called the "Flynn effect" after a study called "Massive IQ Gains in 14 Nations: What do IQ Tests Really Measure?" by J.R. Flynn which appeared in 1987 in *Psychological Bulletin*.

6 However, one can question whether jobs really require more intelligence, or if it is the law of supply and demand which plays a role: after all, the rise in requirements is made possible by the rise in the number of people having a higher degree.

7 This figure, along with the references to all these articles, can be found in the book *Intelligence, Genes and Success* by B. Devlin et al. (1997, Copernicus, New York). Recommended for further reading on the topic of "classic" intelligence.

discussion, we suggest to focus rather on the typical characteristics we could identify in someone who corresponds to our definition of classic intelligence[8]—wherever that comes from. Although little can be done about the origin of this intelligence, we can increase our own intelligence by learning techniques which enable us to act intelligently.

An intelligent person's reasoning is often based on images; they can make connections between different domains and look at a problem from different perspectives. They trust that their unconscious will help them in solving problems. They can see the big picture but can also zoom in on all relevant details and take them into account. This type of person can easily adapt to new contexts and rapidly master a new domain. If they encounter difficulties in finding a solution to a problem, they will translate the problem description and use other knowledge to find an appropriate answer. They tend to base their reasoning on the structure which underlies a problem and organize their response accordingly. They often have a clear vision of the future and of their mission to best contribute to this future.

We may see some new tests taken from the field of neurolinguistics in the coming years. These will measure intelligence according to this description. Such type of study will then probably create even more controversy around the IQ measurements, but that takes us beyond the scope of this book.

Emotional Intelligence

Classic intelligence and rational thinking have dominated Western society for centuries. It was Freud who showed, through his analysis of the unconscious, that there is more to us than rational thinking. Since Freud, the development of psychology has brought us the insight that a person's actions aren't just rational or logical. Emotional Intelligence seems a good term to name our "non-rational" way of thinking and being, even if the source of this intelligence has kept researchers from fields such as psychology, anthropology and sociology busy for the last 150 years.

---

[8]   These characteristics have been developed by Robert B. Dilts in his book *Strategies of Genius, Vol.3*, Meta Publications, Capitola, Calif, 1995.

From our definition you learned that Emotional Intelligence means "to be able to reach your goals by interacting with your environment." But what is it really? In Daniel Goleman's book *Emotional Intelligence* you'll find vague terms such as perseverance, self-confidence, enthusiasm and self-motivation. These elements are connected to your emotional state. If you put yourself in a resourceful state, you can access your perseverance, self-confidence, enthusiasm and self-motivation. The definition of Peter Salovey, a professor at Yale University, adds self-awareness and empathy to these characteristics of Emotional Intelligence. Empathy is "the ability to identify with and understand another's situation, feelings, and motives."[9] Observation skills help you to achieve this: you can learn to "read" what is someone's emotional state and use this information to improve your ability to enter into the part which is required of you.

Summarizing the above, we can say that Emotional Intelligence is a container term which encloses a series of skills one learns more or less intuitively. The best communicators, salespersons, lawyers, politicians and psychologists, etc. have often developed these skills to a high degree and use them unconsciously. This book will bring your abilities back to your conscious awareness and explain to you the structure of these skills, thus giving you more control over them than you thought possible.

All too often, it seems that people lack perseverance when they need it most or lose control over their emotions in difficult situations. Aristotle expressed it this way: *"Everybody can get angry—that's easy. But getting angry at the right person, with the right intensity, at the right time, for the right reason and in the right way—that's hard."* A manager who loses their temper may not reach their goal and instead risks losing their credibility with their employees. A consultant who thinks they can outsmart people while working in a company will create resistance instead of gaining respect. A parent using their physical superiority to impose rules upon a child (because there doesn't seem to be another way) will stimulate anger and resentment in this child. Moreover, as the child grows older the physical advantage disappears and this strategy to "convince" the child will stop working. Finding constructive ways to use your emotions is the key.

[9]   *The American Heritage Concise Dictionary, Third Edition* © 1994 by Houghton Mifflin Company.

Now try this: put down this book, stand up and bend your upper body so that you can (almost) touch the ground with your hands. Now say: "I feel successful." You will notice that it is very hard to feel successful in such a position. This body posture doesn't "fit" with the feeling. And here is a second one: stand up straight, head up, shoulders back, belly pulled inwards and say: "I feel sad." Again you'll notice incongruity between body posture and feeling. We'll investigate this matter in Lesson 4 and you will learn what elements influence your emotional state.

Finally we'd like you to consider the following: the well-known geniuses of this world weren't perfect. Most of them excelled in only one or a few specific areas of life. Walt Disney didn't want to pay tribute to his collaborators for the work they did, claiming he did it all. President John F. Kennedy is known for chasing women around the White House. Martin Luther King beat up his wife, and so on. Given our definition of Emotional Intelligence it would appear that all these public figures had areas in their life where their EQ failed them. They were quite lucky to be able to keep these areas out of the public attention.

The Presuppositions Used in This Book

The philosophy of science stresses the importance of explaining the presuppositions, operating assumptions or axioms one uses when presenting a scientific theory.[10] Scientists themselves say that you can never prove anything right, because an exception may turn up round the corner. Science is therefore built on presuppositions which work well enough until proved otherwise. The presuppositions we discuss below explain the perspective which underlies the models we present in this book and which we daily apply in neurolinguistics. When running neurolinguistics courses, we recommend that our students act "as if" the following presuppositions were true. Whether these neurolinguistic presuppositions are "really" true or not ultimately doesn't really matter.[11]

---

[10] Karl R. Popper, a renowned philosopher of science, writes in the introduction of his book *Realism and the Aim of Science* (Routledge, 1992) that anyone who wishes to defend the empirical-scientific character of a theory has to indicate within which conditions a theory can be proven true or false.

[11] As such, the neurolinguistic model doesn't fulfill the condition Popper demands, as this would seek to apply an objective perspective on a subjective experience. In that sense, the model comes from a pragmatic scientific perspective. To find a way to falsify its presuppositions doesn't prove anything. If you are interested in the reasoning involved, read R.A. Wilson, *Quantum Psychology*, New Falcon Publications, Phoenix, Ariz., 1993.

What matters is that hundreds of thousands of people worldwide have found it very useful to act from them. In fact, such presuppositions may prove to be the biggest secret behind the Emotional Intelligence of some people. Once you start applying these presuppositions, notice how they add to your freedom and thus provide you with even more flexibility than you had to begin with.

Now imagine that you've heard some people express some personal convictions which you'd like to make your own. For instance, the following statement may attract you: *"Whatever is possible for someone else is possible for me."* Of course, it wouldn't be too difficult to find counter-examples to disprove a statement such as this. After all, if you were ever to entertain the hope of running 100 meters in less than 10 seconds, you would need to train accordingly, and is that realistic? Consider the amount of time, money and energy which a world champion has invested in their sport to achieve such feats. Are you ready to do this? The possibility may still be there for you but you may need to change your whole life to achieve it, and the probability of ultimate success would be considerably remote. Of course, if you use the "right" kind of reasoning you'll manage to prove most beliefs wrong. We'd rather consider such examples as exceptions. Instead we challenge you to take another approach, but if you hadn't wanted to be challenged you wouldn't be reading this book, now, would you?

How about accepting the above statement therefore as being "true," at least for now, and trying out for size what it will do for you. If you were to start from the presupposition: *"It's not because somebody else can do this that I could ever learn it,"*[12] would you have as much fun? Many presuppositions we use operate as "self-fulfilling prophecies," as Leonard Orr's law, *"What the Thinker Thinks, the Prover Proves,"* suggests. These become guiding principles which help you to organize your life in one way or another. The more you start using a presupposition, the more it gets integrated into your life, until you become unaware that it is present at all: it has become part and parcel of your "model of the world." In Lesson 2 we present a technique to "empower" a resourceful belief by connecting it to reference experiences, which applies a similar approach.

---

[12] This is emphatically NOT a presupposition we support in neurolinguistics: would man ever have emerged from caves holding such a one?

Now let us explore our presuppositions and illustrate some of them with examples and exercises.

Core Presuppositions

❶ *"The Map Is Not The Territory"* (Alfred Korzybski)[13]
  - People act from within their personal map of the world (as opposed to acting from "the reality").
  - Different descriptions (maps) of the same reality (territory) each have their value, depending on the context where you apply them.

❷ *"We Cannot Not Operate Systemically"*
  (Gregory Bateson)
  - Body and mind form a systemic whole (answer to the philosophical dualistic model). Everything that happens in the body is reflected in the mind (and vice versa).
  - We are *both* whole and parts, and we ourselves are parts of a greater whole.
  - The whole is more than the sum of the parts: you do not know or understand the whole by understanding just the parts.
  - There is no failure in communication, only feedback.
  - People communicate at two levels: the conscious and the unconscious.

Although these presuppositions are explored at length throughout this book, we think that the first one, given its importance to the field of Emotional Intelligence, deserves further elaboration.

The Map Is Not The Territory

"The map is not the territory, but if correct enough it will have a structure that is similar to the territory, which explains why we find the map useful."

Using this metaphor Korzybski sought to point out the difference between the sentences we utter and the experience underlying the utterance. Just as most roadmaps don't indicate where you'll find

---

13   Korzybski, A. (1933). *Science and Sanity*, Lakeville, Conn., Institute of General Semantics.

the next traffic jam, most superficial statements a person shares with you don't have enough depth for you to find out the reasoning which underlies them.

Although Korzybski first formulated in the 1930s, with little direct hard evidence to support it at the time, the idea that we operate from mental maps the progress in neuroscience which has been taking place since then—not least through the use of PET brain scans—has been providing an abundance of confirmatory material.

Over time, Korzybski's metaphor acquired additional explanations:

❏ When we observe reality, we filter the reality and make out our own "map" of this reality. This map isn't "the reality." However, people often confuse their thinking (their map) and the reality it is based upon. Or as Maturana and Varela would say: "*Everything is said by someone. Every reflexion brings forth a world,*" and "*What we say—unless we are lying—reflects what we live, not what happens from the perspective of the independent observer.*"[14]

The following joke nicely illustrates this principle: *A traveler is enjoying his trip through the Scottish highlands, marveling at the sunset ahead, when suddenly the car breaks down. After discovering there is no mobile phone coverage in that area, he concludes that the only solution is to walk to the castle he sees on the top of the hill a few miles further down the road and to ask whether he can use their phone to call for assistance. While walking, he suddenly remembers the Scottish reputation for meanness. "No problem," he says to himself, "I can pay for the phone call." And he goes on walking, only to start thinking that a castle owner living in such a deserted place might be quite suspicious, receiving a visitor at this time of the day. "Oh, I'll manage," he thinks. "After all, I'm quite smartly dressed today, they'll be able to distinguish me from a burglar or some mobster." He keeps on talking to himself like this, and before he realizes, he has arrived at the castle. Much to his surprise, as the gate opens, instead of the grumpy old castle owner he anticipated, he sees a beautiful young lady greeting him with a warm smile. But*

---

14   Maturana, H. and Varela, F. (1987). *The Tree of Knowledge: Biological Roots of Human Understanding,* Boston, Mass., Shambhala Books—Chapter 1: "Knowing how we know."

before she can invite him in, he yells: "Get lost! You stingy Scots are all the same, but we travelers don't need your help. We can manage on our own! You'll see we can!" And, full of anger, he runs off in the dark, on his way to the next village ten miles away. "After all," he thinks, "they might have a public phone there ..."

Or take René Magritte's famous painting on which a pipe is painted, along with the text *"This is not a pipe."* The reaction of Magritte when someone questioned him on this? "I told the truth. The pipe is a drawing. And a drawing of a pipe is not the real thing. Indeed, try smoking using the pipe on the painting ..."

❑ At the same time, we may find that different maps describing the same reality are in existence at the same time. None of these maps equate to the reality. The usefulness of a map depends upon the context you want to use it in. For instance, if you go into the countryside for a ramble, a roadmap describing the whole of the country won't get you very far: it will lack the details you may need to find the direction to take at the next crossing.

Japanese culture deals with "reality" in accordance with this presupposition. They have several kinds of truth:[15] the first is the public truth, which is the explanation an outsider will get. The second is the "private truth," which is what insiders know. Of course, both forms of truth aren't always "compatible": a company may keep up its face and declare everything is hunky-dory, while at the same moment negotiations are going on with the financiers where the survival of the company is at stake. As long as insiders are kept informed of the "private truth," this type of behavior is perfectly acceptable to the Japanese.

What we can learn from this discussion is that it is next to impossible to really know "the reality" or "the truth." This is something that Eastern philosophers have tried to explain to Westerners for ages: much of the emphasis in Buddhism, for example, invites you to gradually peel away the "veils of Maya" (illusion) to gain a perception of reality as uncolored as possible by your own filters.

---

[15] This topic was discussed in the article *"Japan. Wanted: A New Economic Model."* (*Business Week*, 30 November 1998).

Only recently have cognitive scientists begun to take on this worldview. But many scientists still have difficulties accepting that what they consider a "rational explanation" today may be proved invalid tomorrow.[16] Some within the neurolinguistic community have used this as an excuse to stop carrying out scientific research with large field tests. You'll often find that neurolinguistics utilizes just the models which deliver the results we want, without having to worry whether they are scientifically proven. This attitude lies close to the pragmatic approach which you'll tend to encounter in the US.

You may ask: what has all this to do with Emotional Intelligence? Just remember to put things in perspective. For instance, when your opinion is different from your partner's, at least show respect for this difference. Once you realize that the map isn't the territory, this becomes much easier to do. It gives you the freedom to ask questions, so that you can learn to understand the other's point of view, and by comparing the differences, you may end up with a new perspective which combines the best of both worlds. This may explain why Cicero classified "Having others behave just as we do" and "Making others believe in the same things we believe in" as amongst the worst mistakes of mankind. Another "problem" of the human race is that humans tend to resist change. According to J.K. Galbraith, when people are faced with the option of changing their minds or of finding other evidence so that they can keep their opinion, they will choose to look for new evidence rather than change their minds. Reflect on this the next time you think you have a monopoly on wisdom.

Another lesson to draw from this discussion is that it is easier to change your perception of the world than it is to change the world itself. Hence our need to learn to apply the following saying: *"To change the world, start with yourself."* Also, we find that human maps of reality are in constant evolution. People **DO** change their minds. When two people communicate, they cannot help but influence the other party in the discussion in some way.

---

16   We recommend Robert M. Pirsig's *Zen & The Art of Motorcycle Maintenance* (William Morrow, New York, 1974) as a book (easy to read) which discusses these philosophical viewpoints. For those preferring a more rational discussion of the topic we recommend Thomas Kuhn's *The Structure of Scientific Revolutions, Second Edition,* University of Chicago Press, 1970.

Operational Presuppositions

Now that we have discussed the basic presuppositions, let us explain what other elements you can derive from these. A mathematician would say: "Given the basic presuppositions, we can deduce most of the operational rules." As we mentioned before, the resourceful attitude our book promotes is supported by a range of mutually complementary operating postulates. Although these may not necessarily be true, operating "as if" they are true makes a tremendous difference to the outcome of any process undertaken.

So, for each of these presuppositions, ask yourself: "How true is this for me?"

(Absolutely true = 5)

PRESUPPOSITIONS	1	2	3	4	5
1. The brain only learns quickly					
2. Mind and body are components of the same system and what affects one inevitably affects the other: any separation is artificial.					
3. We simultaneously communicate at unconscious and conscious levels.					
4. We continuously process information through our five (or more) senses.					
5. All distinctions we are able to make concerning our environment and our behavior can therefore be usefully represented through our senses.					
6. Recognizing responses requires sensory channels which are clean and open.					
7. The most important information about a person is that person's behavior.					
8. The intention behind anything a person does is fundamentally positive for them.					
9. There is a context in which every behavior has value.					
10. Behavior is geared for adaptation, and present behavior is the best choice currently available to a person within his or her model of the world.					
11. The positive worth of any individual is constant, while the value and appropriateness of their internal/external behavior can be questioned.					
12. A person's behavior is not who they are: we can disapprove of what a person does and yet respect who they are.					
13. Changing the *process* by which we experience reality is more valuable than changing the *content* of our experience of reality					

(Absolutely true = 5)

PRESUPPOSITIONS	1	2	3	4	5
14. The map is not the territory.					
15. We operate from our internal maps rather than from the external reality.					
16. The words we use are not the event or item they represent.					
17. Respect for the other person's model of the world is essential for effective communication.					
18. Rapport is about meeting individuals at their map of the world.					
19. The meaning of communicating is the response that it elicits.					
20. There is no failure in communication, only feedback.					
21. All results and behaviors are achievements, whether they are desired outcomes for a given task/context or not.					
22. Resistance in a person is a sign of lack of rapport: there are no "resistant" people, only inflexible communicators.					
23. We have within us all the resources necessary to achieve any desired change.					
24. There are no unresourceful people, only unresourceful states.					
25. It is when we are at our most flexible that we have the highest probability of achieving the response we desire.					
26. Any procedure carried out should increase the range of choices available.					
27. Behavior and change are to be evaluated in terms of context and ecology.					
28. All procedures should increase wholeness.					
29. Modeling successful performance leads to excellence if somebody can do something, anybody can.					
30. I am in charge of my mind, and therefore of my results.					

Extension

You may find additional presuppositions which will be helpful for you. For all that you know, some may even be hidden in this book. Other presuppositions some of us adhere to are: "You never can have enough fun in life!" and "You never can enjoy life too much." What do you think? Begin to collect your own list of presuppositions. Even ours had to start somewhere, after all! You can turn them into posters and scrolling marquees on your screensaver.

Emotions 101: Understanding the Power of Emotions

"Our emotions are only 'incidents'
In the effort to keep day and night together."
T. S. Eliot

Before letting you loose in the main approaches we want to present in this book, let us begin by making some observations about Emotional Intelligence and by explaining to you why emotions are so important to all of us.

Managing Your Emotional Budget

Some people just seem to get more life out of life. Could it have something to do with the perspective they have about living? How is it that people can do so many different things in life and never seem to tire? We have seen some people in their early seventies who are full of dynamism and look like they are 50, or even less. Sometimes, just looking at them can tire you. We also know of many young people who give the impression that they were born old ... Some people seem to live to the full to a ripe old age, as if they were driving in total safety on the fast lane of life. Others seem to be just chugging along in the slow lane below the speed limit. You could understand that, to some extent, if the first ones were driving a Ferrari and the second ones a Trabant, but sometimes it's the other way around! Haven't you ever seen Mustangs and other power cars driven at unreasonably low speed on a clear road?

Have you noticed how, when some people are around you, particularly if they are suffering from a depression or a burn-out, they just seem to suck out your energy in minutes? OK, some of it can be explained by looking at a person's metabolism, and indeed techniques like bio-energetics can help us to raise the amount of energy we have available, but even people who practice bio-energetics don't always seem able to avoid burn-outs. Maybe some of this is genetically determined, but how do you then explain differences between siblings, where one can do weird and wonderful things while the others are stale and boring?

Some people are able to pull through extreme hardship or physical trauma and emerge virtually unscathed, while others are crushed by an apparently trivial matter. What's the difference between those people? This is the real question. If you, like us, are interested in accessing and modeling excellence wherever you find it, you'd want to know what makes some people succeed against all odds, now, wouldn't you, because that's what YOU want to do also. So what's all this about? It's about Emotional Intelligence.

Your Personal Dashboard

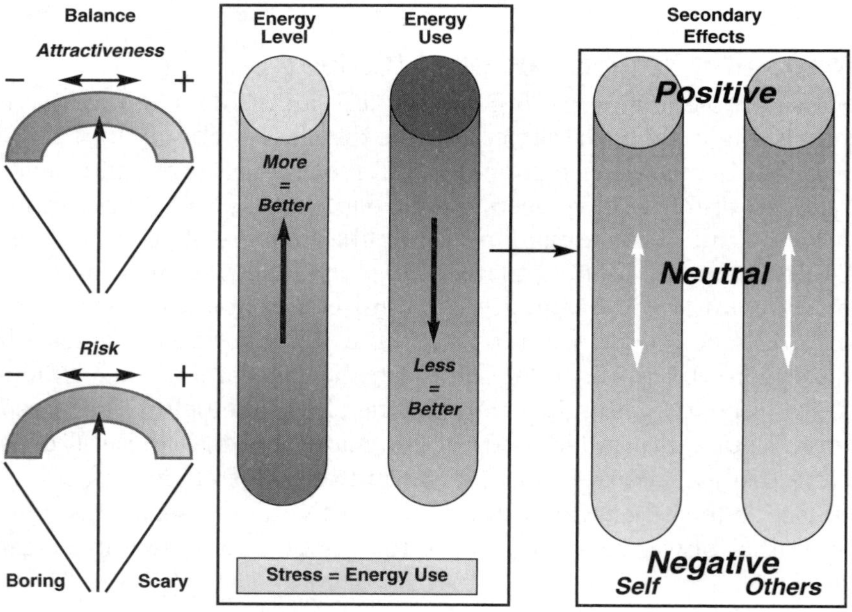

Figure 1: Managing your emotional budget

That figure above gives you a first glimpse at some possible answers. The *Energy Use* indicator determines how much energy one requires to make it through the day. Having more energy (*Energy Level*) available may be a solution, but that doesn't stop you from wasting energy.

Something which is more attractive makes you want to expend more energy. While something that is unattractive may make you spend energy just to get going at it.

Managing risk is another element in the equation. Activities containing too much routine, or too little risk, could be considered "boring," as they may not be satisfying enough: you dissipate energy just to "motivate" yourself to keep at such activities. On the other hand, activities which move too far from what you know may have too high a risk content and may make you feel anxious: managing this anxiety requires emotional management and thus drains energy. Or you might not be able to fall asleep at night, because the worries over what's waiting for you the next day keep you awake. This may limit your ability to "recharge" your battery through a good night's rest.

In both "Attractiveness" and "Risk," the middle areas indicate your "comfort" zone. The level of risk or attractiveness this zone represents depends on your personal motivation patterns, linked to your experience and expectation. What seems risky for someone may be daily routine for someone else, etc. For instance, if you wanted to experiment with nuclear fusion, having only Physics 101 as current knowledge, that would seem a high-risk activity. However, if you were to tell us that you are a nuclear physicist, this might be close to a routine activity for you.

Secondary Effects

How well or badly you manage your emotional budget will be reflected in the way you and the world which surrounds you are affected by this management. People will see you as the Trabant on the fast lane or maybe as the Ferrari on the slow one. The activities you undertake may put others at risk. For instance, the brakes of the Trabant may not be engineered for the speed you're driving at. This leads us to wonder whether, as is the case in Belgian traffic law, someone causing a traffic accident solely through their unreasonably high driving speed should be condemned for murder or manslaughter just because they put others at risk. What effect does your management of your emotional budget have on you? What effect does it have on your surroundings? Would you label this effect overall as rather negative or rather positive? And are you the best judge of that?

Superconductivity of the Mind

Managing your energy budget, therefore, involves not a simple figure but a ratio between how much energy is available to begin with and how much of it you need to use. Developing your Emotional Intelligence is about learning to optimize this ratio, so that whatever amount of fuel you have within yourself will be sufficient to achieve whatever you set out to accomplish, and more.

Energy use depends on the amount of resistance one has to overcome. If you carry out a task you don't like, there is much resistance owing to the friction which is generated, which dissipates much of the available energy in the system; and, there may be a positive consequence, there may also be many side-effects for you or others. However, if you are busy carrying out one of your favourite activities, or attaining a state one has during a peak experience, it's as if you encountered no resistance to it and your internal wiring worked to perfection. And, as is the case when one has superconductivity (no internal or external resistance), hardly any energy expenditure is required to sustain this state.

In the literature, such a state is also known as a "flow state" and the world of sport knows it as being "in the zone." In a flow state you are so absorbed and productively working on your task that all your attention goes to it and you tend to "forget" that there is an outside world behind you and the activity. A programmer in a flow state may forget any notion of time and hunger, and keep on working, to notice only in the middle of the night (falling out of the flow state) how late it is and how hungry they actually are. Cyberneticists, who study the properties of systems, call such a flow state *Synergy*: this is a special condition where the energy available in a given system is greater than the sum of the energies provided by the individual components of this system. "Magic" happens.

Flow states can also occur in the company of other people, for example when an orchestra works as one, or when people are so attuned to each other that they fire each other's creativity and imagination and enjoyment is both effortless and inevitable. For instance, when running a training session in a flow state, the trainer may feel they have more energy after giving the seminar than before starting it! In all likelihood, the participants in the course of this trainer were also in the flow state. You may recall such a state when something wonderful happened in somebody else's company and you can't remember who said or did what, just that it was done.

This book, therefore, will enable you to achieve and sustain such "flow" states, such "superconductivity of the mind" longer, more often and with more people, because that's what Emotional Intelligence is about.

Emotions, Health and Well-being

The medical community still doesn't agree whether and to what degree conditions such as asthma, allergies, headaches, stomach aches, backaches, but also more life-threatening diseases such as heart attacks, multiple sclerosis, diabetes, cancer, etc. are related to psychological factors. Often, a psychological explanation is reached only when no other is to be found. In addition, the medical treatment rarely leaves room for the emotional and mental aspects of the healing process. Unfortunately, the time to teach these aspects in medical schools has, until now, remained limited as well.

Still, if we consider the full implications of our presupposition that "mind and body are a cybernetic system," we know there is a relationship between emotions and health. The question then becomes, what kind of relationship are we talking about? Emotion and health are even linked in our language. The question "How do you feel?" can be interpreted in terms of health or emotions, and only the context will indicate one or the other. Echoing and expanding on Carl Jung, who said: "The unconscious lies in the body," Candace Pert, who discovered the opiate receptor in the brain in the 1970s, states: "The body IS the unconscious mind!"[1]

So, without really discussing whether or not we can prove this, which we leave for other, more academic minds to do, let us instead presuppose that psychosomatic complaints act as a substitute for emotional reactions or as a manifestation of these. Take a

---

1   Pert, C. (1997). *Molecules of Emotion*, New York, Scribner's.

headache, for example. The stress within the head of a patient might be an expression of the hidden desires a person has in a particular context. Instead of acting out their anger and standing up for their rights, a person can choose to bottle up their feelings concerning this potential conflict. One could say that the headache became an instrument to suppress, or perhaps express, rage or frustration.

Another example of this approach comes from an asthma patient one of us (Rudy) worked with: the reaction of "suffocation" had become the way that the body signaled that the patient reacted with too much empathy, losing himself in a relationship with a loved one. The solution came from helping this person to create a personal space and to set some boundaries and have a good feeling within this space at its boundaries. As a result, he didn't have to feel suffocated any longer. The irony of this case was that the asthma gave this person a personal space, because of the desire to rest by being on his own and by traveling (alone) to the mountains "to breathe the fresh air."

Both examples illustrate how an illness can take the place of an emotional reaction, perhaps as a last resort when all other messages have been ignored. Whether you find stress, fear or anger as the underlying emotion, physical symptoms are often an indication of dis-stress or dis-ease. The meaning of the emotion is often tied to the relation the person has with himself or to the relation between self and others. Evidence, albeit anecdotal for the most part, is rapidly accruing about the connection between a range of physical conditions and specific emotional states:

- *Anger* is being associated with cardio-vascular disease and high blood pressure. Heart attacks are being linked with expressed anger and strokes with repressed anger. Interestingly, the incidence of strokes is higher among women than men, perhaps because it is less culturally acceptable for women than for men to express anger. The headache referred to above fits well within this pattern.

- *Sadness* is being associated with depression, low blood pressure, low levels of energy and lower immune response.

- *Fear* is being associated with allergies and overactive immune responses.

- *Guilt* is being associated with suffering from the side-effects of the things one feels guilty about.

- *Shame* is being associated with skin problems.

- *Conflict* is being associated with cancers.[2]

- *Regret* is being associated with Alzheimer's disease.

- Need for *Control* is being associated with Parkinson's disease.

- *Disgust* is being associated with obsessive-compulsive disorders.

So, listening to the messages of our body, of our unconscious, and searching for their meaning is something that can have only positive consequences for us. Indeed, we ignore these messages at our peril. An example we can give you occurred a few years ago to one of us (Denis).

I was shopping in a local supermarket a few years ago, when I observed the following incident. A young woman was doing her shopping, pushing a trolley, accompanied by a little girl. At some point, the woman met a friend down the aisle and they started talking. The little girl was left to her own devices and began wandering in the aisle. She saw something interesting and came back to her mother to tell her about it. Her mother completely ignored her. The little girl then began tugging at her mother's summery blouse and started calling her to draw her attention. Her mother told her off, matter-of-factly: "Be quiet, I'm talking," she said. So the little girl tugged more insistently and raised her voice. "Mam, Mam!" she called. In turn, the mother raised her voice: "Be quiet: I'm talking." The little girl started shouting louder and louder: "Mam, Mam!" and stamping her feet. The mother shouted

---

2   A German doctor, Ryke Geerd Hamer, M.D., carried out a survey in the 1980s about cancer which went even further. Studying about 9000 cancer case histories, he found that the type of cancer people had was directly related to the type of conflict they had experienced about three years prior to the manifestation of the cancer.

back at her: "Can't you see I'm talking? Be quiet!" At which point the little girl stopped and rolled on the floor, screaming her head off. By this time all the nearby customers had stopped doing what they were doing and were observing the interaction, looking alternately at the little girl and the mother with accusing eyes. The friend with whom the mother had been talking muttered a few words, probably to the effect they'd continue the conversation at a better time, because she left. The mother then went down on her knees and pacified the little girl and gave her a good cuddle. The screams finished as quickly as they had begun, as the mother lifted the little girl onto the seat of the trolley and peace was restored to the supermarket.

The above incident is a strikingly perfect example of the relationship we tend to have with our unconscious. We receive messages from within all the time and, by and large, we ignore them. As a result these messages get more and more insistent, some times so much so that we seek to repress them with anything that comes our way, knocking them out with work, alcohol, drugs, medicines, etc. At some stage a crisis ensues, like a heart attack, or a car accident, at which point we have to take stock and re-evaluate our priorities in life. Just count out the number of people in the past you've heard saying words to the effect that: "In retrospect, that heart attack/accident/crisis was the best thing that could have happened to me. It forced me to take a hard look at my life and where I was going and to change direction." Such stocktaking is all to the good, but do you actually need to reach crisis level to intervene in your life and make necessary changes? What would it be like to become more aware of your inner messages, so that you can notice all the warning signs and respond to them accordingly? The crisis need never occur.

We see this approach as complementary to conventional Western medicine. Discovering the meaning often won't be enough. Especially if the underlying emotional conditioning has been in place for a long period of time, the physical damage may be considerable, requiring medication to heal it, or even causing permanent damage.

We have known for a long time that many so-called psychosomatic conditions have been shown to arise from a lack of communication with our unconscious. We are only now beginning to realize the extent to which this is also the case with many other health conditions. Although heart attacks, strokes, infections, cancers, or even Alzheimer's or Parkinson's diseases appear to have little in common with psychosomatic conditions, these may be the last and most intense message we get from our unconscious to do something about a deeply troubling matter which needs remedying. This counsel of despair is even more poignant when you realize that your unconscious is actually in charge of maintaining your life 24 hours a day, so that you keep breathing even when you're asleep. It may be a matter of considering which is the lesser of two evils. As we tend to hear more about the people who responded and changed their lifestyle, we'll never know what those who did not listen thought about the matter. Maybe their last thought was: "If only ..." Will it be yours, or would you rather do something about your life instead? If you do, our book will show you how.

Lesson 1:
Managing Your Emotions

"One must have a reason to be happy.
Once a reason is found, however, one becomes happy automatically."
Victor E. Frankl

Goals

- Recognize and control emotional impulses, so that you can stop your emotions from managing you.
- Learn to manage your emotions.
- Relive experiences and be able to dissociate from them so that they don't affect you and you can learn from them.
- Re-access the emotions you like and have more of them more of the time.
- Choose your emotional state: e.g. confident, resolved, easy-going.
- Motivate yourself.

Neurolinguistic Assumptions

In this chapter we apply the following assumptions:

- *Your mind and your body are inseparable and operate as one single system. What affects one affects the other and vice versa.*
- *An emotion is something you do, a specific product of human functioning. They can be charted and organized.*
- *There is a context for which anything you do may be appropriate.*
- *You have within you all the resources to achieve what you want. You just don't know how to access these resources as much as you'd like, yet. If somebody can do something, so can you!*

Why this Lesson?

At this stage, the biggest challenge you encounter may be to control your emotions. By learning to do this you will be able to manage them and restructure them in the way you desire.

- Emotions can be used as *a goal on their own* (e.g. being relaxed, having fun, power). Ideally you should be able to remain in a resourceful state in an ongoing fashion, as it will act as a filter[1] which will color your everyday experiences in the best possible manner. For example, an established religion like Christianity promotes the adoption of a total and unconditional love for one's fellow human beings. Likewise, Buddhism encourages the adoption of dispassionate compassion.

- You can also use emotion as a *resource* for reaching a goal, i.e. use it as a means to an end. For example, although anger is often perceived as negative, provided it is in the right proportion, focused on the right person, in the right place and at the right time, it may be an appropriate emotion to have. By learning to separate an emotion from the context where it emerges spontaneously and to consciously apply it in other, perhaps more appropriate contexts, you can develop your emotional competence.

Introduction: A Plea for Self-management

Sometimes we think our environment is responsible for our mood. For example, some people are troubled when it rains, and blame it for affecting their temper. Others have an early morning mood when they "get out of the wrong side of the bed." Others are troubled by the shortness of winter days … And yet others need alcohol, pills or drugs to feel OK.

It is now well established that loud music, with a rhythm of 130 beats per minute or more, works as a stimulant or provokes aggression in traffic, by directly affecting the fluids in our inner ear, in our organ of balance, the vestibular system. Soft, classical music on the other hand, with a rhythm of 60 beats per minute, has been shown to stimulate the memory.[2] Many religious rituals across the world use the effect that music has on emotions. Think

---

[1]   L. Michael Hall, the neurolinguistic scholar, calls such a filter a "canopy of consciousness."

[2]   This is discussed in the book **Superlearning 2000** by Sheila Ostrander, Lynn Schroeder, and Nancy Ostrander, New York, Delacorte Press, 1994.

for example of the black Christian churches in the United States, with gospel songs and melodious sermons. New Age movements search for a quiet place for meditation, such as nature, retreats, etc. … After a while, your state changes and you feel different.

What kind of feelings, words and images are activated in your mind by expressions such as *sad, insulted, aggressive, cheerful, merry, being in love, curious*? Try it. Experience each of these words for one minute. Write down the effect they have on you.

The conclusion of a recent study of students' success was that their hope of passing is a better indication of their results than their scores on competence and intelligence tests. According to another study in the insurance sector, the results of optimistic salespeople were about 37% higher than those of their pessimistic colleagues.

Why is your state so easy to influence? How come some people are more influenced by external factors than others? Well, in actual fact, whether you realize it or not, all this is within your own control.

A very common way people express themselves to describe the impact of this external environment is by using a technical metaphor, such as: "He just knows how to *push my buttons*":

- "It's *a grim day,*"
- "What *a depressing environment!*"

or

- "When they do such and such a thing, *they make me mad!*"

However, when you ask apparently absurd questions, such as: "How interesting! Where are your buttons? What shape are they? How many have you got? Show them to me! Would it still work if they were sliders?" you get very interesting results …

Indeed, such questions enable people to realize that these "buttons" are, in fact, figments of our imagination and don't actually exist. We respond to others or to our environment in a certain manner because, unconsciously, we choose to, usually as a result of previous conditioning. Thus:

- a *grim day* is a day during which we *choose* to feel grim;
- a *depressing environment* is an environment in which we *choose* to feel depressed;
- *When he/she does such and such a thing, he/she makes me mad!* actually means: When he/she does such and such a thing, I *choose* to become angry.

Although this is often easier to say than to achieve, realizing the choices we actually have at any one time frees us from investing other people with some power they have over us. Managing our emotions means that we can choose to have the emotions we want instead of putting the outside world in charge of them.

In this chapter we show you how you can choose your state: so, make your own drugs from the inside and be your own boss at last! It is no coincidence that a famous Belgian cycling champion has the following motto: *Somebody is unhappy because he does not know he is happy.*

As mentioned in the Introduction, Daniel Goleman, in his book *Emotional Intelligence,* discusses rather abstract concepts such as perseverance, self-control, enthusiasm and self-motivation as the determining factors of one's Emotional Intelligence. Well, in this chapter you will discover how you can achieve and control such factors by activating the appropriate state in yourself.

In each experience you have three elements which influence one another: your thoughts, your feelings and your behavior. You can say, for example, that your behavior is caused by your internal state. In other words: when you are in a resourceful state, your communication and actions are more successful than when you are in a limiting state.

But what exactly do you need to do to control your emotions? You can learn to activate a desired state through the use of triggers we call *anchors.* An anchor is the "ignition" key which causes a certain state to occur (just like ignition causes the explosion of dynamite). In the examples we mentioned at the beginning of this chapter, the anchors were respectively: alcohol, drugs, the weather, music, … So you could think of an anchor as a button on the control panel in your head to switch on emotions or to turn them off. Instead of allowing other people to push these buttons, or letting external situations function as this kind of button, it is much more interesting to have these buttons within your own control![3]

This chapter therefore aims to elaborate on the above-mentioned principles and conclusions and to give you ample opportunity to practice: this should be fun.

The Intertwining of Emotions and Experience

In our introduction to this chapter we indicated the relationship which exists between your internal state (feeling, mood or emotion), your internal processing (thinking strategies) and your external behavior. Body posture is part of external behavior. At any given moment in time your whole body posture[4]

> People with a high level of personal mastery cannot afford to choose between reason and intuition, or head and heart, inasmuch as they wouldn't choose to limit themselves to walking on one leg or watching with one eye.
>
> *Peter Senge*

reflects your emotional state. Typically, an emotion is reflected by a specific body posture which will completely differ from the body posture which comes with another emotion.[5] Therefore even small changes in body posture can alter your state.

An emotion, such as anger for example, is made up of a combination of behaviors, sensations, interpretations (labels) and beliefs. In other words, an emotion forms a part of an experience, although it is not the experience itself. This may explain how a change in perspective about an experience can bring an emotional change. An emotion differs from the other aspects of an experience, but in essence it is still related to them. Let's take a look at these differences.

- An emotion is directly linked to *behavior*, and still differs from it. An external behavior which we label as anger may

---

[3] For a few years Richard Bandler, one of the co-developers of the discipline of neurolinguistics has been developing "Design Human Engineering." This, among other things, enables us to install such a personal control panel, although in much finer detail, for greater flexibility and resources.

[4] The way your body posture reflects your internal state is called "psychosomatic syntax" in neurolinguistics.

[5] We say "typically" to refer to the way emotions naturally get encoded in body patterns. However, some specific processes exist, also based on anchoring, which allow the transfer of resourceful states onto postures initially encoded as resourceful. This, however, requires specific work on this very issue.

not necessarily correspond to the emotion "angry." As observers we may say "You look angry," and yet nobody else but the person themselves knows whether or not they actually are angry. After all, no one but you can be in your own head.

- An emotion is directly connected to *physical sensations* and still differs from them. Physically you can describe your rage in detail. Stomach tightening, the tension of your skin, the opening of your lungs, all these sensations are the physiological base of the emotion. Usually we say "I am angry" instead of "I feel a tension in my skin." However, another person may experience similar physical sensations and label them differently, coming to a different conclusion.

- An emotion is thus directly linked to an *interpretation or "label" of your experience*, and it still differs from it. To one person the tightening of the stomach may be perceived as a sign of fear of failure. Another would call it excitement. Yet another would call it anger. Thus, an emotion is an interpretation and at the same time a physical sensation.

Emotions, feelings and moods are called internal states. This physical sensation differs from thinking and behavior. Taken together: internal state, specific behavior and given label form what we call an experience. You can compare these three elements with atomic parts which together constitute your molecule of "experience."

How do you distinguish an emotion from a sensation or mood? We classify the recognizable forms as emotions: anger, fear, joy, loneliness, sadness, pain, jealousy and all kinds of variations. We do not, however, always feel such a strong emotion as these. Nevertheless, we experience an emotion or mood at many times. Thus you may feel responsible, relaxed, strong, etc. Such feelings are present but weaker and less defined than emotions. States relate to such feelings. A state is an internal experience which is vaguely present in the background. Although it can strongly influence your self-esteem it can seem elusive and you may not even be aware of it at the time. Emotions, in comparison, always play in the foreground of your mind.

The concept of developing Emotional Intelligence first of all means managing and using *emotions* in the restricted sense. However, why should we limit ourselves to emotions? This would seem like offering us an impoverished palette or a restricted diet, lessening the range of our emotional life. This is why in this book we henceforth choose to use the generic name "emotions" to embrace the concepts of recognizable emotions as well as feelings and vague moods.

Definitions

- *External Behavior:* What can be observed by other people in our body posture, gestures, in our voice, muscle tension, breathing, etc.
- *Internal Processes:* What we imagine, what we are saying to ourselves (our internal voice[s]).
- *Internal State:* What we feel internally, our emotions, our moods.

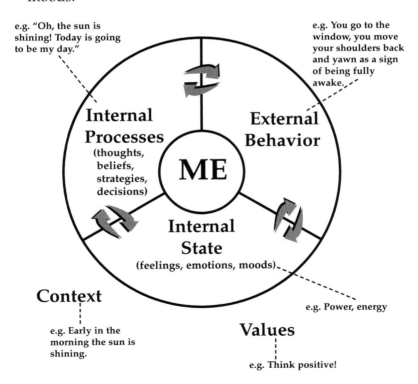

Figure 1.1 : The Structure of Subjective Experience.

The Systemic Relation between the Elements

External Behavior, Internal Processes and Internal State are inextricably bound up together, as the relationship between these elements is systemic. This means that all these elements are interacting and form merely three partial descriptions of an experience:

- Thoughts are systemically associated with emotions.

  e.g.:   —Repeat for yourself many times a number of sayings or slogans (for example "I am worth something") and you will ultimately experience the state these evoke.

  > —Someone who feels depressed will have pessimistic thoughts. You can also reverse this: someone who always evaluates their experiences in a negative way will feel depressed.

- Emotions are skills

  e.g.:   —A self-employed person cannot allow themselves to become ill. This can give them the ability to become resistant to diseases.

  > —Not coping with divorce for ten years implies a skill. What makes him manage?
  >
  > —Somebody has a history of repeat failing. This, too, is a skill. They are *excellent at failing*. What could it be like if they could transfer this excellence onto success, for a change?

- Emotions are decisions

  e.g.:   —After a successful job interview, you feel happy. Your state determines the conclusion you draw about the situation.

  > —A child lacking affection may conclude from their performance that it is better to retreat into their own world of feelings. This is, of course, not a conscious decision at all but it may be perceived in the future as the best solution for the adult who once was this child in a given situation, even though better ones may be available.

- Behavior is emotion

  e.g.:   —Being self-confident = look someone in the eye, shake someone's hand firmly

  > —Doing things in a group = feeling acknowledged.

Many people explain their emotions in a linear manner, linking cause and effect. The weather is depressing. Nothing is working because they are depressed. Or could it be because they think THEIR life is like that their LIFE is like that? Self-fulfilling prophecies are made of such thinking. In reality it is difficult to agree about what comes first, and we personally do not think it matters. After all, in this book we assume we are able to guide and manage ourselves, which is all about being human. Try it out and see how far you get. However, when someone takes on a guiding responsibility over themselves, it does not mean that they understand or have the competence to do so. So we also aim to give you some skills to achieve this more readily.

Any linear causal relation as seen above can easily be refuted.[6] For example, someone who feels depressed blames their environment. If that's the case, why do other people in a similar situation feel really cheerful? Or someone says: "I cannot do anything with my life because I am always depressed." But could it be the other way round? After all, if you are not taking action, you do not have anything to do but just think about yourself and brood. If you stare at the floor long enough, sighing and with your back bent, might you not indeed begin to feel "downhearted"?

Or, as Shelle Rose Charvet[7] said: *"Are you feeling bad enough to change right now, or do you prefer to wait a little longer, until you feel worse?"*

Note: Why you cannot always recognize a state in behavior.
Often, we don't experience a pure state. A basal state we are in may "contaminate" other states and other behaviors. The effect of dominant emotional states can be stronger than the so-called "normal" process of behavior influencing emotions. Thus you may go on experiencing a dominant state, whatever your external behavior is. For example: if someone feels depressed, you will notice that when this person tries to feel happy, or just smiles, the happiness gets flattened out, and the person is less cheerful than

---

6   We call such "either/or" digital type of thinking *Aristotelian*, from the Greek philosopher of the 4th century B.C. In reality an effect may be the result of many causes and a single cause many have many effects in an anything but linear fashion.

7   A neurolinguistics trainer and author.

usual. Concurrently, a person who is naturally cheerful will experience distressing situations in a far more resourceful fashion without becoming affected.

In addition we also have the choice to consciously hide our state or emotions, for example because we were taught it is "indecent" to show your emotions,[8] or because we are playing poker and don't want to show that we've really got good cards.

Sometimes these two exceptions cause misunderstandings in communication. In such a case the intuitively "recognized" emotion of the person you are talking to appears to differ from the emotion the person is actually having.

Interweaving Emotions in Our Experience

The coherence of emotions and sensations, thoughts, behavior and context constitutes an important starting point for working with emotions. Above we pointed out the relation between your external behavior, your internal processes (thinking) and your internal state (emotion, feeling). The old Cartesian division between mind and body has been shown as no longer tenable. Thus any emotion, such as anger, consists of a combination of external and internal patterns. Many scientists have now begun to use the term "bodymind" to acknowledge this understanding.

A conclusion to draw from the above is that any emotional state can be accessed from broadly two categories: the Body End or the Mind End of our bodymind. The neuro-semanticist L. Michael Hall calls Body and Mind *"The Two Royal Roads to State."*

The Body End
- → Search for *the context* where you naturally experience the emotion (e.g. in a dance club I feel full of energy, on stage I want to be a clown, …).
- → Activate *external behavior*: body posture, gestures, voice, etc.
- → Activate *internal sensations*: breathing, warmth, muscle tension, etc.

---

[8] A very common English trait in a culture which values a "stiff upper lip" and where anything emotionally related is derogatorily labeled, e.g. "Happy-Clappy," "Touchy-Feely."

The Mind End

→ Activate *beliefs, values* and *internal representations*. This includes those of situations where we naturally experienced an emotion and even where we imagine what it would have been like if we had experienced it or would be like if we do.

Gateways to the Creation of States and Emotions

Many people believe that, in order to experience an emotion, they need to be in a situation which will provide it for them, like the thrill of the chase. However, whenever you need a context for evoking emotions, you remain dependent on an external gateway. This, by definition, lies out of your own control and Emotional Intelligence is about self-empowerment. Therefore, we will focus on the other three channels for activating emotions. Of course, you can choose at a particular moment to leave a situation and to do something by yourself. This book will help you to use your emotions independently of the context you are in.

An example: consciously use the gateways!

Which emotion would increase your joy of life and your job satisfaction? First of all define this emotion. Secondly, imagine how you can activate this emotion (matching external behavior, internal sensation, belief, etc.). Use these gateways several times a day. Start now!

In order to give you a range of choices, we will show you below how to access emotional states from the Mind End and from the Body End. You may want to record the text of the processes with as much feeling as you can muster or let another person take you through them. Preferably carry these out standing up, closing your eyes, all the while trusting that your unconscious will keep you awake and upright.

How to access a state from the Mind End

The easiest way to access a state is from the Mind End. Think of a state you would like to re-access: let's say, Confidence.

If you haven't had much first-hand experience of Confidence, think of a person you know who behaves confidently and imagine how this person experiences this state from the inside.

If you can't think of anybody directly, you may have seen a person on the television who behaved with Confidence; imagine how this person experiences this state from the inside.

If you can't even think of one of these, pretend you know what Confidence is like from the inside, and imagine how it would be to experience this. Children are very good at this in their playing. So, re-access your inner child and enjoy the play!

First note that, if you recall only a so-so state, you get only a so-so state back, so go back in your mind to a time when you felt really **confident**, I mean **REALLY** confident. It may have been very recently or a long time ago. Whichever it is, re-access this memory in its full "sensorama":

- Seeing with your mind's eyes what you saw at the time …
- Hearing what you heard at the time, including the internal dialogue you might have engaged in …
- Smelling what you smelt at the time (if anything) …
- Tasting what you tasted at the time (if anything) …
- Feeling what you felt at the time …

Notice what happens as you re-access this memory in more and more detail. What happens to the emotional state you're experiencing?

How to access a state from the Body End

You can do this when you are so familiar with a state that your body remembers it for you. Conversely, you can also do this when you are so unfamiliar with a state that you are putting yourself, as it were, "in the shoes" of another person, or even that you are allowing yourself to access your body's natural wisdom. It is interesting to notice at this stage how similarly emotional states are expressed in behavior across cultures, which shows how the expression of emotions is innate. We will revisit this idea in Lesson 7.

↓ So, give me the posture of Confidence …

↓ Give me the stance of Confidence …

↓ Give me the way you are balanced on your feet with Confidence …

↓ Give me the shoulder position of Confidence …

↓ Give me the neck position of Confidence …

↓ Give me the head position of Confidence, the way your head is balanced on your neck with Confidence …

↓ Give me the jawline of Confidence …

↓ Give me the facial expression of Confidence …

↓ Give me the eyes of Confidence …

↓ Give me the tonality of Confidence …

↓ Give me the language of Confidence …

↓ Give me the icon/symbol/metaphor of Confidence …[9]

Notice what happens as your body accesses this state with ever-greater precision. What happens to the emotional state you are experiencing?

Anchoring

An anchor is a very concrete signal which evokes a corresponding state. Although you might not always realize it, your world is full of such signals which elicit a state. For example, you change states many times a day, although you may return to the same one time and again. In the case of strong emotions you may find it easier to define what exactly is triggering this state. By summing up the range of anchors and illustrating how they work, we want to help you to use such anchors as instruments which work for you and which you can consciously use to manage your state.

Types of anchors

An anchor helps to create a state. We can create anchors based on the four gateways for the activation of emotions (or states) which we identified above. Here are a few you will recognize:

---

[9] This invitation to access a state from the Body End is derived from L. Michael Hall.

1. External means

e.g.:
- Picking up a stick when you see a dog in order to feel safe.
- Running water gets you going.
- Taking a shower or soaking in a bath, in order to wash stress off.

2. External behavior

e.g.:
- Crossing arms and standing centered, well balanced on your feet, provides protection.
- Clenching one's fist gives strength.
- Looking up makes you feel good.
- Standing straight, shoulders back, results in confidence.[10]
- Bending your head back makes you feel relaxed.

3. Internal behavior

e.g.:
- Filling your lungs with air and then exhaling slowly will help you to regain calmness.

4. Thoughts, words

e.g.:
- Eureka!
- Thinking of warmth activates a loving state.
- When driving the car, when you say to yourself "I am in charge of driving myself" it helps you to feel more in control.
- The image of a panoramic landscape.

Turning Daily Life Anchors into Rituals

Make a habit of noticing the numerous spontaneous anchors in your daily life which activate corresponding resourceful states. For instance, if you notice that stretching in the morning helps you and gives you strength, you can turn this into a morning ritual in order to be less troubled by an unresourceful morning state. Research has shown that people who do not have problems falling asleep make a ritual of the last few activities they carry out before they go to bed. Brushing your teeth can be part of that.

Many people do not realize to what extent their emotions and states are linked to very specific gestures or other specific body

---

[10] It is no coincidence that soldiers have to take this body posture when they have to jump to attention.

language. Feedback on body language can be useful. When somebody is talking about an experience which is linked to a strong state, you can see which body signals (e.g. gestures) are typical of their state. These body signals are the state's natural anchors. By memorizing these signals, you can begin to use them consciously and experience the state. Many Eastern disciplines like *t'ai chi* and *yoga* make use of this pattern. When somebody, for example, tells you spontaneously about a harmonious experience, they may join hands and slow down their breathing. Their body posture becomes symmetrical and centered. By memorizing such gestures, breathing and postures, you can learn to replicate them easily. When you begin to do this, you can choose what state to experience, what emotion to feel: what once was a spontaneous expression of your emotions becomes a tool to manage your emotions. (You may like to know that you can still continue to experience such spontaneous expressions, so that nothing has been lost but much has been gained!)

Tip: **Re-access Your Spontaneous Anchors**

(a) Choose a resourceful state rich in sensory information and investigate which stimulus triggers access to this resourceful state.

(b) Select three undesired states and look for the stimulus which causes each state.

(c) Find an example of a situation in which you spontaneously correct your own state, and find which anchor changes your state.

A Reference Experience as Resource

A reference experience is a specific experience which occurred at a specific moment in time and at a specific location in your own life, and which you refer to if you think of a specific emotion. For example, if you went to work with a feeling of being "relaxed," you can refer to the moment you were traveling and completely calming down.

In a reference experience there is always a strong connection with the sensory experience you were having at the time, i.e. between what you were seeing, hearing (possibly smelling and tasting) and what you were feeling at that particular moment. Such an experience can be so strong that you have only to think back and the emotion immediately returns as well. These experiences often come over you spontaneously. You remember something and plop! the feeling is back, taking your body into another emotion.

Every one of us has a wealth of such experiences available. Moreover, these experiences can immediately change your state. So why don't you take the time to consciously search and access memories like these, your inner Hall of Fame, so that you can use them more often to manage your emotions? This way a reference experience becomes a resource of self-control.

Milton Erickson, a world-famous hypnotherapist, used this as the basic assumption in curing people: he assumed that each person has sufficient resources inside themselves to solve all personal problems. Unfortunately, only a few of us can consciously access this storehouse of resources, because nobody has taught us how to do so or given us permission. Therefore Milton Erickson used hypnosis to facilitate his patients' re-accessing of past experiences.

After a few weeks, people who consciously start on the quest for their own referential experiences are often surprised by the powers they (re)discover inside themselves. Think, for example, about the states you can observe in children. They are able to show such amounts of affection, have so much fun, can be so shamelessly assertive, have such thirst for learning, are so wholeheartedly spontaneous, and so much more. Which similar experiences can you remember from your childhood? Had you really forgotten about this aspect of you? Notice how the more you do this the more it will come back. It's as if we all have Mary Poppins's carpetbag inside us. Just open it and find out.

Association/Dissociation

To access a desired state and utilize it you need to realize exactly what kind of physiology, thoughts and behavior the state requires. **Association** and **dissociation** are two ways of becoming aware of your experience.

Dissociating means separating, detaching, distancing yourself from an event or situation. You watch a movie, as it were, in which you can see yourself as a protagonist. *Associating*, on the other hand, means being a part of an event and experiencing it from the inside. You are on the set and are playing your own part.

Figure. 1.2: The man on the right (on the lounge chair), is associated and is living the experience. He is enjoying the peace, while he can smell the grass, hear the birds and feel the sun's warmth. The man on the left (with the telescope) is dissociated, watching himself relaxing next to the lawnmower.

Associating into a memory—At a given moment in time, going through a chosen event and fully experiencing the emotional and sensory perceptions available.

Technique to stimulate association:

Ask for ***sensory-specific information.***   e.g.: Someone says: *"I feel at my best when it works."*   Question: What are you seeing/feeling/hearing, as you are doing this NOW?   Answer: *"I feel my lungs opening up, more air is coming in. I am breathing deeply."*

Dissociating from a situation—Watching a chosen experience from a distance. I am observing myself.

Technique to stimulate dissociation:

> Help the person *to watch themselves from the outside,* perhaps inviting them to step aside.
>
> e.g.: Someone says: *"I feel at my best when it works."*
>
> Questions: What is this person doing over there?
>   What can you say about their behavior?
> Answer: He is walking with his head up straight.
>   She is looking people in the eye.
>   He is standing there firmly.

Additional questioning techniques to enable dissociation:

1. **Another place:** *You are standing next to a situation, observing. From a safe distance you can watch yourself, dispassionately …*

2. **Time-related:** *Imagine we are one year ahead in time and you are looking back to this moment and seeing yourself there. What do you think of the you over there?*

3. **Another point of view:** *Imagine yourself being a video camera recording this event. How do you look at the situation?*

These questions invite the person to observe from another point of view, every time "distanced" from the event: first physically distanced, secondly distanced through time and thirdly by looking through somebody else's "eyes."[11]

> *Tip:* When the person is dissociated, invite them to speak of themselves saying "he/she … over there" and to refer to themselves over there using their names, as if they were somebody else. Anything that you can say which brings distance, in space or time, will be useful.

---

[11] Notice the emotional difference between "watching an event as a camera" and "watching an event through a camera." "As a camera" implies you becoming the camera and having the feelings and thoughts of the cameraman, i.e. somebody else. "Through a camera," on the other hand, means you keep retain your own thoughts and feelings.

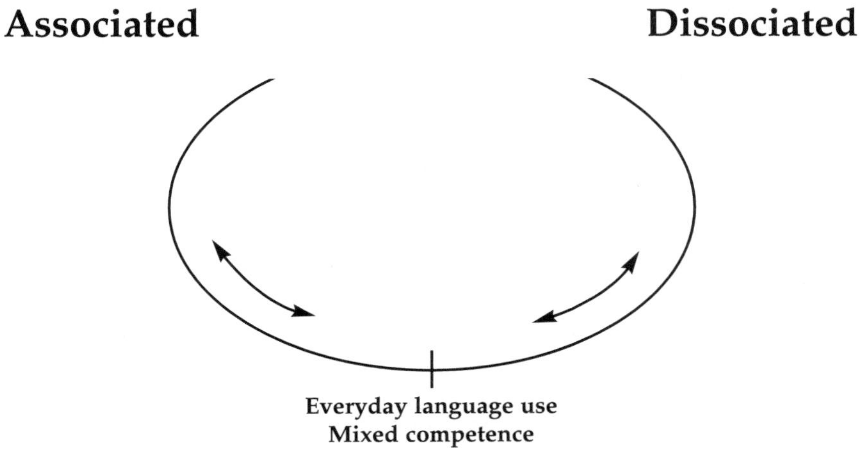

Associated   # Dissociated

Everyday language use
Mixed competence

	Association		*Dissociation*
Advantage:	Going through the experience in all its richness. Being yourself.	Advantage:	Discovering meaning and patterns. Knowing what is inside you, knowing how to behave.
Disadvantage:	Being too deep into the experience to actually work with it.	Disadvantage:	Being too far away from the experience to work with it.

Figure 1.3: The Association-Dissociation Continuum

Figure 1.3 shows the two extremes in the association/dissociation continuum:

- Being so deep inside your emotions that you are not conscious of your own behavior and its effect on other people (e.g. somebody who is furious).
- Being so dissociated from your own emotions that you consider yourself a stranger or that you do not realize you have emotions (when you repress them).

> **In conclusion to this we can formulate three key skills for an emotionally intelligent person:**
> - *Being able to choose at a particular moment to completely access your emotion.*
> - *Being able to choose at a particular moment not to access your emotion.*
> - *The skill to experience your emotion at a particular moment and, at the same time, being able to describe it or to reflect upon it.*

Using Association and Dissociation

It is good to distance yourself (dissociation) from unresourceful events to learn from them dispassionately and it is nice to relive the good memories from within. And why shouldn't you?

Research shows that depressed people neither have more bad luck nor experience more unfortunate events than people who feel good. However, people who are troubled by depressions often dissociate from good events and associate into negative experiences in their life. So they constantly relive their bad feelings. If you want to have a depression, success is assured.

Example: Using Dissociation and Association to Increase Your Self-Confidence.

Being frightened every now and then is natural. However, anxiety can sometimes block people, without any "rational" reasons. In *The Naked Ape*,[12] Desmond Morris suggested that anxiety may be a remnant of our prehistoric instincts, where it served as a kind of self-protection. Still, we can also acquire anxiety following a significant emotional event. Neurolinguistic research about phobias, such as fear of heights or spiders, tells us many anxiety patterns can often be traced back to childhood experiences, some of which may appear insignificant in retrospect, but which had a profound impact at the time.

When you are afraid of something, distance yourself from it (dissociation) and examine the problem in a sensible way.

---

[12]   Morris, D. (1994). *The Naked Ape*, London, Vintage.

Rationally check what risks are linked to the problem. If you rationally think you can handle the situation and cope with the risks, this means you don't need the anxiety any more. So it is time to feel different about it. Remember a past event from which you can draw a lot of self-confidence. Associate into that event and if you feel that your self-confidence is coming back, think of your problem.

Another way is to represent yourself *after* the issue about which you used to feel anxious, was resolved to your satisfaction. How does it feel to know it *was* resolved to your satisfaction? Experience fully how this feels. When you have accessed this experience fully, allow all the events between then and now to re-evaluate themselves in the light of this realization, so that the steps to this satisfactory resolution manifest themselves easily and you know what to do to achieve this successful resolution.

The process below applies the two preceding principles: on one hand, the anchoring pattern stimulates your associating with experiences which are linked to positive emotions. On the other hand, "V-K dissociation"[13] uses the resourceful state to increase the feasibility of your plans.

Anchoring

Procedure
1. Describe your aim (desired state) and present state.
2. Determine which resourceful state might help you to achieve this aim.
3. Search for a moment in time when you experienced that particular state. What anchor is linked to the state, or what triggers it?
4. Apply the anchor in the here and now until you feel you can do it.

Figure 1:4 illustrates this:

---

[13] "Visual-Kinesthetic" dissociation: this means a situation where visual representations and feelings are separated.

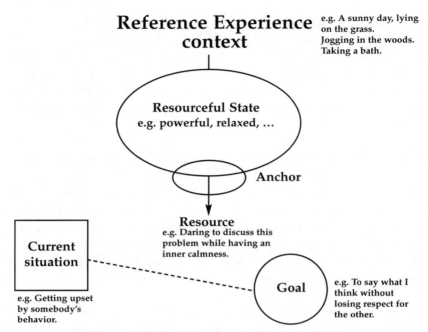

Figure 1.4: The Transfer of a Resourceful State

Some examples

The resourceful state makes the difference in the following:

- A salesman feels unconfident about the new product. Therefore he misses a lot of opportunities. Such an uncertain state thwarts his plans. He used to feel confident. He knew the product inside out. Hence the belief which prevents him from feeling confident: "If I do not know my product, I cannot feel confident."
  Procedure: In a situation with a new product, trigger the physiology associated with the state of "confidence."

- "When the sun is shining, I feel good. Now it is raining, so I do not feel OK."
  Procedure: Think of sunshine when it is raining. When it is raining you can say yourself "What a beautiful day" while looking at the sky or into the distance.

- Somebody needs other people's appreciation to feel confident. Whenever criticized, the person feels inferior.

Procedure: Search for a context in which you feel OK and confident. Remember this context. Associate into this state's physiology. Anchor the physiology in order to be able to activate it when you get into a situation in which your self-confidence is undermined.

- An educator is able to keep calm when mentally disabled children start yelling at work. When her own child is being a nuisance in the car, however, she is unable to keep cool and collected.
  Procedure: Reflect upon how you manage to keep calm in your profession. Anchor this ability and use it in the car. In this case, the educator seemed to know the trick of completely associating into something else in that context. Therefore, the noise of the children became emotionless, the noise turned into information. That is what she did from then on, while driving: she observed billboards, trees along the road, etc. She anchored her emotion thereto and the crying of her own child became information to which she could respond appropriately.

Whether you like it or not, your emotions influence your life. If you do not control your state, it will control you. Which would you rather have? Choose now.

The Transfer of a Resourceful State in 11 Steps
Note: See figure 1.4 about the resourceful state, (p. 52).

Step 1: Choose the situation in which you know you are not in the best state. Write this down in the "current situation" box.

Step 2: Reflect upon what state you would like to be in. (Write down in 'goal.') Which state would be a better resource for you to reach your goal in this situation? (Write down in the "resourceful state" box.)

Step 3: Search for a past experience with this state.

Step 4: Choose an area on the floor—say, a circle in front of you—to step into in order to associate.

Step 5: Remember the experience in which the resourceful state was available. Allow yourself to enter the circle and to relive the experience fully in just the way you want to have it. The guide asks questions such as the following.

> *What exactly happens when you feel this?*
> *(e.g.: Are you calm, do you feel strong?)*
> *What do you see?*
> *What do you hear?*
> *What do you tell yourself?*

Step 6: The explorer steps out of the circle and shakes off the experience. The guide and the explorer look for a physical anchor which elicits the state.

Step 7: Step back into the circle and associate into the experience. (Activate the state of the resource.) Every time you step again into the circle, amplify the state further. Refresh your chosen anchor.

Step 8: Step out of the circle and shake off the experience. In addition to the anchor, select a keyword (e.g. "yes") which will trigger it.

Step 9: Step back into the circle together with the physical anchor and the keyword.

Step 10: Repeat steps 5–7 several times to strengthen the anchor.

Step 11: Think of a situation in the future similar to one in the past, when you might have been in the problem state. Imagine yourself triggering the anchor. How does it feel? How does that change the situation? Repeat this mental programming several times.

Changing One's Emotions: a New Culture?

"Managing" your emotions is an essential part of Emotional Intelligence. First, because your emotions are resources in achieving your outcomes (e.g. controlling your anger, helping you to be assertive); second, because having emotions is a goal in itself.

We often define our final outcomes in terms of feelings. You want to be happy, you want to feel satisfied, you want to feel relaxed, you want to have self-confidence, you want to be proud of yourself, etc. We would do anything to activate the feeling in question. Some people spend a lot of money to be acknowledged in this society. Some go on expensive trips in order to relax while others follow strict diets just to feel all right, etc.

But did you ever wonder whether you could directly activate such feelings, without the efforts you thought were required? Can't you just feel proud of yourself without having to work late every night? Can't you feel good even when it is raining? Can't you feel full of vitality even when you are overweight?

Of course you can and many already do. Still, we often take a detour. And this detour in turn often causes new problems. Why do we always have to take a detour when there is a shortcut? The only explanation we can think of is that our behavior is embedded in a cultural pattern. You think that you have to work at being happy, that you can't get it for free. We raise our children in an "if then" pattern. ("If you ... (*study well*), then ... (*you will be appreciated.*") Always the if, if, if.

This markedly differs from African and Asian cultures. We have a lot to learn from them. How can Africans have fun when they are living in what we call "extreme poverty"? How do Indians and Buddhist people manage to be satisfied with what they have? The current increasing interest in Buddhism we are experiencing in the West is not surprising. We want to feel well again, unconditionally. We want to be pleased here and now.

The critical discerning reader that you are may say: "Easier said than done!" Indeed, we experience a lot of resistance when we invite people to activate a particular feeling. After all, self-management means you are responsible for your own feelings. Imagine somebody is feeling depressed and you invite them to feel cheerful. Or when you are sad over the loss of a loved one, and we invite you to dance and laugh at the funeral. No, that is impossible, or is it? Even well meant advice often fails to help. "Oh, get over it." "Do not let it get to you." And then we often resign ourselves to it: "It has to wear off." "It needs time to heal." "It will take the time it takes."

This demonstrates not only a lack of knowledge about the skill of recognizing and changing your emotions, but it also shows a deep belief that this is not possible or even wrong. Our Western culture does not allow us to "play" emotions. Emotions must not be controlled. They have to remain spontaneous. Emotions are a part of our inner person. An emotion is real. Research shows, however, that emotions are acquired to the same extent as a belief or a conviction. We only *pretend* they are natural. Does our culture really benefit from our taking a detour to happiness? How could it benefit even more by our using the shortcuts other cultures are aware of?

If you still want to learn to work with your emotions, there are several possibilities: we presented some of our approaches in this lesson. But you could also choose to take drama classes, where you access sadness or happiness at will, or you put yourself in the shoes of an angry person. Through practice you learn to activate emotions and to let them disappear again. Yoga, meditation and breathing techniques also help you to achieve immediate control over your physical feelings. In fact this is quite easy to learn. Whatever you ultimately choose to do, our initial question remains: "Are you prepared to learn how to manage yourself?"

An Emotion is a Choice: Reap What You Sow.

Choosing positive emotions is like self-fulfilling predictions. Deepak Chopra says:[14] *"Every action generates a force of energy that returns to us in like kind. What we sow is what we reap. When we choose actions that bring happiness and success to others, the fruit of our karma is happiness and success."*

---

[14] Third law from *The Seven Spiritual Laws of Success: A Practical Guide to the Fulfillment of Your Dreams,* by Deepak Chopra, Amber-Allen, 1995.

So, why not constantly put yourself in a state you like?

Apparently depressed people brim over with (self) criticism. They expect failure instead of success and are pessimistic regarding the future. Compliments are understood in a negative way. They are in search of additional negative information in order to confirm their negative self-image.

Others cut themselves off from their feelings. If you behave like a computer you will think the whole world looks like one. In that case you look at life like James Joyce's Mr. Duffy, who "lived a short distance from his body." This is the kind of person who functions rationally and walks through life like a computer. However, nobody dares to call a computer intelligent, let alone emotionally intelligent.

Research has shown the influence of self-esteem in sales, in a job interview or in a presentation. When taking exams it can be helpful to a certain extent, though its influence should not be over-estimated. Apparently, male students were more self-confident concerning the results of a psychology exam than their female colleagues. Actual figures, however, showed that the female students had better results.[15] In any case, the male students had enjoyed the exam more and the following exams were not affected by negatively brooding about the results. This is why, in some sales training, they advise you to begin with the most difficult client. If you fail, it can only get better. And if you succeed, nothing can ruin your day any more. Collect all your fears and replace them by joy!

Some people manage to be constantly cheerful and in a good state, while others are good at motivating themselves. They can urge themselves to look for distraction or comfort. And what is to stop you from taking a rosy view? Not against your better judgment, but positively committed to having a go: nothing ventured, nothing gained.

However, you need to be careful. The emotional "being at one" in New Age courses, as well as pep-talk in sales courses, can cause a whirl of manic emotions. Will these last? Are they effective?

---

15   *Psychological Reports,* Vol. 81, pp. 76–78, 1997.

Having an emotion is a choice. Decide for yourself about your optimal state. Combine the best parts of several states. Devise your own emotional cocktail! Do you like a certain feeling? Double its power, its intensity. Feel it in your body. What happens when you feel it twice as powerfully? And who is to say you can only double it?

There is nothing wrong about being "guided" by our emotions.
We cannot help it. The only question is,
"What emotions?"
Are they the sterile, stultifying, fearful emotions of inhibition, or are they
the free, healthy, vigorous, and rewarding emotions of excitement?

Andrew Salter in Conditioned Reflex Therapy, 1949

Cases

We have gone through some of the mechanisms which help you to manage your emotions and you probably already have several cases of your own in mind. To illustrate the principles mentioned above, we give you four worked-out cases. We're sure you will find many more. Keep us posted!

Case 1: Managing Distractions

Enjoy whatever you do! Mihaly Csikszentmihalyi writes in *Flow*[16] that happiness is caused by bringing more harmony and coherence into your daily life. This corresponds partly to the Zen philosophy. Once you have a particular aim and you are trying to reach it, the point is to concentrate on what you are doing. While doing something, you fully focus on it and you learn to enjoy what you are doing. We will show you in Lessons 2 and 3 how to make sure your plans fit into your life context and how to increase your likelihood of success. But let us first focus on concentration.

Can you concentrate in a noisy environment? When somebody or something disturbs you, can you easily start again where you left off? What if the phone rings? If this kind of distraction makes you

---

[16] Csikszentmihalyi, M. (1990). *Flow: the Psychology of Optimal Experience*, London, HarperCollins.

lose your concentration, you can do something about it by means of the anchoring technique.

Recall a moment of absolute concentration, of being completely engrossed, absorbed by what you were doing, whatever that was. Associate into that experience (what are you doing, what do you see, what do you hear?). Which anchor can you use to remain concentrated? Have you got one already? Trigger it. Can you remain concentrated? If not, strengthen this anchor by associating into a similar experience of concentration.

Do you like these moments of concentration? If not, what do you need to change to get to like it? For example, how would you like to be able to concentrate on mowing the lawn or doing the dishes and enjoying it at the same time? Can you imagine that? Adapt your anchor to get this "pleasant concentration."

What happens if something disturbs you and makes you lose your "pleasant concentration"? In a nutshell, your state changes. The first step in the process is to get back into your optimal state of concentration. After all, the most important thing to do is to get back to where you left off. And for that you now have an anchor.

In the following case we apply the same principle to studying.

Case 2: Using Emotions in Study

Imagine a subject which you haven't yet felt able to master completely, or which you do not feel comfortable with when studying it. What could you do to bring yourself into the optimal studying state? As we explained, we look for a resourceful state and we add it to a problematic situation.

Step 1

First let us evoke a situation which you can say: "I mastered that subject completely." Associate into that experience. (What are you completely mastering? What do you see? What do you hear? How does it feel?)

Now, associated in the experience, look for the moment of the breakthrough, the moment you realized: "That's it! I've got it!"

(What do you see? What do you hear? How does it feel?) Anchor this moment by pressing lightly on one forearm with a finger of the opposite hand.

Look for two more of these learning situations and repeat Step 1. Each time you want to anchor a state, choose a different (slightly higher) place on your forearm with the next finger.

Now you have three anchors for the states experienced in successful learning situations.

Step 2
Think of the subject which you hadn't been able to study easily. Use the anchors on your forearm to activate the optimal learning situations. As these situations are thematically connected, you can activate first one, then the next, then the third, or all three at once.

Discussion afterwards
Did the anchors work?

If not: Associate again into the situations and experience them even more intensely and vividly, then refresh the anchors. Or look for still stronger learning situations that gave you even more the impression of "Wow, this is it!" (variant: choose other things which might be able to help you, e.g. power of concentration, the feeling of doing well, ... and anchor them as above).

If so: Each time you get to a learning situation you acquire a new learning aid. Subsequently use the three anchors on your forearm or add another.

Try it: Think of three occasions in the future where you will be able to use this aid. Associate into each of these future experiences. Use your anchors. What do you notice?

We encountered a salesman who used this very technique of successive anchors to intensify an activated state. When he had to demonstrate a product in his company's office, he walked from his office to the demo-room. Whether it was Monday morning or Friday evening, he had always reached the optimal state to give the presentation by the time he got there.

What did he do? Well, with each step he took he consciously thought of other successful demonstrations he had given. Each step actually was an anchor for his resourceful state! Like him you can find many ways of anchoring.

Tip: Think of three situations in which you can build a good resourceful state by using successive anchors.
If these situations are of different intensities, place the one with the lowest intensity furthest away from you and the most intense closest. This way, when you trigger the anchors one at a time, you will feel the state build up in you, increasing in intensity with each anchor.

Case 3: The Walt Disney Creativity Strategy

The creativity strategy is an excellent example of the application of the neurolinguistic model for studying a successful strategy. In addition, by explaining the strategy we kill two birds with one stone: on the one hand your classical intelligence increases because your creativity is stimulated. On the other hand your Emotional Intelligence increases, because in this creativity strategy we use the emotional side of the resourceful state.

The creativity strategy we present here is based on the modeling project of Robert B. Dilts.[17] Robert found his inspiration in Walt Disney, the well-known genius who, together with his brother and their team, created an incredible series of cartoons and finally founded the Disney amusement parks.

Robert Dilts distinguishes between three phases in the creative process:

1. Starting from the "Everything is possible" attitude the *dreamer* develops a general vision: what is your goal (in positive terms!)? What will the result look like in general?

---

[17]   A prominent developer and author in the field of neurolinguistics. The complete description of this modeling project can be found in Dilts's *Strategies of Genius, Volume I*, Meta-Publications, Capitola, Calif., 1994.

What are the most important benefits? The idea remains general but you approach the subject through an overview, a synthesis.

2. From the perspective that this dream can become true, the *realist* develops a plan of action. You determine which action you should take to make this vision become true: how will you reach your goal? What will you do, which steps will you take (possibly elaborating in great detail)?

3. To make decisions when you are in a critical mood, distance yourself from the project and subject it to a meticulous analysis. The *critic* uses logic and analysis in order to avoid potential problems, pitfalls and shortcomings. He checks whether the realist's work is complete: whether it meets the criteria you formulate, whether he has missed out risks, ... (Why do you take part in this project? Why do you do what you do? What if situation X occurs?) The criticism you give is constructive, which allows the dreamer and the realist to continue their work. Formulate your criticism as questions, to which dreamer and realist will find answers.

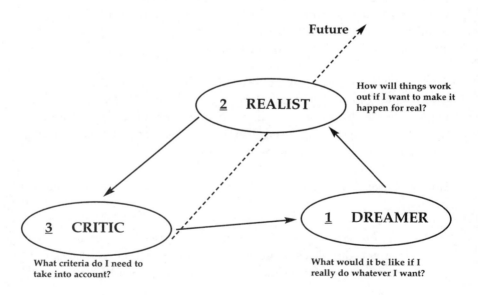

Figure 1.5: The Walt Disney Creativity Strategy

The creative process consists of a combination of these phases. The dreamer gives ideas to the realist who will develop them into a "prototype." The critic evaluates the result, etc. If you have reached the third phase (the critic) and you are not satisfied with the result, then let the dreamer adapt the vision and/or have the realist complete the details. Go through the cycle until you are satisfied with the result.

Lying behind the "reality" of what the Walt Disney Company is doing, you will also find this model expressed in its core values: creativity, dreams and fiction, a fanatical eye for consistency and details and a lack of cynicism.

The Walt Disney Creativity Strategy in six steps

Step 1: Preparation. Select three locations in a triangle (as depicted in Figure 1.5). Anchor each of the three resources/"resourceful states"/abilities to one of these three locations, perhaps using a piece of paper. Each time associate into an experience.

> **1. The Dreamer**. Remember an experience in which you gave your imagination free play. Construct images of yourself (visual constructions). You can appeal to past experiences, other models, images from movies, etc. Select parts as well as the whole. Take on an appropriate body posture.

> **2. The Realist**. Remember an experience in which you were perfectly able to formulate a plan and to implement it. Link the visual constructions to the external visual information. Take on the appropriate body posture. Check your feelings to see whether it will work.

> **3. The Critic.** Remember an experience in which you could easily weigh up the values of ideas and plans, in which you could look for possible obstacles. Use visual memories and talk to yourself. Take on the appropriate body posture.

Step 2:   Aims. Distance yourself from the three locations that you have taken. Imagine what you look like in each of these locations. Decide what you would like to achieve. Make sure your aim is clearly defined (see Lesson 3).

Step 3:   Step into the **Dreamer** position. Imagine what it would be like if you do what you want to do. Visualize yourself realizing your aim. See yourself doing what you want to do.

Step 4:   Step into the **Realist** position. Search for a specific context in which you want to achieve this. Feel what it feels like to put this behavior into practice.

Step 5:   Step into the **Critic** position. Evaluate the behavior. Is it OK? Does it meet the criteria you have set up? Do you need to add or change anything? What would be the consequence, positive or negative, of doing this? What suggestions could you make to avoid the pitfalls?

Repeat: Step back into the **Dreamer** position. Change your dream according to the information acquired. Go through this cycle a few times, if necessary. You know you can stop when the critic is satisfied with the plan.

Step 6:   Write down your solution. To implement your plan, use a TOTE (see Lesson 3) or the questionnaire which you will find at the end of Lesson 3 (exercise 3.2).

Managing Creativity in Groups

The skills of the dreamer, the realist and the critic are not always equally well developed. Some people are rather critical, while others may be more of a dreamer. With a bit of exaggeration you can draw the following caricatures. The critics accuse the dreamers of fleeing into the future, of dreaming, floating, refusing to be realistic. The dreamers refuse to co-operate with the critics because there is nothing to be done with them, as they are so pessimistic, etc. The realist has to separate the two fighting parties and to show the critic that the ideas of the dreamer can be useful, given the necessary adjustments.

Nevertheless you can call the critic creative, even though they tend to use their creativity, their ability to imagine things (to dream), to find reasons why something will go wrong. On the other hand the dreamer can be critical, although their criticism is mainly directed at other people's lack of creativity.

The emotionally intelligent solution lies in leading creativity and criticism in the right direction, in order to give a chance to the total creativity strategy, with its three strategy components of dreamer, realist and critic, in due course. This has regularly been acknowledged since the 1960s, not least within Total Quality Management (TQM), where the steps for brainstorming and problem-solving are used to distinguish creativity and criticism.

We can achieve the same effect in a group by using the Walt Disney strategy. Note here how the addition of the pragmatic down-to-earth realist as buffer between dreamer and critic significantly enriches the models above. First we define the aim of the working group and, as soon as we agree about it, we can get started.

1. In the first phase we are collectively creative. We use brainstorming to generate ideas.
2. Then we collectively change to a realistic state: based on the results of the creative state we divide the tasks scheduled for the first phase.
3. Finally we become critics. We get together to discuss and to evaluate the results.

We repeat these three steps until the group has found a solution we can all agree with.

Simulation of different creativity states in a meeting
Minimum four people. Make sure every participant gets to play every part.

Person A elaborates on a project they wish to realize (this can be a project at work, but it can also be a holiday, for example). Person B plays the dreamer, Person C plays the realist, Person D the critic.

1. Person A presents their project.
2. Asking questions: in turn B, C and D ask a question, reacting as they would in their respective role of dreamer, realist and critic. Person A answers their questions.
3. Finally, Persons B, C and D, in their role, make a sketch of the project, as they see it.
4. They explain their sketches to Person A.

Case 4: The Secret of Brilliant Speakers

Did you ever wonder why some speakers are so fascinating? While other speakers have the ability to make their listeners fall asleep? The answer is simple. A capable speaker is a master at manipulating emotions.

So, what are the most important techniques to apply to become an excellent speaker?

The first and most important secret you need to realize is that the excellent speaker associates into their own experience. No matter what subject you want to discuss, while mentally preparing your speech you should look for the points in the subject which fascinate you. You can already imagine how enthralling you will be while speaking. Restore this personal connection when speaking and you will see: you will use more body language, your voice will be more expressive, livelier, warmer. Your public will get involved in the subject without any problems, BECAUSE YOU YOURSELF ARE INVOLVED IN YOUR OWN SUBJECT.

Second, the excellent speaker shamelessly manipulates their public. Focus your attention externally and do not worry too much about what you will say. Look at your audience's reactions. If you hear a buzzing of voices on the right-hand side of the crowd, focus your attention more on those people and speak as if what you are saying is especially relevant to them. If you perceive some kind of general fatigue or lull, put more variation into your voice, perhaps clapping your hands every now and then or making some sort of sound effect. In so doing you will communicate your own energy to your audience so that they revive and respond more to what you are saying. In turn, they will repay the energy you have just invested into the system with added interest.

Third (but we will elaborate on this in our last chapter), gear up to your public's interest and especially to the way they receive information (see Lesson 4). For example, when talking to engineers, you may want to use short sentences, lots of figures, visual terms, etc. When telling a story to children, use distinct and exaggerated facial expressions and lots of sensory details.

As you can see, it is not all that difficult, in fact, to present an event you are emotionally involved with in an interesting fashion.

Exercises for this Lesson

Exercise 1.1: A general task

This chapter includes several processes already. Go through the chapter again and see how you can apply them in your everyday life.

Exercise 1.2: The power of association and anchors

A. Remember a moment when you had the impression "I can do anything." Relive this experience. Choose your anchor. Aim to retain this emotion for one day (if you lose the state, activate the anchor again).
B. Remember a moment when you felt really healthy. Relive the experience and keep the feeling for one day.
C. Search for a strong positive experience in your life which is linked to another resourceful state. Associate with this state and keep this feeling for one day.

Exercise 1.3: Resourceful state

A. Search for seven areas in your life where you look at things too seriously. What will change if you look at them in a humorous way?
B. Search for seven areas in your life where you think (and/or feel) in a conservative way. What will change if you look at them in a creative, dreamy state?
C. Search for seven areas in your life in which you feel anger, frustration or impotence. What will change if you explore them with a feeling of loving (aimed both at yourself as well as at other people)?

Exercise 1.4: Improve your external attention

In this exercise we seek to maximize the sensory perception of our context. In the initial phase do this one sense at a time. The best place to do this exercise is a place where nobody will disturb you and where you have a wide view (e.g. a dune with a view of the sea, a forest on a quiet day, an apartment block with a panoramic view, etc.).

> Look around at your environment; change views, from short to long distance, focused as well as panoramic. Notice the colors, the range of brightness, of contrast. Do this all the way round.
>
> Listen to the sounds, hearing the tones, pitch, speed, etc.
>
> Touch objects, feel their texture, moisture, temperature, etc.
>
> Smell the air.
>
> Taste whatever you can taste in this context.

Select an anchor which is variable in strength, and which you can modulate, e.g. by making a fist, opening your arms, etc. The modulation comes from relaxing a fist one finger at a time or gradually opening your arms. With each sensory channel activation, vary your anchor. The exercise concludes when all channels are open at the same time. *Example: beginning with a tightly closed fist, I open my hand a little, while focusing on the image, relaxing one finger, then I open it a bit more while I add the sound, relaxing the next finger, and finally, when all channels are present, I have a wide open hand.*

Exercise 1.5: Programming your intention
For two people: Person A helps Person B to go through the steps by asking questions.

1. Access a relaxed state
   - Search for a moment in the past which was very relaxing. Relive this moment (what did you hear, what did you see or feel?), anchor this state.

2. Choose a well-defined outcome (see also Lesson 3)
   - Determine what you want. Write down this aim with as much detail as possible.
   - Check whether you really want it. If you are having mixed feelings, adapt your aim to make sure you can fully support it and that all parties involved get something out of it, not just you.

3. Combine the relaxed state with your outcome
   - Go back to your relaxed state. Ask your unconscious to help you to achieve your aim. Imagine how you will achieve it. Anchor this representation. Let go of the aim and thank your unconscious for its co-operation.

4. Write down your outcome and the anchor you used
   You may want to keep this as a reminder to revisit regularly. Put it in a place such as your bedroom, so that you can think about it before you go to bed.

Exercise 1.6: Editing formats
Step 1: Select a context with limited options.

Step 2: Activate an optimal physical state
   e.g.: —an optimized way of walking
          —a meditative soft-focus attitude
   How can you improve this state? (just like an editor edits text)
   If, for example, you choose walking, you can optimize your way of walking or ask a partner to help you. For example, how powerful or springy are your steps? How quickly do you walk? Do you have an erect posture, relaxed shoulders, etc.? And so on.
   Anchor this optimized state.

Step 3: Introduce elements of the problem by thinking of the problem situation. Maintain your resourceful state while the elements of the problem are added. By the end of this you should experience the problem situation and still be in a resourceful state.

Exercise 1.7: Circle of excellence
1. Imagine a circle on the floor in front of you, big enough for you to step in. Fill it with your favourite color, the one which makes you feel at your best.

2. Go inside yourself and recall a time when you were particularly wonderful, witty, bright, confident, capable, and displayed all the qualities of excellence you know you have.

Even if you don't have any personal history of excellence that you can remember, pretend you have one, using real or imaginary people who display qualities of excellence you would like to have. As you don't need to tell anybody, nobody will know!

3. Develop a holographic representation of yourself in the circle displaying that state of excellence. Make it as realistic as you can:
   - seeing yourself being wonderful and displaying those marvellous qualities,
   - hearing yourself responding wittily, speaking with assurance,
   - feeling yourself gushing with pride at that undeniable state of excellence. Then, when the representation is as real as you can make it ...

4. Move into the circle of excellence, stepping into that representation of yourself and taking its posture and physiology. See what you see in that state, hear what you hear in that state, feel what you feel in that state, fully and completely. Intensify it further, doubling it, trebling it until you are about to reach an absolute peak. Then, anchor this state with a resource anchor, so that you can bring it up as required at any time.

Then step out of the circle, bringing the state with you.

Exercise 1.8: Increase your emotional strength

This exercise is inspired by a similar exercise from Jeanne Segal's book *Raising Your Emotional Intelligence*. She recommends you do this exercise 20 minutes per day[18] for a period of 28 days, as this will give you enough time for the pattern to be integrated in your body.[19] In the context of this book, the purpose of this exercise is mainly to help people to activate a state and to hold on to it more easily. This is a warming-up exercise in which you learn to live with your emotions.

---

[18] Segal, Jeanne (1997). *Raising Your Emotional Intelligence*, Henry Holt. It is of little use to spend more time on this exercise than the amount we suggest. If you are afraid of losing track of time during the exercise Jeanne advises you to use a cooking alarm set to 20 minutes.

[19] Some will be able to do it faster. If you notice, for example, after one or two weeks, for example, that you can hold on to a feeling for 10 minutes without any problems, you can call this exercise a success. Keep doing the exercise until you feel comfortable with it.

Steps

1. Preparation
Make sure you are in an environment where you can relax and exercise without being disturbed. Sit down in a comfortable position which you can sustain for about 20 minutes.

2. Relaxing and managing your attention *(about 5 mins)*
Begin the exercise by focusing on your breathing. Inhale deeply so you can enjoy the air filling your lungs. Exhale slowly. Let peace take over while doing so. Focus on every part of your body, going from head to toes. Each time you exhale, feel tension fade away bit by bit. At the same time, let all thoughts slowly fade away so that you really calm down.

3. Choosing a feeling *(about 5 mins)*
Focus your attention on the various parts of your body. Become aware of your current present perceptions[20] and matching emotions, and where you experience them in you. Each time you come across a feeling, pay attention to it. Intensify the feeling and give it a name.

4. Give a feeling a moment *(5–10 mins)*[21]
Select the feeling you want to work with (e.g. the strongest feeling). Focus your breathing on the part of your body where this feeling is located. Focus on this feeling, finding out which experiences are linked to it in your mind. Once you have found an experience, ask yourself the following questions: "What is happening? What do I see? What do I hear? What do I think of? What do I smell/Which smell comes into my mind? What do I taste/Which taste comes into my mind?" Focus your attention on the feeling again.

---

[20] If this initially appears to be difficult, be patient and carefully scan various places in your body until you notice the differences between them. Jeanne mentions the story of a person who needed three weeks before he could give his feelings enough space to manifest themselves.

[21] After a month of practice, you should be able to concentrate on a feeling for 10 minutes. If you have problems doing this, and other disturbing thoughts keep popping up, continuously repeat the words "Thank you, feeling" (as if it were a mantra).

Steps (continued)

---

5. Finishing the exercise
Thank the feeling for having been able to pay attention to it. Get up and walk around (in the room where you are, or in a different place). Then start the next planned activity.

Variation: Focused Process
If a problem has been troubling you today, instead of focusing your attention on your body, focus on the feeling which the problem evokes in you.

Lesson 2:
Levels in Experience and Communication

"We think in generalities, we live in detail."
A.N. Whitehead

Goals

In this session you will achieve the following five objectives:

- Learn how to better understand your own emotions and those of others, using some specific questions;
- Learn how to map the relationship between your behaviors and values with the "neurological levels" model;
- Set targets for your self-development on a range of such levels;
- Relate the neurological-levels model to your thinking and that of others to map its internal logic (and question it appropriately);
- Learn how to use beliefs in an emotional way to make them work for you.

Neurolinguistic Assumptions

In this second step we will enable you to apply the following ready-made presuppositions:

- *Emotions do indeed have a positive intention and serve a positive purpose.*
- *You have within you the necessary resources to achieve whatever goal you set yourself.*
- *If others can do it and succeed, so can you. You can map the behavior of a person from a structural perspective. Success and happiness are skills you can acquire. Human behavior has its own logic which you can chart out and summarize.*
- *What a person does is not who they are. You can dislike what they do and still respect them as human beings with human rights.*

Why this lesson?
What is the purpose of this chapter?
1. You will use the model of neurological levels to map the structure of your mind and that of others, and achieve greater understanding thereby. You will identify the values which motivate your behavior.

2. The neurological-levels model will contribute to your personal development so that:
    ● By realizing who you are and what matters most to you, you will learn to harmonize your internal processing to respond to others and the world more appropriately.
    ● You will reach an understanding of the logical level at which you need to change and/or operate for a given context.
    ● You will become aware of your identity and mission in life, so that you can fulfil these in the fullness of time.

3. The neurological-levels model will enable you to improve your interactions with other people:
    ● By tuning into the relevant neurological level you will learn to pace the emotional state of the people you communicate with and demonstrate your interest in them.
    ● By understanding the relationship between someone's behavior and their underlying values, you will achieve better rapport with them. In discussions or sales pitches you will be able to attune your arguments to the values of your partner.

Introduction: The Levels of Your Functioning
Emotions are not just there. They play a role in your functioning. The first step towards managing your emotions the way you want is increasing your self-knowledge. When you feel an emotion, pleasant or unpleasant, ask yourself: *"Why do I feel this emotion?" "What does it do for me?"* For example, you can feel you are in love or you can feel passionate about working hard. Conversely there may be some situations when you do not feel confident or resourceful. Do you know why?

How many times have you felt an emotion without actually understanding why you had it? How many times have you had the impression that you and the person you were talking with were at cross-purposes? How many times have you experienced how a discussion about a rather innocent subject escalated into a heavy argument? So, what is the function, the purpose of a given emotion? What does having it do for you?

Your Emotional Intelligence will spectacularly increase if you apply some techniques to understand the function of your emotions in your own performance and that of other people. The model of the 'neurological' levels, to which we will shortly introduce you, will help you to understand the meaning of emotions and, among other things, will help you to disentangle communication knots.

Before going any further, we'd like you to fill out the questionnaire of Exercise 2.1 on page 110.

Basic Model of the Neurological Levels of Experience

In the 1980s, Robert Dilts developed the model of the neurological levels which identifies the operating levels you can distinguish in your language and that of others at any given time. This model is inspired by the general model of Logical Levels which the ethnologist, philosopher and systems theoretician Gregory Bateson developed in the 1980s.

The basic principle of Logical Levels is that lower level concepts and modes of operation are embedded within higher level concepts and modulated by these. In descending order of leverage, Dilts distinguishes between the following logical levels:

	Level	Typical Concept/Concern	Function
6.	*Spirituality/ Connectedness*	How do I relate to my culture and society? What is our society heading for?	Vision and interpretation
5.	*Identity*	Who am I?[1] Why I am here?	Role and mission
4.	*Values/Beliefs/ Convictions*	What is important to me? What is my conviction? Why?	Motivation and permission
3.	*Competencies/ Capabilities/ Skills*	How do I do things? What can I do?	Perception and direction
2.	*Behavior*	What do I do?	Action and reaction
1.	*Environment*	Where? When?	Limitations and opportunities

As you can see, each lower neurological level is embedded in a higher one.[2] For example, all the possible behaviors of a person include all their environments, and the identity of this person incorporates all their values, etc. We will begin with a discussion of the different logical levels and in turn will show how you can use them in practice.

Your External Environment/Context, in Terms of Both Space and Time

What surrounds you?

Where you live and work, in terms of both the locations themselves and of the people you interact with there, your colleagues, family, friends, and also of the wider context, the country you belong to ... This environment can also be expressed in terms of time, i.e. how your surroundings have evolved through time: it includes the current economic climate, literally *"the times you live in."* Ask yourself how this environment affects you: for example, are you concerned about what is happening outside your country?

---

[1] Your own formulation of your sense of identity is distinct from your daily actions (your behavior). It is also more abstract. That is why one often needs to use images and metaphor to describe identity.

[2] Several persons do not agree with Dilts in this area. They say that, from a strictly logical point of view, these levels aren't "really" logical levels. In this book, you may find that, when trying to make sense of experience, or trying to decode communication, distinguishing between those levels is useful, even if they may not follow totally strictly logical rules.

To what extent do you feel related to the political problems of your country? How does the Internet revolution affect your life?

Your Behaviors
What do you do?
Actions such as talking, looking, walking, ... Notice how, since people have no idea what goes on inside your head, this is the only neurological level which is visible to the outside world. It is unconsciously modulated by your skills, values, convictions and your identity. New behavior is easily acquired (see below).

Your Skills
How do you do what you do? How can you do it?
What skills have you got? What are your core-competencies? Something you are used to doing becomes a skill: for example, the skill of driving, the successive actions you engage in, such as turning the wheel, accelerating, watching the road, shifting gear ... To begin with you had to learn these individual actions separately. Later on you learned how to combine them and use them in a sequence until you did it well enough to get your driving licence. Provided you have enough opportunities to practice, you improve your skills on an ongoing basis. Communication training is mostly situated at this skill level: sales course, a course in meeting techniques, how to delegate, assertiveness training, etc.

Your Values and Beliefs
What is important to you? Why is that?
What is your opinion about how things are going or should be going? Values and beliefs regulate whether or not you acquire skills or behave in one way or another. It is a myth that you can easily impose a belief on someone, let alone change convictions. You can acquire a new behavior or belief only when it is compatible with the already present values and beliefs. The strongest values and beliefs are shaped before the age of 21. Many beliefs and convictions even take shape at the imprint phase, before the age of 6. You draw conclusions based on events which affect you. The more moving the event, the stronger the impact it has on you and the more difficult it becomes to change the value or conviction. For

example, a child may have learnt at a very young age that initiative yields appreciation and attention. You may not want to change some values and convictions because they serve you. On the other hand, other values or beliefs acquired at a particular time may limit you and what you seek to achieve, and therefore need revising.

Here are some examples of values: being nice, freedom, creativity, quality, success. A belief is a connection of meanings, often expressed in *"if … then"* or *"A = B, somehow,"* such as: *"If I react spontaneously like a child, I am bad,"* or *"If I take the initiative, I will be appreciated."* When somebody says, for example: *"I think women in managerial functions are more capable than a man,"* then the formula may be: *"If a woman is managing, then she is more capable than men."* Such values and beliefs obviously have an enormous effect on the direction of your life. Whether they are well formulated or "well-formed," as we say in neurolinguistics, is contingent upon how well they serve you and other people around you, i.e. their ecology.

Your Identity
Who are you?
Such an easily asked question which people can find hard to answer. Learn to distinguish between a person's role-identity and their core-identity.

Your *role-identity* refers to who you are in relation to a given context, a role you are playing within society. Every single one of us has a range of roles: private, professional, social, etc. Your role-identity can be distilled from your answers to questions like *"Who are you within your family?"* *"Who are you perceived as where you live?"* or *"Who are you as a salesman?"* It ultimately relates to the hat (or mask) you are wearing at any one time. Incidentally, the very word "personality" relates to the "persona," which is the name for the masks actors wore in classical antiquity.

Your *core-identity* refers to who you are, apart from the roles and titles you are given. If you take away the roles, what is left? Or: *"What is common to all those roles?"* Your experience of identity, the way you see yourself, shifts and evolves throughout your life. People usually experience "Mid-life crisis" as the consequence of not being satisfied with the answer they were given or gave themselves—usually as an teenager—to their core-identity question. Many problems arise when people confuse their role-identity and their core-identity. Retirement problems usually occur as a result of confusion between role- and core-identity: *"Who remains when you take away the professional part?"* Conversely your core-identity may not fit or may even conflict with the identity you assume within a role. We have met several highly skilled and motivated employers who admit in private that, within their job, they are not themselves. This common misalignment between role- and core-identity is at the root of much stress and can often lead to serious health problems.

Identity is strongly related to the question of what we understand by a "meaningful life." It also invites questions eliciting your purpose in life, such as: *"What is my **reason** for being here on earth?"* or *"What is my mission, my purpose in life?"* In order to remain in a situation in which they are not themselves many people often find it necessary to dissociate from their mission. After all, if such questions are at the root of your actions, you may

> **"If we didn't have something worth dying for, none of us would have anything to live for."**

find yourself face to face with the challenge of having to align your values and make important life-choices. For example, on one hand you do not want to have a stressful job or want to work part-time, but on the other hand you want to earn a lot of money. How will these values relate to each other? You will need to make a choice. Which will win? Incidentally, did you know that survivors of concentration camps often mention an urging, future-oriented mission as the most important reason for their survival?

Your Spirituality/Connectedness
The spiritual level again forms the link between you and your surroundings and the circle is closed. A social being, Man is at the centre of a network of connections linking him to his surroundings, fellow humans, nature, and the cosmos. At this level the following questions emerge: *"What will our society look like in five years?" "Why do we live?" "How does mankind evolve?"* ...

Remarks

1. Detecting logical levels in people.

   Noticing at what logical level people are operating is not always obvious when based on a single sentence. Look at the following example:

   "I cannot achieve that here."

   I = Identity
   CANNOT = belief
       ACHIEVE = competence
           THAT = behavior (what you are doing, your activity)
             HERE = environment

   The only way to identify the level at which a person is operating is to listen for the words on which they put the emphasis in a sentence, either in vocal expressiveness or in body language. For practical purposes, look for the prevailing logical levels in a discussion by listening for such emphasis and observing their gestures.

2. Beliefs and prejudices.

   The media are showering us with beliefs and values, hoping that we will take them on. A particular type of beliefs, *prejudices*—also known as *preconceptions*—can easily be acquired from other people in communication. Prejudices are generalizations of one's own experience and applying them can easily harm someone else or even ourselves. If you start from a prejudiced position, you "forget" to question your own way of thinking. The question you could ask yourself to avoid preconceptions in ordinary communication is: *"What should be true in order to make this utterance meaningful?"*

3. Honesty, safety, friendship, freedom, peace, wealth are nonexplicit words. How do you know what they really mean to anyone? However, such value- and belief-laden expressions are reflected in people's behavior. Before deciding whether or not a person shares your belief, you may want to carry out a number of observations. You already know that, by regularly

observing a person, you can ascertain whether they have a specific skill; their success at a relevant task enables you to deduce that they actually have this skill, or not, as the case may be. You can also do this to identify their beliefs and values, although these can be less obvious. To do this, you need to find skills and behaviors which support their beliefs or you can try it the other way around, by asking the person what beliefs underpin these behaviors.

As John Grinder, a world-renowned neurolinguist, often likes to repeat: "One behavioral observation is an 'incident', two behavioral demonstrations invite an hypothesis: it takes three examples to see a pattern." Once we have seen three behaviors, we may infer from that the pattern occurring at capability level. Similarly, once we have three capabilities, we may ask ourselves, again in a Batesonian tradition: "What's the pattern that connects them?" From these three capabilities, we can derive the supporting belief.

Example
Behavior:
A person listens to the news a lot, reads many books and papers about all manner of things, he gives lectures and asks relevant questions. He also published a number of articles, gives reading hints to other people and at the moment he is writing a book …

Capabilities:
He can join in conversations about current affairs, is well informed about trends and news, and is able to connect different fields of study.

Belief:
Knowledge is power.

We remember that, in order to know whether a person really has a particular belief, in fact you need to have at most nine observations of behavior or 3 times 3, see above. In practice, however, you and I often generalize much faster, based on just a few examples, with all the consequences this entails.

4. If you are already familiar with the self-analysis system known as SWOT analysis—where the initials stand for: Strengths, Weaknesses, Opportunities, Threats—you may have noticed how the level of Environment relates to external Opportunities and Threats, while all the other levels relate to your internal Strengths and Weaknesses. We suggest you adopt our enriched model of SWOT analysis as shown below. *(Note how all the questions are deliberately couched in positive terms, to move a person from a problem state to a solution state. See Lesson 3.)*

		ENRICHED *SWOT* ANALYSIS		
	Level	**Strengths**	**Weaknesses**	
		What am I good at?	What could I be better at?	How could I achieve this?
INTERNAL	Spirituality/ Connectedness			
	Identity			
	Beliefs and Values			
	Capabilities and Skills			
	Behavior and Activities			
	Level	**Opportunities**	**Threats**	
		What supports me in achieving my goal?	What could prevent me from achieving my goal?	How could I remedy this so that it doesn't prevent me any more?
EXTERNAL	Environment and Context			

5. Among the values that you hold, some are rather secondary while others are essential. Your essential values are closely linked to your identity. One way to identify core values is to ask the following question: *"What do I consider important in life, regardless of what I do?"* or *"What belief is worth dying for?"* Ask yourself in what way the outcomes you are striving for are helping you to fulfill your core values.

> **"It is never too late to become what you might have been."**
> *George Eliot*

Aligning Neurological Levels

The way people or organizations think about themselves at higher levels influences their operating lower levels. If you change something at a higher level and are consistent in everything you do, this change will percolate down to the lower levels. If it turns out that your behavior is incompatible with your beliefs, you will experience internal conflict. In this case we say that your behavior is "non-aligned" or "misaligned." And this is exactly where the idea of aligning logical levels arises: by aligning your logical levels, you are able to resolve conflicts within yourself and, as a result, with others also. Since organizations also respond as if they were people—after all, the law even considers them legal entities—aligning logical levels in a business will greatly enhance its effectiveness.

Example:
I choose to accept the belief that *"the map is not the territory."* The moment I decide to adopt this belief, circumstances where I enter into a discussion about "religion is the opium of the people: Yes or No" no longer apply, as it does not matter whether this saying is "true" or "false." In any case, as we saw in the section about neurolinguistic presuppositions (p. 12) in our Introduction, it will be impossible to convince the other of the fact that you are right.

Sometimes people confuse neurological levels. This creates thought patterns which "jump" from one level to another. You come across utterances such as: *"I was not qualified enough to get the contract, I am a good-for-nothing."* The above example combines the level of capability (qualification) and that of identity (being a good-for-nothing). In a given situation which refers to capabilities, a person will draw a conclusion about their identity instead. This is when we talk of confusing logical levels. Another example: a child comes home and says: *"The teacher told me that I am stupid because I did not shut up."* In this case the teacher confuses behavior (not shutting up) and identity (being stupid). Both examples appear to be "logical rules" (if A then B) but, the level of utterance A differing from the level of utterance B, both the first expression and the teacher's statement are illogical. A logical and more resourceful way of rephrasing these could be: *"I was not qualified enough to get the contract, I must acquire new skills or qualifications to improve my chances of getting the contract next time." "Not shutting up when you're told to is a stupid thing to do: do keep quiet next time."*

The Role of Logical Levels in Feedback

Feedback usually comes in two forms: criticisms and appraisal. The way we receive these is directly related to our sense of self-esteem. How do you receive these?

1. If somebody gives you a piece of criticism, do you think:
   (a): "I'm no good,"
   or
   (b): "I must do this better next time."?

2. Do you:
   (a): receive this criticism straight in and feel deeply wounded by it,
   or
   (b): look at it dispassionately and appraise its validity?

3. On the other hand, if somebody pays you a compliment, do you:
   (a) just shrug it off, like water off a duck's back, and say; "Oh, it's nothing,"
   or
   (b) feel good and answer with a compliment yourself?

4. Do you:
   (a) receive it with suspicion and keep it "at arm's length,"
      or
   (b) receive it wholeheartedly and allow it to "nourish your soul."?

If you responded (a) to questions 1 and 3, chances are that you probably have a low sense of self-esteem. You habitually receive criticisms at the level of identity and compliments at the level of behavior. Realizing this, is it any surprise that your self-esteem is as it is? It is likely that you also answered (a) to questions 2 and 4, which shows that you associate into criticisms and dissociate from compliments. It's as if you are permeable to what could hurt you and impermeable to what could nourish you.

To remedy this situation, represent your logical levels in front of you perhaps as a set of shelves. Notice how you have been receiving criticisms at the level of identity and compliments at the level of behavior.

1. Now closing your eyes, take hold of your compliments "folder" with one hand and your criticisms "folder" with the other, as if they were real.
2. Now physically reverse them so that the next time somebody criticizes you, you receive their criticism at the level of behavior, and when somebody pays you a compliment you receive it at the level of identity. Notice how it feels to have made this change.
3. Imagine a situation in the future when somebody criticizes you: how does it feel to receive it at the level of behavior?
4. Imagine a situation when somebody pays you a compliment: how does it feel to receive it at the level of identity?

Chances are that reversing these levels will also reverse the association/dissociation we identified above, so that you can keep criticisms at arm's length to appraise them dispassionately and learn from them how to improve your performance, and that you can now receive compliments wholeheartedly and allow them to nurture your spirit.

Incidentally, if you feel wicked enough, you could apply this even to false compliments, receiving them as if they were real and kindly meant. There is nothing more disarming than paying somebody a false compliment, expecting the person to feel the hidden barb and to be wounded by it, and instead to see it accepted as if it was true, and even honestly reciprocated! That would be real Emotional Intelligence, now wouldn't it?

So, both in discussions and in therapy, clarifying and separating logical levels has proved to be of great value. This is because placing each expression at the right level creates freedom. Learning to do this gives you greater control over your emotions and greater choice in life.

Where Emotions Fit within this Model

Emotions are related to both our internal behavior, namely physical sensations, and to important values. In the neurological-levels model an emotion occurs at the level of behavior and the meaning of this emotion appears at the level of values.

An emotion can be acknowledged and experienced by somebody as within their control. If the emotion is contained, it will remain a physical sensation at the level of behavior. Much of its emotional impact will be limited or channeled and used as a resource.

If the emotion is not contained, however, but dominates the person, this emotionality indicates that something really important is occurring which is directly connected to their core personality. Such emotions relate directly to the higher logical levels of values, beliefs and even identity. They pervade, as it were, your complete experience.

For example, a person experiences the emotion *"afraid to fail"* as a specific behavior inside their body—literally so, as it is a result of a surge of particular hormones and neuro-transmitters, which leads to the contraction or relaxation of a range of muscles, etc. Meaning itself occurs at the level of beliefs. Even if only unconsciously, a belief is directly present in a given experience. Only after deliberately querying this belief, however, will it be expressed in linguistic terms. Let us ask this person the following question: *"What does having this emotion mean to you?"* An answer you could receive might be, for example: *"If I fail, I am not worth living."*

People often react emotionally in discussions or conflicts. Why do they? After all, it is just a question of words, isn't it? Yet such discussions affect us deeply. Because we identify with particular values and beliefs, our body releases adrenaline, testosterone or cortisol when these are questioned. We may even drastically reorganize our lives to abide by our own values and mission. And many a war has been caused by differing opinions and beliefs.

There is a direct correlation between a person's emotions and their core-identity. Somebody may feel depressed when, having been working for their boss for years, that boss does not appreciate their work. You become passionate about defending your own point of view. Our emotions impact our everyday behavior. And what can happen when

> "To be completely honest with oneself is the very best effort a human being can make."
> *Sigmund Freud*

you fall in love again? Suddenly you are more confident, you could tackle anything, you walk on air.

The Meaning of Emotions

In order to get to know ourselves and other people, we apply two principles: induction and deduction. When we draw conclusions from observations of behavior and situations, we use *induction*. When we draw conclusions based on generalizations or patterns we use *deduction*. In your everyday interaction with other people you use both induction and deduction, spontaneously drawing conclusions about what the person is like and how they will behave in given circumstances. Interpretation mechanisms in our perception are extremely automatized. Such a process, however, is not without its hazards. The danger is that many people distinguish between only the people they like and those they don't like at all, an extreme form of polarization which we call a digital response. A more emotionally intelligent person will begin to use a wider range of categories in order to describe somebody or something. After all, the world is not black and white, not even just all the shades of grey in between, but full Technicolor. And what about the colors we can't detect above and below our range of vision, like infrared, microwaves, or X-rays? By limiting yourself to just black and white you constrain yourself to a very limited universe. We give you an example of this case in Lesson 4.

What can you do to avoid such spontaneous conclusions? The emotionally intelligent person that you are can and will be willing to constantly question your own interpretations. If you easily allow yourself to think *"This person is unreliable"* you can ask yourself the following inductive question: *"On what observations or feelings did I base this conclusion?"* And when you think: *"I will not ask this person, they will refuse anyhow,"* you can ask yourself *"How do I know that this person will refuse?"*

In other words, a person who is emotionally intelligent has available to them a range of examination tools in order to get to know themselves as well as other people. We will closely study this examination technique, which follows the previously mentioned model. The first three questions are inductive and go upwards, from specific towards more abstract, from the outside to the inside. The last question is a deductive one and goes in the other direction.

So, instead of writing a thick book, bulging with generalities about the meaning of emotions, we recommend that you investigate the specific meaning an emotion has for each individual, by asking appropriate questions of each of them individually. Since this meaning is linked to an experience, you will find a different meaning for each person, and will be able to tailor your own response accordingly. We offer you some guidelines on how to ask such questions further on.

Guidelines for Discovering the Meaning of Emotions

To identify the role of emotion in the way a person functions you need, first of all, to acknowledge that everything you do has both a rational and an emotional component. Establishing rapport with yourself or with another person is essential for successful communication: without rapport you can't get any further. You will find you are on the right track when a person's body language corresponds to what they are saying, i.e. if, instead of just pretending to please you or to hide something, you can deduce from their response that the person you are communicating with is actually meaning what they're saying. We call this internal harmony "Congruence." The closer their response relates to their core-identity, the more emotional their responses will be.

For example, somebody asks you: *"I am afraid of failure: why is that?"* You could find possible reasons for this in a great many books. And since you are an expert you could feel flattered you've been asked and tell them what you learned from such books. But is this kind of answer useful to the person if they can't relate it to their own experience? As intellectual answers often seem to drown in a morass of explanations, experience has shown that it is far more effective to start working immediately with this person instead of working at a cognitive level. Because the question "why?" invites a rationalization, aim to avoid using it.

Imagine yourself asking *"Why are you afraid of failure?"* and the other person may say, *"Because, in the past, my father was too tough on me."* So, what can we do about it? Sometimes rationalizations are so challenging that the person gets stuck in them. In such a case you need to change the rationalization before the emotions can be changed. Once we came across the following: *"I am impulsive because it is in my nature; after all, I **am** a Sagittarius."* This is a rationalisation at the level of identity. How are you going to change the impulsiveness of *Sagittarius* if a *Sagittarius* really wants to stay a *Sagittarius*? After all, whatever you do, they will still have been born under this star sign. If, however, you could make them think of *Sagittarians* who were NOT impulsive, the person might realize that impulsiveness is not an identity issue, but perhaps one which belongs to lower logical levels, like behavior: if they do it, they could also NOT do it.

You can also identify a qualitative answer in somebody's language. Imagine the person replying, *"I think I may be afraid of failure because I think success is very important. Could that be the reason?"* This is not a qualitative answer, but an intellectual one. It has too much *"I think," "maybe," "could that be?"* Someone who really gets in touch with the meaning of their emotions will look out with soft focus, will talk cautiously and, above all, will be associated in their experiences.

Questioning
1. This first set of questions will help you to explore emotions and the values which hide behind them:
   What is important to you?

What does feeling like this do for you?
What value do you meet by feeling or behaving like this?

Possible answers:
—I am afraid to walk alone on the streets at night. By this I avoid dangerous situations. *Safety.*
—I feel unsafe when thinking of working part-time. I think I will be sorry for not having made a career for myself in my life. *Success.*
—I am in love. I want to enjoy life. Enjoying. *To live.*

2. The second set of questions will enable you to explore the relationship between emotions and the beliefs which hide behind them:
What is causing you to have this emotion/to feel like this?
Why do you have this emotion?

Possible answers:
—If I feel under stress just before a deadline, I can motivate myself.
—When I get angry I feel strong enough to actually say what is bothering me.
—When I feel shy and start blushing when I am in a group, I am protecting myself against possible criticism.

3. To help you find a connection between emotion and identity, you can ask a third set of questions:
What does feeling this say about yourself?
How is feeling like this typical of you?
Who are you, having this emotion?

Possible answers:
—This frustration is typically me. I want to save the world.
—Being impulsive is my way of loving. I am a Sagittarius.
—I am melancholy and solitary.

4. The following questions will enable you to identify the relationship between expressions of identity (I am ...) and specific levels:
How do you know you are...?
Why do you deduce that...?

How did you come to the conclusion that...?

Possible answers:
—Criticism often hurts me: I am of the sensitive kind.
—I am the romantic type: I keep looking for things to escape in and to dream away.
—I am a born leader because I feel strength and wisdom inside me.

The Positive Intention of Emotions

From time to time an emotion seems unwelcome or appears to interfere with your performance. However, we assume that no emotion is totally negative, that having it has a positive intention for the person who has it. Emotions serve purposes. They have a function. They are doing something for you, or, at least, aim to do so.

Sometimes people worry about particular emotions. In such cases they may feel as if a particular emotion is alien to them, an unwelcome visitor. They'd love to see this emotion disappear. But this emotional reaction IS there and has probably been present for many years. So, what does it achieve? This is where we distinguish between the *Positive Intention* and the *Secondary Gain* of an emotion.

—The *Positive Intention* is the function which this emotion has in your behavior. The consequences for you or others of feeling sad may be negative but the intention is good. For example, the positive intention of this sadness may be to remain connected with something which no longer exists. The positive intention of a depression may be the avoidance of pain. The positive intention is the place the emotion has in the person. The positive intention can explain the reason for this emotion being there. The emotion is doing something for you.

—*Secondary Gain* is what you end up with after you have experienced an emotion. If you are feeling sad, for example, the people around you may respond by comforting you. The fact that people react to you in a particular way will be a consequence of your sadness. This profit is secondary to the response itself.

We assume that emotions do not occur accidentally, and that, no matter the side-effects they give you, you have them for a reason. Only when you accept this basic assumption and search for this reason will you notice that everything in your life has a function and can be a starting-point to change and to learn.

We will now give you some examples of the positive intention of emotions, divided into desired and undesired aspects.

EMOTIONS	*UNDESIRED*	*DESIRED*
Doubt	If the person doubts so long that it affects their power to decide, then the question arises: "Why do you keep on doubting. Why don't you just decide?" After some self-examination this kind of answer often follows: "If I don't take any decisions, I will not make mistakes. And if I don't do anything I avoid the risk of being punished. Taking no risks is a way to protect myself."	Somebody may doubt a lot before deciding. The positive intention is that the person wants to build up security and to hedge their bets.
Stress and Fear of Failure	When the person's fear of failure paralyzes them, they may stop what they are doing before actually finishing their work. They may not take an exam or may become ill, etc. By doing this, the person avoids being confronted with the fact that they would not succeed. They are in charge of the result.	Stress and fear of failure may activate your mental and physical capacities to fulfill a job. The fear of failure can often motivate somebody to carry out a work very well: many actors actually like their stage fright.
Emptiness and Exhaustion	Depressed emotions which cause long-term inactivity are often caused by the need for self-protection and the avoidance of frustrations and pain. It is like a polar bear hibernating, comfortable in his den. The world is too hard. The question is how does the bear know spring has returned?	Emptiness and exhaustion are familiar feelings when you have worked hard. Some people become ill because their body seeks to recuperate, to really enjoy having to stay in bed. The emptiness after a period of exams or on a Sunday and holidays are similar indications that the body is recuperating.

EMOTIONS	UNDESIRED	DESIRED
Loneliness	Undesired loneliness can cause frustration as you miss interacting with others. It may indicate your desire for company. If the loneliness is ongoing, you could ask yourself what other reasons prevent you from seeking or enjoying company.	Loneliness can be positive when you enjoy having your own free space. It may motivate you to get in touch with other people and to meet them.
Anger, Aggressiveness, Dominance	Aggression becomes a problem when you can no longer control it. Impulsiveness may be the only way somebody may know to be themselves. In any other kind of relation the person is not really appreciated. It may cover a fear of being controlled.	Anger may stimulate you to be honest, or give you the energy to stand up for what you deserve, and it also may be used to protect you and your values.
Sadness, Grief	Being stuck in sadness can be due to pathological mourning. Lasting sadness may be due to clinging to another and assuming this is the only way to keep in touch and to control it.	Sadness may enable you to keep in touch with something which no longer exists.
Shame and Guilt	Shame and guilt may be a way to control whatever is happening around you. Feeling guilty implies a causal connection with something occurring in your environment.	Shame and guilt may be protecting you and enabling you to evaluate whether or not you are adapted to your environment.
Being in Love	This may be an urge to possess people and objects. Being in love can be a way to vitalize oneself.	The mechanism inside you which enables you to be connected with somebody.
Jealousy	Jealousy may be the urge to possess another to avoid being hurt. It can be used to manage your self-esteem.	Jealousy could be a healthy way to express your love and to bind yourself to another.

Advanced study: suggestions for finding the positive intention of an emotion

According to Abraham Maslow, self-realization[3] is the ultimate motivator. However, many emotionally intelligent people link achieving their own self-realization to activities which involves helping other people to realize themselves. We therefore include some ideas below to help yourself by helping other people as well.

> *Principle*: If a person cannot find the positive intention behind a behavior or emotion, do not press the case but just explain that your question suggests possible avenues for their further development. Rapport is very important to ensure the client is willing to consider the question. Be patient while the person works out the answer and remain silent, so that the person has time to think.

If the other person does not accept the existence of a positive intention:

1. Turn believing that there is such a thing as a positive intention into a first sub-goal. Question how positive intention relates to their perception of being human. (Example: Apply this step when somebody says: *"This is not my emotion. I want it to disappear."*)

2. Turn the belief in a positive intention for this emotion into a condition to proceed. You could say: *"If you do not accept this emotion as having a meaning, we cannot continue because I am not a surgeon who can amputate a part of your body."*

3. Look for a reference experience. Invite the client to search for possible situations when they identified that something they had done had a positive intention for them. Beginning with a positive behavior, make them realize how it relates to a need or purpose. Then invite them to search for a time in which they changed their behavior after they had realized why they acted that way. (Example: *"I remained angry because I wanted to stand up."*) Make them think of a time when they changed their opinion about somebody else's behavior after they had realized the positive intention which was behind their behavior.

---

[3] For a detailed discussion on self-realization we would like to refer you to Maslow's book *Towards a Psychology of Being*, John Wiley & Sons, 1961. These principles were developed for use in companies in the book *Eupsychian Management* which was reissued in 1998 as *Maslow on Management*, John Wiley & Sons.

(Example: *"When I realized he was doing it because he felt power-less, I was no longer angry."*)

4. Give a personal example of how discovering the positive intention of an undesired behavior changed your own relationship towards this behavior.

5. Give them permission to imagine what it could be by saying: *"You may not be aware yet of the positive intention for doing/feeling this, but if there was one, what might it be? If you knew, what would you say?"*

6. Suggest: *"You may not believe there is a positive intention behind what you did/felt, but how would you feel just knowing there was one? How would you feel if you could just pretend there was one?"*

7. Use humor, laugh, provoke, with love in your heart and a twinkle in your eye. Blow it out of all proportion. For example, to a person who is allergic: *"What! You think it has got nothing to do with you? It has everything to do with you! You are one big allergy!"* Make them laugh.

If the other person cannot find the positive intention:
1. Continue to ask variations on the question. Example: *"What could be the consequence of not behaving like this? Imagine yourself not behaving like this."*

2. Use what we call Cartesian logic, playing with four possibilities (+/+, -/+, +/-, -/-) as shown in the table below. This is very good at ferreting out all the options of an issue and highlighting the ecological consequences of the decision.

   - *What would happen if you did this?*
   - *What wouldn't happen if you did this?*
   - *What would happen if you didn't do this?*
   - *What wouldn't happen if you didn't do this?*

What Would/If I	Do Not Do This	Do This
Not Happen	- -	- +
Happen	+ -	+ +

3. Have the person associate with an extremely specific experience.

4. Let the person give you a number of experiences and ask them for the common elements. Example: *"In these three cases I have the emotion in response to a person who is looking at me in an authoritative way."*

5. Take an example and analyze the construction of the emotion. Look at what is immediately before the emotion. Example: *"Immediately before my fear there was a voice inside of me which said: 'I cannot do this.'"*

6. Look for the moment when the person behaved undesirably for the first time, assuming that the behavior was the best way to deal with the situation. (You might want to use a timeline.[4])

7. Put yourself in Second Position (see Lesson 5) place as a guide and discover the positive intention yourself. Give your opinion and check whether or not the person recognizes it. After all, if you're wrong, they'll tell you.

The relationship between emotions: the sequence of emotions

The positive intention of an emotion often lies in another one. When experiencing a situation, and in the coping process which follows this experience, many emotions come in quick succession. In order to find the positive intention you have to start looking for the underlying cause. For example, anger can be a way to channel disappointment. This disappointment could be a way for a person to realize they are hurt. Feeling hurt might be the consequence of a strong desire. At the time, or even afterwards, you may be aware of only the most immediate emotion.

ANGER ➔ Disappointment ➔ Hurt ➔ Desire

---

[4] For more information on working with timelines, you might want to consult books such as *Time Line Therapy and the Basis for Personality* by Tad James and Wyatt Woodsmall, Meta Publications, Cupertino, Calif., 1987 and *Time-Lining: Patterns for Adventuring in Time* by Bob G. Bodenhamer and L. Michael Hall, Anglo-American Books, Carmarthen, 1997.

The Power of Emotional Beliefs

There is a relationship between emotions and meaning. You could consider them two sides of the same coin, two aspects within a single experience. An emotion without an explicit meaning is perceived as alien to our behavior, like the proverbial hair in the soup. Earlier on in this lesson we discussed the reflection by an emotion of a value which may or may not be explicit.

On the other hand, knowledge and beliefs may appear abstract and distant in our lives. For example, think about physics or mathematics. To most people such subjects are void of emotion; they leave us cold. When asked: *"How does it feel to believe that gravity is holding you down?"* *"Nothing at all,"* is the usual answer. Therefore it may be worthwhile to investigate why many people do experience emotions about physics and mathematics.

Just as we proceeded to understand the meaning of emotions we can enliven any belief, connecting it to experience. In so doing we work in the other direction, looking for what makes a belief emotional. So, how can we turn intellectual beliefs into emotional ones? How can we embody beliefs, giving them a place in our lives as something *"e-motional,"* something which puts us into motion, preferably in the direction we want to go?

Let us, for example, take the subject of Positive Thinking. Many people have been inspired by the concept and they went through the following process. First they would read a book[5] full of fantastic ideas. Then they would use affirmations (daily repeating positive utterances to yourself), hoping to develop the power needed to achieve control over their emotional responses and personal empowerment. Many people, however, do not achieve their goal with these affirmations. Why is this?

There are two answers to this:

Any emotion you experience is a sequence of neuro-psychological steps. This sequence needs to be broken. To do this we discussed the dissociation technique in Lesson 1.

---

[5] Books about Positive Thinking, for example Dyer's *The Sky's The Limit,* HarperCollins, 1982, or Norman Vincent Peale's *You Can If You Think You Can,* Simon and Schuster, 1991, are mega bestsellers.

The repetition of positive utterances and beliefs, in and by itself, does not guarantee the embodiment or the emotionalizing of these beliefs. The following is a more effective technique.

Technique: emotionalizing beliefs

Step 1. *Formulate your beliefs.*
Read or listen to a belief which strikes you, which makes you think: *"This is the vision which can change my life, my emotions and my state of mind."* To start with, write down the belief you want to work with. Just as some positive thinking courses suggest, you can stick them to the wall and read them every day.

Step 2. *Charge the belief with consequences at the behavior level.*
Imbue this belief with meaning by identifying its positive consequences, for yourself, others, your organization, community, the world. As using the belief as a filter will be your target, make sure it has only positive consequences at all levels. Are there any new experiences in which you can experience believing this? How does it feel to realize this? Think about next week and ask yourself: *"How does believing this affect the way I'll behave in the future?"* *"How do I need to behave to put this belief into operation?"* *"Will I interpret the events differently if the belief is true for me and how will that be?"*

Step 3. *Charge the belief with purpose.*
Look for additional arguments, elements of proof, to support this belief: with this belief in place, how do you represent yourself, other people, mankind, the world, and your relationship to these? What is your perspective on life? What has to be true which will ensure this vision becomes true to you? What values does this belief imply and where would you locate these in your hierarchy of values? (See Exercise 2.5, p.112)

Step 4. *Charge your belief with emotions.*
We presented this process in the previous chapter. A referential experience is an event in your life when a state or belief was already operational, when you already believed or experienced this. Look for a referential experience and associate again with it, revisiting it in your mind as you experienced it at the time. Feel to what extent this belief was already present as a physical experience, what having this belief felt like at the time. Hear this belief

resonate in your mind. The belief was functioning as an assumption. By associating into this, your belief becomes again an experienced reality, instead of a purely intellectual expression.

Step 5. *Anchor this belief in you in the most appropriate way.*
If you have done the previous steps properly, you should already be able to access this belief at anytime. However, if this belief is as resourceful as you want it to be, you want to have it without even thinking, don't you?: you want to live it, to breathe it, to demonstrate it in each and every behavior and activity, in any environment. So connect this belief in your mind with something you do automatically, without even thinking, like breathing, or your heartbeat. After all, these continue even when you are asleep, don't they? We hope so too!

Applying Logical Levels to Enhance Your Emotional Intelligence

We have already shown above how neurological levels relate to you so that:

—You can see how neurological levels are structured and how emotions are linked to them.

—You can change logical levels and, by doing that, actually manage your emotions.

—Your higher logical levels (vision, mission and beliefs) are the key to your self-motivation.

You can also identify neurological levels in other people and even in organizations. Such observations are useful in dealing with the people you interact with. You can disentangle logical levels in a conversation or, for example, use another person's core values to strengthen the emotional bond between you. You can show them how such values matter to you also and take them into account when you want to explain something to them or ask them something.

Example:	John's core-value is *peace*	Peter's core-value is *happiness*
Asking for help	If you help me now, I will leave you in *peace*.	You don't half know how *happy* you make me by helping me.
Letting out a house in the Ardennes	It is really *peaceful* over there.	Your whole family can be *happy* there.

Application 1: Neurological Levels in Organizations

You can use the model of the neurological levels with individuals, for example, in the context of their job, as well as with groups, with a business as a whole.

Use at a company level
Identity

The mission statement expresses the identity of the organization. A good statement describes what the business is, what keeps the people in the organization together.

An example:

"Better things for better living.
We are a science and technology-based global company of people
who make products that make a difference in everyday life."[6]

Values and Beliefs

An organization also needs to have a clear set of values and beliefs which are shared by all staff and which guide the organization's decisions.

Examples of values important to an organization:

Focusing our business
Commitment to the environment
Empowering people

---

[6] Slogan and mission statement of international company *du Pont de Nemours*, as it was printed on the top of their home page in December 1997. The company Du Pont is almost 200 years old. A similar, though less explicit, statement could be seen in their 1992 annual report.

The identity and values of an organization are often presented in their annual report. However, the proof of the pudding comes from eating it! Check how these statements are put into practice: are the skills and behaviors of the organization in accordance (aligned) with its mission, values and beliefs? Is the organization consistent in applying its values and beliefs? (What will they put in the annual report in a few years? Are the board's decisions in accordance with their values and beliefs?)

Individual use

Example: a salesman.
— Environment: *This area* is the perfect market to sell my products.
— Behavior: In my sales talk I *ask* a number of *questions, I explain, ...*
— Skills: I have *mastered all techniques.*
— Convictions: *If* I sell more, *then* my salary will go up.
— Identity: I *am* a compass, showing the way to the solutions people need.
— Spirituality/connectedness: I *expect the world to change a lot* in the next five years, because of the sales of computers.

Individuals within an organization

Finally we can check how the logical levels of the organization and the individual are related to one another. This leads to questions such as: is the identity of an individual aligned with the organization's mission? Are their personal values and beliefs in accordance with the organization's?

For example, when an organization aims for customer satisfaction and long-term customer relations, it can question whether it would be useful to have an aggressive salesman who is aiming for as big as possible a turnover. Either the organization is not completely honest about its values, or sooner or later the salesman and the organization will clash. As an employee too it might be better to ask yourself whether or not the organization and you are a good match.

> "46 percent of the people that left their jobs last year did so because they didn't feel appreciated for their work."
> *Ministry of Labour, US*

Mergers and business cultures

Whether or not they take place, mergers are the best moment for headhunters to pinch good employees from the companies in question. In Belgium, for example, this was the case when CERA and Kredietbank merged into KBC in 1998. Sometimes employees leave the organization because they are asked to work in another city (for example, in Brussels instead of Leuven). Mergers also create a lot of instability. The question often arises as to whether and how the "atmosphere" within the organization will develop.

Important mergers between companies fail with unsurprising regularity. For example, in October 1998 it was announced that the fusion between American Home Products and Monsanto was called off. The explanation was that their respective business cultures were not compatible. The same had happened before between Glaxo-Wellcome and SmithKline Beecham. Glaxo's business culture was too aggressive for their new partners. It took some changes in the management team before merger talks could resume about 28 months later. And when, in 1997, the fusion was announced between KPMG and Ernst & Young, many of the employees anticipated problems because of their differing business cultures. Eventually the merger failed, officially because of "government resistance."

Even if a merger works out technically, it takes a while to see whether it was a success. To form a new entity you need to develop a new and common vision of the future and an adapted mission for the new organization. And one should identify which beliefs are important to the organization. Ultimately, a merger works out only when employees can adapt to the culture of the new organization.

Some beliefs to think about

In 1960 Abraham Maslow and Douglas McGregor formulated six important assumptions for organizations.[7] These are partly known as "Y-theory for management."

---

[7] These are described in *Maslow on Management* which was reissued in 1998 by John Wiley & Sons. In his book Maslow implies a whole series of assumptions which are useful to an "enlightened" company.

1. Co-workers deserve to be trusted.
2. They look for and take responsibility.
3. They want a useful job.
4. They want to learn.
5. They do not oppose changes but they refuse to be changed.
6. They prefer to work instead of doing nothing.

> **"Profit is like health. We need it, but we do not live for it."**

Even today, however, the application of such principles often seems radical. The very idea of putting people first generates emotional concerns. The slogan in the frame comes from St. Luke's, an advertising agency in London, where the complete capital is divided amongst all its employees. Although it is usual to work 60 hours per week in the advertising world, according to the agency, a 40 to 45 hours' working week for the executive staff is realistic. In addition they profess the principle of hiring a person for life.

Note: "logical levels" within quality management
In addition to the neurological levels model, explained above, there are many different models which function according to the principle described by Bateson.[8] For example, we have the Quality Function Development (QFD) model, which separates the client's needs from the solutions which are given, as these start from the actual need, separated from the technical possibilities.

Application 2: Neurological Levels and Changework
Although the neurological levels model is primarily an analysing instrument to map a desired situation and rather than an intervention strategy in itself, it nevertheless offers a number of interesting principles about change.

1. At which level is someone's problem located?
Example: Somebody says "I am depressed." Notice how different this is from a person saying "I have a depression," or even better, "I have been having depressing feelings since I was fired." In the first case the person is experiencing the emotion at the level of identity: he IS like that. In that case people say: "That is who I am."

---

[8]   Bateson, Gregory (1972). *Steps to an Ecology of Mind*, New York, Chandler Publishing Company (reprinted University of Chicago Press, 2000).

An utterance such as this offers fewer possibilities for self-control and change than when the emotions are located at lower levels. The best way to deal with your emotions is therefore to consider them as parts of you which occur at specific times in specific situations. You can say, for example: "At night, when I come home after a day of hard work, I feel empty and lonely." We will see in the next chapter what you can do with this.

Example: a difficult marriage.
Filling in information at all levels provides a synthetic overview of the total actual situation.

—Environment: I have been *with my partner for ten years*.
—Behavior: I have *followed* him for ten years by supporting him in everything he did.
—Skills: We have *never been able* to talk very well.
—Beliefs and values: *If* we had shared our feelings with each other, *then* I would have felt more related to him. Since we didn't do that I now feel alienated and therefore I want a divorce. I have always missed good contact.
—Identity: I *am* a failure in the field of relationships. To other people I *am* selfish because I do not think about the children.
—Spirituality: I *expect* there will be more alternative ways of living together which give more space for individual freedom. This strengthens me.

Having elicited this information I can ask the following questions:
—You have been following for ten years. But are you a follower?
—If you are no follower, what are you?
—Which value is the most important to you and how can you use this one as a criterion in your next contacts?
—Why have you never been able to talk well?
—Why did you follow? Which value was the most important then?

2. At which level does change need to occur to resolve the matter?

The principle is that, to resolve a problem situated on a specific level, the changes should take place on a higher level, at it has more leverage. As Albert Einstein stated: *"We can't solve problems by using the same kind of thinking we used when we created them."*

Example:

—A person who took an assertiveness course and who is able to say "no" at the training, will not necessarily be able to say "no" to their boss. Why not? Because the problem did not reside in saying "no," but in the belief that you can say "no" and still be accepted by other people.

—If somebody does not believe they have musical talents, it is no use sending them to a school of music, unless you can convince them that they are talented.

—If employers do not feel that their organization has a responsibility towards society, they will not be inclined to give their personnel more training than necessary.

Appendix to Lesson 2:
The Theory Behind The Model

Dilts's model was inspired by the "logical levels of learning" model which was developed by Gregory Bateson[9] in the 1960s. This model is based in its turn on the *logical types* of Bertrand Russell.[10] You will find below the rules which logical types meet:

—On the one hand a class of objects cannot be a member of itself. For example: Muhammad Ali is a member of the class of boxers but the class of boxers is not a member of itself.

—On the other hand an object's *name* does not correspond to the *object itself*. For example: the *name* Muhammad Ali does not correspond to the *object* (the person with this name). You can hit a boxer in the face but you cannot literally hit the name. Again, the map is not the territory.

—In the case of logical levels the concepts on a lower level are *enclosed* by concepts on higher levels. For example:

● The class of boxers is on a higher logical level than Muhammad Ali.

---

9   Gregory Bateson, *Ibid.*
10   The first discussion of the logical types was written down in Bertrand Russell's *The Principles of Mathematics,* which was published in 1903. The theory was developed by Russell and Whitehead in *Principia Mathematica* (1910–1913)

- The class of sportspeople is on a higher logical level than the class of boxers.

- The class of people is on a higher logical level than the class of sportspeople.

Levels of emotions

Let's apply the above-mentioned principle to emotions.

I can have emotions about something which is happening around me ("ordinary emotions"). I can, for example, feel anger when I have to wait at a red traffic light when nobody is coming from the other side. But I can also have emotions about my emotions ("meta-emotions").[11] I can be angry with myself, for example, because I cannot wait patiently at a red light.

Levels of learning

People are intelligent beings who can learn on various levels. This is how our traditional and Emotional Intelligence is continuously growing. By definition learning implies change, although it can be quite difficult to say what specifically is changing. Based on these changes, Bateson distinguished between subsequent levels of learning:

Learning 0:

A change in response to a stimulus (behaviorist idea of learning or unlearning a particular response to a particular stimulus).

Example: The school bell teaches me the class is over. I quit paying attention.

Learning I:

A change in Learning 0: the subject learns versatility in behavior. Depending on the situation they will react differently to the same stimulus. To do this they use information which is derived from the context. It is not always exactly clear how this information is derived.

---

[11] Concerning this conclusion L. Michael Hall developed a theory about "Meta-States" (**Meta-States,** Empowerment Technologies, Grand Junction, CO, 1996).

Example:
1. The school bell rings: I can run out of the classroom or wait until the next class will start. At the end of the day I will choose the first strategy. When I know another teacher will enter soon, I will choose the second one.
2. It depends on my mood which road I will take to go to the station.

Learning II:
A change in Learning I or "learning to learn": a change in the process of learning.
Example:
1. From a number of experiences of "learning I" (school bell, the organization's time clock, the army call ...) I decide about the best way to learn how to react to new time signals.
2. From my experience in various exams I decide about the most efficient way to study.

Learning III:
A change in Learning II: what are the various learning systems? What can I learn by means of these systems?
Example:
1. In acquiring information from an expert, for example in order to build up a planning system or credit analysis, I check first what kind of knowledge the expert is using. Depending on the types of critical knowledge, I decide what kind of learning strategies would be the best to apply.
2. When developing the concept of the learning organization within a company, I think about the key relevant factors which are important in learning. The Human Resources manager makes sure that these factors are stimulated in order to make type learning possible.

Exercises for this Lesson
Exercise 2.1: Questionnaire "Your role within your professional context"
Individual: Fill out this questionnaire

1. What kind of business (company, school …) are you working in? What kind of organization is it exactly?

2. What is your function within the organization?

3. What do you think the environment (in its widest sense) of your organization will look like within five years, socially and economically?

4. How does your organization think its role will be five years from now? What strategy is your organization planning to use to interact with the future environment?

5. Who are *you* within your organization? Who are you elsewhere? What is your personal mission in your professional life?

6. If you were to apply for a job with your present employer, what beliefs would you emphasize because you know they would suit your employer?

7. What beliefs would you rather not talk about, because they are not completely compatible?

8. What is important to you in what you are doing? Why is it important?

9. What are the core-skills of your organization? Which of these core-skills match your own core-skills? Which ones should you develop?

Exercise 2.2: Find the neurological level
What neurological level is this on?

	SAYING	NEUROLOGICAL LEVEL
1.	*A newspaper is more than a collection of articles.*	*Belief*
2.	I would love to do it but something prevents me.	
3.	I am a mediocre salesman.	
4.	I cannot keep up a relationship.	
5.	If I make a contribution to society, my life will have been worth living.	
6.	What are you going to do to solve it?	
7.	Where is the bathroom please?	
8.	I am in trouble. How can I get out of it?	
9.	I am out.	
10.	I know I will manage some day.	
11.	I have difficulties following.	
12.	We received many facilities.	
13.	We are good at having meetings.	
14.	Everybody was trying real hard.	
15.	When I am not in a relationship, I feel worthless.	
16.	We are a perfect team.	
17.	Nowadays you have to protect yourself or everything will be taken from you.	
18.	I get my strength from the idea I am contributing to the improvement of the universe.	
19.	This room is not suitable for this training.	
20.	I think this exercise is an easy one.	

Exercise 2.3: How your identity is reflected in your actions

Sum up three things you can do well, that you have. The counsellor asks the following question: *"Why are these things important
to you? What do they give you?"* Keep asking until you obtain replies
at the level of identity.

Identity ....

                 ↑   ↑

Belief ....

                 ↑   ↑

Skill ....
(what I am good at ...)

Exercise 2.4: Values underpinning other people's behavior

Find some examples of other people's behavior which you do not
understand (for example: piercing, camping, gambling, collecting
things ...). Try to find out what personal characteristics and values
these uphold. When you understand this, does it make it easier for
you to accept the other person?

Exercise 2.5: What are your core values?

Sum up ten values which are very important to you and put them
in order of importance.

VALUE	*ORDER*

Imagine you would have to renounce these values one by one in order to survive. Which one would you renounce first and which one wouldn't you renounce at all? To put them in order you might want to compare them two by two and weigh them in your mind. Number the values in the chosen order. Having completed this, how do you feel with your choice? If you're not happy with the order you can choose to reorder them. If you do so, what does that do to the way you perceive yourself, others and the world?

Exercise 2.6: Write down three expressions of the form: "I am ..." or "I am someone who ..."
The counsellor asks: *"How do you know this?"* The explorer looks for the behaviors and beliefs which underlie these expressions of identity. On which level is identity granted?

Identity ....
(I am ...)
(I am someone who ...) ↓   ↓

Beliefs ....

             ↓   ↓

Values ....

             ↓   ↓

Behavior ....

Exercise 2.7: The levels of criticizing
Formulate a criticism about a person and try to fill out the different levels.

Exercise 2.8: Analyzing personal failures

Take one of your own failures (unachieved goal). At which level is your spontaneous expression of failure located? Complete the other levels.

Exercise 2.9: Business analysis

Take a look at the organization you are working for. Formulate a number of striking facts for each neurological level. Begin with your own environment and continue until you have reached a formulation of the organization's identity and mission.

Exercise 2.10: Secondary gains of undesired situations

1. Pick an undesired behavior or a challenge. What are you doing even though you do not want to do it?

2. What do you want to do this for? What is the positive intention of the part which is generating the undesired behavior?

3. The counsellor inquires about the gain: "If you had achieved this, what would it have given you?" The counsellor continues until the explorer comes across an important value.

4. Associate with this important value. Intensely experience having it. Focus on re-accessing the appropriate posture and breathing which defines it. Fix the experience by associating a word, an attitude, an image, a sound and a feeling. Realize you do not have to do anything to be inside the experience. The experience is already there, right at that moment.

5. Stay in the experience and think again of the problem you started with. In what way has the experience been able to help you change the problem?

Exercise 2.11: Hierarchy of values and criteria

1. What am I seeking to achieve in work, life and relationships? What am I seeking to avoid?

2. Draw up two series of values, one for each, and order them according to importance.

3. Test the hierarchy:
   a. What is more important than …
   b. If I have to choose between value A and value B, which is the more important one?
   c. Compare the values to achieve and the values to avoid: what should happen in order to make value B acceptable?

4. If the hierarchy is correctly arranged, answer the following questions: "Does the present hierarchy lead to the choices I want to make in the future? What changes do I need to make in the hierarchy to achieve these choices?"

5. Ecology test. If I swap X and Y, what could go wrong?

6. If the change seems to be necessary, it can be accomplished by changing the submodalities, by using the submodality Switching or Change Beliefs patterns (presented in Lesson 4, pp. 180–181).

Exercise 2.12: Criteria for a job or friend

Two people try to find their criteria for an interesting job. Person A will invite Person B to fill the vacancy, initially by using the personal criteria of Person A, secondly by using those of Person B. Calibrate the difference.

Example:
   —Criteria of Person A: *"I think you will find this an interesting job. It is challenging and you will learn a lot."*
   —Criteria of Person B: *"I think this is an interesting job for you. It is a permanent job in a company with qualified management."*
   —Reverse roles and use the criteria for a friend.

Lesson 3:
Planning for Success

"To who does not know where he wants to go
there is no favourable wind."
Seneca

Goals

In this chapter you will achieve the
following four goals:

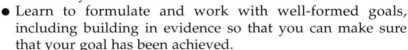

- Establish a framework which will
  enable you to clearly understand the
  difference between your current
  state and your desired state.
- Learn to formulate and work with well-formed goals,
  including building in evidence so that you can make sure
  that your goal has been achieved.
- Obtain an understanding of potential obstacles and sources
  of help to overcome them.
- Create the appropriate attitude to bring about the changes
  you want, both in yourself and in others.

Neurolinguistic Assumptions

In this chapter we will mainly apply the three following
assumptions:

- *In a learning process, there is no such thing as failure: each result
  is a feedback.*
- *At any given time, what you do is the best choice you are aware of.
  We therefore do not take away or replace choices, but add more
  choices.*
- *A person with the greatest flexibility of behavior stands the best
  chance of achieving the result that they wish.*

Why this lesson?

- In our definition of Emotional Intelligence we made you
  realize that, in addition to dealing with yourself (the intrapersonal), a significant proportion of your focus is directed
  towards achieving solutions in your environment and with

other people (the interpersonal). The Well-Formed Change model and especially the TOTE model we present below will help you to understand how you can set to work.

● Many people suffer from "undesired" emotions which they would rather be rid of. Very much has been invested into achieving desired emotions and yet undesired emotions stubbornly continue to occur. Working with an appropriate "means-end" structure will increase your effectiveness. Changework needs to meet a number of "well-formedness" principles. If these are respected, you will significantly enhance your effectiveness at managing your emotions.

Our approach is twofold in this chapter. On the one hand you will learn to work with your emotions within the framework of a planned and purposeful approach. On the other hand you will discover broader ways of changing your conditioned responses and emotions. We present a staged plan below which you can apply to deal with undesired emotions.

Introduction: Models for Effectiveness

Emotional Intelligence is necessary to achieve your plans. If you have not realized this yet, consider the number of people who go for interviews or take exams, who may have all the facts at their fingertips and yet break down or underperform under stress. A sound engineer said once that the best sound system you can have is only as good as the speakers you have plugged into it. You may have all the intellectual resources or qualifications to achieve something, but if you are let down by your emotions, what use were they to you? Your output was not up to what you had planned.

In life we make many more plans than we are aware of. What is actually involved in the planning process? List for yourself five projects (professional, personal, hobby, holiday, personal development, small or large …) you were concerned with over the past six months. Were all these equally successful? If not, what's the difference between those you consider achievements and the others?

In relation to your accomplishments, ask yourself the question: "How did I do that?"

In relation to the less-than-successful ones, ask yourself: "Why did my plan fail?" Could it be that:

- Perhaps you were not really sure about what your goal was, or it did not lie within your personal range.
- Perhaps the goal seemed so distant to you that you could not represent in your mind the intermediary steps required to achieve it.
- Perhaps you did not know which actions were the most appropriate to reach your goal, or you were simply unable to take the necessary actions.
- Perhaps the way you planned prevented you from taking possible changes in circumstance into account.
- Perhaps you did want to achieve your goal but, in contrast to Machiavelli, found that the end did not justify the required means and was not worth it.
- Perhaps your goal was incompatible with others you had set, or with the requirements that your environment placed upon you.
- Perhaps it was something else we have not mentioned yet.

The subject of this chapter is to optimize your chances at succeeding in your plans. The first requirement for any successful plan is therefore to know what your goal is. So, what do you actually want to achieve? Let us draw inspiration from the Cheshire Cat in *Alice in Wonderland*:

Alice:	*"Can you tell me which road I must take?"*
The Cat:	*"That depends: Where do you want to go?"*
Alice:	*"I don't know."*
The Cat:	*"Then it doesn't matter which road you take."*

In other words: unless you want to wander about aimlessly, set yourself a goal. If you have an aim in mind and take a step in

> **If you don't know where you're going, how will you know you've got there?**

the direction of your goal, then you are further ahead than if you had taken a step in another direction. However, the direction in which you step depends on where you stand now and where you set your focus. So identify your starting point and your finishing point, as this will define your trajectory. After all, if an Englishman wants to go from London to Brussels, he will travel in a different direction from a Frenchman who sets off from Paris.

Once you know where you stand now (current state) and where you want to go (your goal or the desired state), you need to determine the steps (actions) you need to take to achieve your goal. When you're on the way, you need to be able to monitor whether your actions are taking you in the right direction; if not, you must adapt your actions (your plan) to get back on track. By constantly adapting your plan, you take into account the famous pronouncement of Dwight Eisenhower: "A plan is useless, but planning is essential." Whereas a plan is a description of the path that you want to follow from a current state to a desired state, planning is the process that you go through to come to a plan.

> **If you're not going anywhere there aren't any obstacles.**

Finally there are the resistances, the inertias, that your plan generates, both in yourself and in others. Is the path that you have mapped out for yourself actually acceptable? What do the people around you think about it? Do they unconsciously agree also with your rational explanation, or do you encounter active or passive resistance? The former is usually better than the latter as you, at least, know what you set yourself up against. The English comedy series "Yes, Minister," where a well-meaning Minister of the Crown faces the inertia of Civil Servant bureaucrats seeking to preserve the status quo at all costs—better the devil you know— perfectly demonstrates both styles of resistance. In the business world and elsewhere, you will often see people nodding their heads in agreement and actually doing the contrary in practice. The 18th century French king Louis XV is reported to have said: "Après moi, le déluge," or "After me, the Flood."[1]

The TOTE Model: The Structure of Flexible Plans

If somebody proffers you a hand, you have the choice of shaking it or refusing to take it. The traditional, strictly behavioristic stimulus-response model appears too limited to explain this choice in

---

[1]   There is no proof that he actually made such a statement, which may have been a piece of revolutionary propaganda at the time. However, the French Revolution DID occur 15 years after he died.

behavior. According to this theory you should respond to the extended hand (the stimulus) in an invariant fashion (the learned response). In practice we are rarely conscious of the intermediary steps involved between the stimulus and the response, but we at least know that we have a choice in our way of responding.

Elaborated in 1956 by Miller, Galanter and Pribram, the TOTE model expands on the stimulus-response model by adding choices made on the basis of feedback loops. The initials T.O.T.E. stand for: TEST(1)—OPERATION—TEST(2)—EXIT.

> *"... a TOTE is essentially a sequence of activities in our sensory representational systems that has become consolidated into a functional unit of behavior such that it is typically executed below the threshold of consciousness."*[2]

The feedback loop concept had been used for many years in engineering, but for the first time the authors applied a similar model to human thought patterns. Adding the principle of the feedback loop to the behavioristic model allows us to take the results of our previous actions into consideration when carrying out a task. A thermostat observes the same principle: by testing whether it deviates from a desired result and taking action depending on this result, namely switching the heating on or off time and again as required, it controls the temperature in your house.

The great merit of the TOTE model is its *systemic character.* The model allows us to take all peripheral events into consideration when taking action, and thus also to take into account the results and consequences of our previous actions.

---

[2]   Miller, Galanter, and Pribram (1960). *The TOTE Model: Plans and the Structure of Behavior,* Henry Holt and Co.

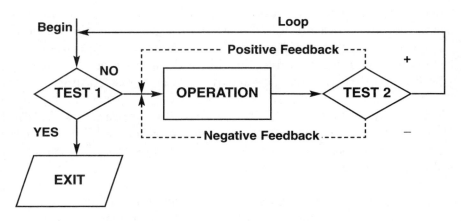

Figure 3.1: The TOTE model as feedback loop

Here is a simple example:

Start: Subject of the Plan: I want to travel from London to Brussels.
TEST 1: Am I already in Brussels?
Answer: No
Operation: I start to travel.
TEST 2: Am I getting nearer to Brussels?
Answer: No *(Negative feedback)*
TEST 1: Am I already in Brussels?
Answer: No

> All journeys lead to Rome, but some take longer than others.

Operation: New action (on basis of feedback): travel in another direction
TEST 1: Am I already in Brussels?
Answer: No
TEST 2: Am I getting nearer to Brussels?
Answer: Yes *(Positive feedback)*
Operation: Same action (improve on basis of feedback): Travel somewhat

> Go slow, Jean, I'm in a hurry.
> *Talleyrand, to his barber*

faster (or slower, depending on the speed limit)
TEST 1: Am I in Brussels? Answer: YES
EXIT: I am there, so I can stop.

We can now extend this example to a general definition:

Step 0: Preparation

(Formulate your well-formed goal)

Step 1: Go through the feedback loop:

- **TEST 1**: measurement of the difference between current and desired state
- **OPERATION:** the step, the behavior or the activity which you carry out to achieve your goal, or to come nearer to your goal.

  To determine your operation, use any information (feedback) which you have obtained from previous operations. (Remember the neurolinguistic assumption: *There is no failure, there is only feedback!*)
- **TEST 2:** After the "operation," test to determine whether the set behavior leads to your goal—if relevant, use this information in the subsequent operation.

Repeat Step 1 until the goal is achieved.

- **EXIT:** Stop if at "TEST 1" you no longer have any difference between the current and the desired state.

Let us now examine more thoroughly the components of the definition.

Formulate your well-formed goal

The above model presupposes as its starting point that you have already formulated your outcome and that you know how to achieve it before you start to carry out your plan. Practice shows, however, that formulating such a goal

> The journey of a lifetime begins with a single step.

in a way which optimizes your chance of success is not as easy as it appears at first sight. However, we recommend five criteria below to help you formulate your goal in a well-formed way (Figure 3.2).

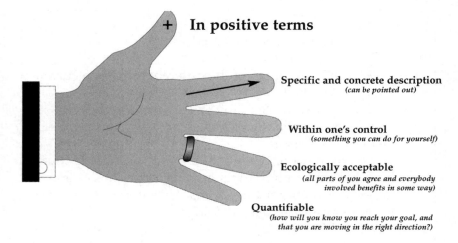

+ **In positive terms**

Specific and concrete description
(can be pointed out)

Within one's control
(something you can do for yourself)

Ecologically acceptable
*(all parts of you agree and everybody
involved benefits in some way)*

Quantifiable
*(how will you know you reach your goal, and
that you are moving in the right direction?)*

Figure 3.2: Five criteria of well-formedness

By offering examples and counter-examples, the following table expands on the well-formedness criteria presented in the figure. It also indicates what questions you can ask to make a goal "well-formed." If the following criteria are not met, there is a good chance that your plan will not work. On the other hand, if they are, knowing that the power to change, to grow and to move forward lies within your own control should give you much cause for optimism.

Criteria	*Examples: NOT*	*Ask the question:*	*Examples: YES*
1. Positive terms	• I do not want to be depressed any more • I no longer want to react so sensitively when I receive criticism • I no longer want to fail in a job application	What do I want then?	• I want to feel alive • I want to maintain a good feeling about myself when I receive criticism • I want to come across as self-assured in my application
2. Specific and concrete	• I want to start my life again • I want a good team spirit on my shift	What do I want to achieve precisely? Where, when and with whom do I want to achieve it?	• From tomorrow I want to look for a job that matches my possibilities • I want people to laugh and have their say
3. Under your own control	• I want my boss to be friendly • I want my neighbours to give us some peace	What can I do to achieve this?	• I will talk informally with my boss in a friendly way to convince him that … • I will talk to my neighbours so that they give us some peace
4. Quantifiable	• I want to sell more • I want to get rid of my asthma	How will I know that I have achieved my goal? What will I see, hear, feel? By when exactly and realistically?	• I want to increase my sales by 20% by (give date) • I want to reduce my asthmatic reaction by six points (plotted on a subjective scale)
5. Ecological (Personal ethics)	• Tomorrow I will actually start to work again (after a heart transplant) • I want the same blind trust in my new relationship	What could be the disadvantages of achieving my goal? What advantages can I lose by achieving my goal? Are there other things which I need to take into account?	• I will see how I can continue my work and still respect my heart • I want to have trust and also to be careful so that I do not repeat the same mistake

Other preparations

Well begun is half won ...

- Determine also the present state. Although your goal is the desired state, you can extend the preparation by describing the current state. On what foundations are you planning to build?

> **Patton's Law:**
> A good plan today is better than a "perfect" plan tomorrow.

- Determine what the possible risks and side-effects are.
- Determine what else you could do (this list does not need to be complete. However, think of the neurolinguistic assumption that the more choices of possible behaviors you have, the more chances of success).
- Determine how you will find out the positive or negative consequences of your goal.

Note: The SMART principle

You also come across the principle of well-formed goals outside the field of neurolinguistics *per se*. The SMART principle, which largely corresponds to what we have described above was developed in the context of quality management:

S.	*Specific*	*cf. 1. Positive terms & 2—specific and concrete*
M.	*Measurable*	*cf. 4—quantifiable*
A.	*Acceptable*	*cf. 5—Ecological*
R.	*Realizable*	*cf. 3—under your own control*
T.	*Timed*	*an addition in comparison with the principles of well-formedness*

You know the expression "Time flies: use it well." What the SMART principle adds to the criteria of well-formedness is the Western emphasis on *timing*. Since the beginning of the industrial period and with the advent of the railways, our way of life has continuously put the focus on time. In Europe, in the Middle Ages, the emphasis still lay on the permanent, the timeless. God stands outside time and  nothing changes for eternity ... Humans, on the other hand, are ephemeral and bound in time. Were you aware that clocks began to show the same standardized time only with the spread of railways? In 1880 the British Parliament decreed in the Time Act that all cities in the UK should display "London Time." Until that time noon was determined locally, by the way the sun was at its highest in the sky at each location. The local time in Bristol, for example, differed by 17 minutes from London time. So, in order for all railways to use the same time, a "time-check" was transmitted via the telegraph every morning at 9 o'clock. This standardization allowed for progress in communication and the set-up of timetables, such as Baedeker, so appreciated by Sherlock Holmes and many more real people. These, in turn, allowed industries and individuals to plan and schedule travel and transport well in advance.

This Western emphasis on deadlines, however, can also be counter-productive, as it operates at the expense of the quality of the result one gets. Often deadlines are set up unrealistically or without taking into account the imponderables which could delay or derail a project. Crippling penal-

> **Hofstadter's Law:**
> It always takes more time than you think,
> even if you take Hofstadter's law into account.

ties are often imposed for projects which miss the deadline, forcing people to cut corners: they may thereby neglect safety factors essential to the success of the initiative and afterwards gloss over aspects of the plan which have been neglected in order to cover their tracks. Along with cost-cutting exercises, recent setbacks in several Mars missions carried out by NASA have been shown to be of this type. The alternative, namely to dare request a postponement in order to achieve a better result, generally appears unacceptable. In addition, deadlines, which are attempts at ironing out natural rhythms of life, have been shown to have a negative effect on people. Stress and many health complaints are often the consequence of unrealistic or inappropriate deadlines.

So, put emphasis on result, rather than on date of completion. Combine this with regular evaluation: "Measurability is knowledge!" This type of combined attitude allows space to consider additional measures for achieving the planned goal.

> *Tip:* Set a flexible deadline: when do you expect, realistically, to achieve the result? Schedule moments of stock-taking: when do you evaluate how far you have got?

The relevance of your goal

Have you ever worked hard the whole day and had the feeling in the evening that you hadn't made much headway? Are your priorities right? What happens if your plan is not carried out? How does this plan relate to other plans that you still have? Intuitively we have the tendency to do first the things which appear urgent.

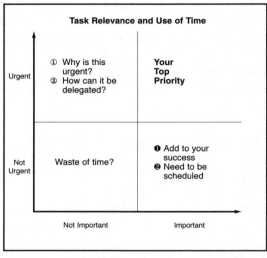

Task Relevance and Use of Time

	Not Important	Important
Urgent	① Why is this urgent? ② How can it be delegated?	**Your Top Priority**
Not Urgent	Waste of time?	❶ Add to your success ❷ Need to be scheduled

We often forget to ask ourselves whether the matter is important. Matters that seem urgent, but not important, sometimes do not need to be done at all! Work smarter, not harder! Of course, you require a fair amount of Emotional Intelligence to see this. If others are involved in this urgent matter you may need some additional EQ to get the message across.

How much time do you devote to work, hobbies, family life, friends, your health (a healthy mind in a healthy body)? Divide your time across all areas in your life, so that all receive a fair and equitable share of your focus. If one of them is prioritized at the expense of the others, you may literally suffer the consequences of doing so, like the manager who wanted to be promoted to a national level within the year: by the end of that year, he had indeed been promoted nationally but had been caught for speeding, had had two car accidents and a heart attack, and was about to divorce his wife and lose his kids, who complained they never saw him any more! Was it all worth it? To use a neurolinguistic expression derived from systems theory, he had seriously compromised his ecology. Take this into account when planning objectives! Shift from the concept of maximization to that of optimization. After all, more is not better: better is better!

Tip: Determine your **priorities**: What is important for you? Where do you deliver optimal instead of maximal added value?

Step 1. The feedback loop

Once you have made a well-formed plan, you need to have enough self-confidence to put it into effect. If you know what you are doing, your plan stands a good chance of succeeding. You also know the respective advantages and disadvantages of your decision and are prepared to live with the consequences of this decision. Therefore, you do not need to assume an arrogant or defensive attitude.

"The proof of the pudding is in the eating," goes the saying. You will know how good the plan was only when you have the result in your hand. During the feedback loop you continue to carry out activities until you achieve your goal. By using the information you obtained through or during the activities you carried out as part of your learning experience and feedback, you are now able to make your next step even more effective.

We live in a culture where failure is absolute. Is it ever? Remember the saying: "success is 99% failure." There are often many more learning opportunities in a situation where you failed than in one where you succeeded, especially if you don't want to make the same mistake again. Progress is based on trial and error: many scientific discoveries and even cookery recipes were discovered as a result of a mistake. Our blame-oriented culture does not allow for failure, not realizing that it is integral to the learning process: thus people who have often never carried out a particular task are expected to get it 100% right first time. If the first time a baby learning to walk falls on his backside he entertains the thought: "I have failed at walking: I shall never try it again," he will never be able to walk. And where would we be if, likewise, our distant ancestors, having burnt their fingers when trying to pick up a burning ember, had thought "Ouch, never touch that stuff again!"? So, if you make mistakes, do not consider that as a failure, but learn from them!

More Choice EQUALS More Success

The wider the range of activities you can carry out, the more flexibility you develop, and the greater your chance of success. "If you only have a hammer, then you tend to perceive every problem as a nail," said Maslow. To be able to genuinely speak about choice you need at least three possibilities: with one possibility it is clear that you have no choice (and act like a robot), and with two possibilities you are faced with a dilemma.

According to Harvard historian David Landes,[3] flexibility explains why, from the Middle Ages to the 19th century, Europe was ahead in the social, technological and economic evolution. In the same period, in China, state interference weighed lead-heavy on society. "Mandarinism suffocated the entire life beneath rules. Every deviation or renewal was nipped in the bud," as when the exploring navigator Zheng Ho, who, at the beginning of the 15th century, had reached the

> **If You Have NO Choice, You're DEAD!**
> **If You Have ONE Choice, You're STUCK!**
> **If You Have TWO Choices, You're In A QUANDARY.**
> **If You Have THREE Choices, NOW YOU'RE UP TO CHOICE: Choose To Have AT LEAST FIVE Choices!**

east coast of Africa and set up commercial links, and upon returning to China was forbidden to travel again.

Remember also the operational assumption: "If somebody can do something, then so can I." This should give you extra strength and self-confidence to take others as an example and to do things that you have never done before.

---

[3] Landes, David S. (1999). *The Wealth and Poverty of Nations: Why Some Are So Rich and Some So Poor,* W.W. Norton & Company.

Further discussion
Make your plans manageable

"The secret of making progress is to get started. The secret of starting is to divide your complex, overwhelming task into small, manageable tasks, and then start the first," says Mark Twain. Some years ago a book based on this principle appeared under the title *Eating the*

> **Knagg's derivative of Murphy's Law:**
> The more complicated
> and grandiose the plan,
> the greater the chance
> of failure.

Elephant.[4] According to this book, eating an elephant is easy: first cut it into small chunks, and then eat them one by one. With that we mean that you split up a large goal into manageable steps, and for each step establish a separate TOTE.

Learn from your plans

In a time management course you learn how *others* make and carry out plans. So, be your own teacher: learn what went well from your plans and use this experience when making new plans. Ask yourself the question: "What could I have done more efficiently?" or "Which steps could I have missed out?"

If it appears that you do not achieve some specific results and continue to put off specific tasks, ask yourself what this means, as it may indeed reveal something about your personal "Ecology." If, say, you had planned to contact particular people and did not, ask: "Was the goal really acceptable for myself and the other persons concerned? What does this say

> **Logic makes people think.**
> **Emotion makes people act.**

about my relationship with these people? Is my behavior based on rational thought or on emotions? How do I know the difference between the rational and the emotional?"

---

[4]   Rainer, Thom S. (1999). *Eating the Elephant: Bite-Sized Steps to Achieve Long-Term Growth in Your Church*, Broadman & Holman.

Trust your own unconscious

The experience that we have built up with the TOTE model in neurolinguistics shows that you can utilize this way of setting goals to program your unconscious in order to achieve the results you desire. The approach works as follows:

> You get what you focus on, so focus on what you want.

- Draw up your goal, taking care that it is well-formed and that a few activities have been set in its direction.
- Then set aside your preparation and work on this goal in parallel with another one that you have already set for yourself.
- Some time later revisit your goal and notice how far you stand with regards to the implementation of your plan. You will be surprised how much you have already achieved.

An ideal application of this is to set yourself some key learning goals for a somewhat longer term. If opportunities present themselves, or if there is some time left over, choose to focus it on learning goals. After some time make a list of all that you have accomplished, small things included, which has contributed to your learning goal. You will realize that you are already much further than you expected!

There is a difference between "doing good things" and "doing things well." If you carry out a plan according to the letter, and achieve the result you desire, then you have done things well ... However, remember that the world around you does not stand still. Thus you may realize that, despite the fact that you have achieved the result you expected, your plan now appears irrelevant or even obsolete!

Flexible Agenda:
1. Leave time for unexpected and spontaneous activities.
2. Be willing to adapt your agenda to new opportunities.
3. Take others into account while planning.

A fine example of this is Microsoft's "MSN" service. When this service was first planned, in 1994, the Internet was still quite unknown. They had barely even heard of it at Microsoft. MSN was set up as a closed communication network, intended as a competitor against America Online and CompuServe, then the two largest closed networks of computer users. By the time the plan was implemented, at the launch of Windows '95, the product already appeared overtaken. While Microsoft had carried out its plan, the rest of world had discovered the Internet! Other private networks had already begun to open up in abundance on the net. As a result, MSN did not become the success they had anticipated, and it was repositioned as an Internet website a year after its launch. The physical network was dismantled in Europe and limited to the role of Internet provider in the United States.

Another, more recent case, is that of the Iridium satellite telephone network. Mobile phones were in their infancy when the project of connecting people together by direct satellite access to a mobile telephone unit was conceived. The unit was cumbersome, though, and costly to support. By the time the whole network of satellites had become operational, the market of mobile phones as we know them had exploded, at costs, speeds and ease of use far better than that which Iridium could hope to provide, and the network closed in 1999.

Morality: Do not carry out your plan with blinkers on! Regularly step out of your feedback loop and check out your plan with the external reality. Continually ask yourself the relevance question, taking into account the changes which may occur around you.

Regularly distance yourself from your daily pursuits to reflect on the actions that you carried out during the elapsed period. How did you allocate your time in relation to the different result areas in your life? Did they all receive an appropriate share of your energies? Review the activities you have planned for the coming period. Are

> The Past is history,
> The Future is a myth,
> But NOW is a gift,
> Which is why we call it
> The Present.

you so focused on the short-term that you neglect the long-term implications? Are you, on the other hand, so busy thinking ahead that you can't relax and enjoy just the present?

> ***Tip:*** Block off a weekly period for review. Spend about 15 minutes going over what you have done in the previous week, and appreciate the results! Make notes of your findings.
> Allocate an evaluation day each quarter: what results did you achieve over the past quarter (on the basis of your weekly notes/compared with your objectives)? What are your plans for the following quarter? Take note!

Plans and stress management

Without Stress Management

How much pleasure do you experience in your job? Do you agree with Bertolt Brecht when he said, "Work is everything from which you don't derive any pleasure?" In our culture, enjoyment of work and stress appear incompatible.

Not everyone, however, seems to suffer equally from stress. Among the ways which have been identified to protect yourself better against the consequences of stress, your general condition (your weight, the amount of sport you do, etc.) and your mental health (how much you learn from it, do you get enough training?) appear at the top. Professor Cary Cooper, in his book *Living with Stress*[5] (1988), points out the causes and consequences of stress. Quite a few symptoms of "dis-ease," such as headaches, stomach problems, back complaints and sleep problems often appear related to stress. According to Cooper and his colleague Richard Lazarus, stress depends on how you perceive a particular situation—if you consider it as threatening, for example—and how you deal with it. In particular, situations in which you feel powerless or helpless are identified as causes of stress. Research on rats shows that even they develop stress if they have no sense of control over their situation. Some people never learn how to cope with a situation, while others "discover" that their normal way of responding does not work for particular problems, and thus they learn to become "helpless." Extreme forms of learned helplessness lead to depression.

5   Cooper, Cary (1988). *Living with Stress*, Harmondsworth, Penguin.

People feel helpless if they have no control over their situation, regardless of whether this is actually so or not. The source of their stress seems to be their perception of reality. Note how "under one's control" is one of the well-formedness principles that we described above. The crucial question to ask is whether it is actually the case that people really have "no control" over their situation. An investigation of some 60 participants in courses on the probability of success of plans showed that most were able to redefine their plan in such a way that they felt their result was within their control.[6] Those who do not think this generally perceive the block as relating to assertiveness, or lack thereof. They obtain an assignment and dare not redefine this in mutual consultation as something which lies within their control.

Can you guess the consequence of such a response? That's right. It is likely their stress matches the definition that the neurolinguist Richard Bandler offers us: "Stress is the uncontrollable urge of your body to wring one or more idiots' necks."

With Stress Management

Stress management includes the following steps:
1. Estimate and evaluate your emotional state (see Lessons 1 and 2).
2. If you decide that you can get more enjoyment out of life, decide how you're going to go about it.
3. Promise yourself to really take action.
4. Carry out the actions you have committed yourself to.
5. Evaluate whether the actions you took are having their effect.

Each of these five steps requires specific skills. If somebody suffers from stress, you can also use the above model as a diagnostic tool (so that you know about the subskill you need to work on).

---

[6] 7EQ training sessions organized by Patrick Merlevede in 1997–1998.

What happens if you do not make any TOTEs?

Instead of setting up goals in our future, we can also look back at our past. Paul Watzlawick[7] describes in a cynical way how you can make yourself miserable. We summarize here a few of his rules of thumb:

> **Whose agenda do you follow? Plan your life or it will be planned for you!**

1. Imagine that everything was better before. Compare this to the way everything has gone wrong since.

2. Use your past failures as an excuse not to work on your future. After all, it can only go wrong again.

3. Remind yourself that your situation is hopeless and is the consequence of your past choices, about which there is nothing more to be done but to feel bad.

4. Realize that there is only one correct way of doing something and if that does not work, then you have to go on doing it, only harder. Of course, never doubt for one moment that your approach is the only correct one.

We personally do not think that such "rules" are very compatible with the principles of well-formedness. Although the situations they describe appear somewhat ridiculous or even far-fetched, at least to an observer, are they?

In the same vein, Michael Hall, one of the foremost new thinkers in the field of neurolinguistics, often remarks on the way that people who feel stressed experience their stress in relation to issues that they perceive as Personal, Pervasive and Permanent, which he calls the three Ps. He is fond of saying: "When you P all over yourself like this, is it any surprise you experience stress?" On the other hand, what happens to your stress levels when you realize that your problem (another P) is not about who you are but just about what you do, and that it is both contextualized in space and limited in time?

---

[7]   In his book *The Situation Is Hopeless But Not Serious*, W.W. Norton & Company, 1983.

A few examples:

1. Somebody hears a report on the radio on the rise of the oil price. He gets worked up over how expensive life is and says: "In a few years we won't be able to afford our caravan holidays in France." (Taking into account inflation and the rise in income, a litre of petrol in Western Europe in 2001 costs less than it did before the 70s oil crisis.)

2. A man says: "I don't want to alter my house any more. I won't start on it any more. Those workmen always make mistakes. After the previous alteration there was a leak in the water pipe!" (His previous water plumbing still had lead pipes, and his wife wanted to replace them with plastic—plastic pipes leak less, and, furthermore, lead is toxic ...)

3. "When I was 16 I wanted to leave school, and now I am unemployed. Uneducated people are no longer needed. But now, of course, it is too late ... (Different training programs for long-term unemployed persons have proved that you are literally never too old to learn a new occupation.)

4. A woman finds that her husband does not help enough with the washing-up. She does not want a dishwasher, "for it's really nice to do the washing-up together." Then she moans until he comes to give her a hand instead of lying on the sofa in front of the TV. (Solution: what, besides washing-up, could you recommend as a suitable activity to have an "enjoyable chat"?

In each of the above examples the person fails to make a plan to get out of their situation, owing to their respective negative "thinking viruses." However, none of these thought patterns in and by itself forms a real hindrance on your road to successful plans. Consider this for yourself!

> The choices you make determine how you will spend your time.

Emotions as conditioned reflexes

In order to better manage your emotional resources, we invite you to reflect on the following presuppositions:

1. Emotions are connecting links in a chain of mental and physical operations.
2. We can map out each of the links of this chain.
3. We can change the links to improve the chain or create a different one.

In that they seem to occur as a direct and instinctive reaction to a given impulse, many emotional reactions resemble reflexes, seemingly outside our direct control. If you consult the literature on neuroscience, you'll often read how they are considered innate biological reflexes emanating from the limbic system, our so-called "reptilian" brain. The most quoted examples are the "flight or fight"[8] responses.

However, when you analyze an emotion, you often find that this so-called reflex is actually an acquired one. After all, if they were innate, we'd never be able to enjoy indulging in activities like rock-climbing, bungee-jumping or watching fireworks. When you compare the way different people respond to similar stimuli, you can actually identify a range of differences which would not occur if emotions were innate:

- **Individual differences:** in the same family or even between identical twins, one child may respond to a challenge with fear or anxiety, while a sibling will seek to rise to such a challenge and even search for them.

- **Differences between families:** having absorbed the behavior patterns of their parents from a pre-verbal stage, children will usually repeat such patterns unquestioningly. Their emotional responses will depend on what is permitted, encouraged or repressed in a family, such as freely expressing anger as opposed to always showing a

---

[8] These should more accurately be called *"Face, Flee or Freeze,"* as you can face something without having to fight it, or run away without having to be afraid, as occurred in the Roman war against the Sabines when the last Roman champion Horatius ran away to better trap the three Sabine champions, the Curiatii. But the above expression is now in common parlance and, as such, perpetuates metaphors such as *"Argument is Warfare."*

smile. As no two families are identical, so the spectrum of *"embraced —encouraged—acceptable—frowned upon—unacceptable—taboo"* emotions will vary between families.

- **Cultural differences:** in the same way that cultural differences will vary from family to family, these will also prevail in extended families, communities and cultures. For example you find a higher incidence of guilt in Judeo-Christian cultures, which emphasize such concepts as sin, while in countries such as Japan, shame will be much more common.

In Lesson 2 we demonstrated how emotional reactions are characterized by an *embodied feeling* to which we give a meaning/label. Emotions change over time, dwindling, vanishing or sometimes mutating into other emotions, and the fact that some eventually "wear out" is related to a process of "deconditioning." Such deconditioning often occurs as a result of new behaviors, learnings and beliefs that the person acquires and incorporates into their "personality." So, change IS possible, especially when you keep working at your self-management and apply techniques such as the ones we present in this book. The extent to which you will invest in this self-management remains a personal decision. Whereas some people might choose to limit themselves to carrying out some superficial polishing by reducing the suffering caused by "unwanted" emotions, you might prefer to strive to achieve happiness, pleasure and control over your "self" and thus work to optimize your emotional potential.

In addition to deconditioning processes, a second, complementary way of changing emotions consists of finding their meaning and thereby changing the effect each has on us. Even if the emotion is related to a conditioning acquired during early childhood, applying some of the processes presented in this book will enable you to identify their meaning for you. Although a three-year-old child may have difficulties in expressing such a meaning cognitively, they may be better able to demonstrate it physically in their body language. Of course, this doesn't make it easier to find the meaning of such conditioned emotions hidden in deeper layers of one's being. For example, Stanislav Grof, who founded the field of Transpersonal Psychology, postulates that many uncontrollable emotional behaviors, such as anxiety, fury, rage and loss, arise out of the perinatal period of life—the period immediately before, during and after childbirth. It is indeed striking, when working with clients, how commonly they identify this period as the time when such primeval emotions began. Occurring so early in the life of a child they would not have been encoded in language terms, but in purely behavioral ones.[9]

Such conditionings arising in early childhood may also be hidden behind a chain of emotional states. To give you an extreme example, let us refer to some cases of alcohol abuse we have worked on.

As we did in the last lesson, we ask the following questions:

- "What is the positive intention of the desire to drink?"
- "What exactly occurs when this desire surfaces?"
- "What does this desire want for you?"
- "What happened just before this desire surfaced?"

In one particular case, we found that the person had difficulties coping with frustration. As soon as something didn't work out as planned, he'd get lost. He would complain about each boss he ever had, and basically run away from one job to the next. This was a clear case of an "avoidance strategy." He literally "fled into alcohol." Drinking kept him from feeling frustrated. In fact, the moment frustration appeared, the desire to drink would ensue.

So the question became: "Why is this person in pain? Where does this frustration come from?"

Finally, after tracking this reasoning down a chain of meanings, the answer came from deep within the person: "I want the world that surrounds me to be good, because I want to feel good myself."

L. Michael Hall has recently identified such chains of meaning as Meta-States, or States-About-Other-States. He identified that there are some states which we experience *in response to the world*: these are outwardly focused and he calls them Primary States. Others,

---

9   Grof, S. (1993). *The Holotropic Mind,* San Francisco, HarperCollins.

by contrast, do not arise in response to the world, but *in response to our response,* and he calls such inwardly focused states Meta-States. Most of the emotional states we experience every day are thus not Primary States, but Meta-States. These occur as a result of our ability, evolved through language, to reflect upon ourselves and on our reflecting in a seemingly infinite regress. Michael has been developing his discipline of Neuro-Semantics,[10] an offshoot and expansion of neurolinguistics, from the mid-1990s to study and work on such Meta-States and has developed many patterns for working with them.[11]

So, at an identity level our client who abused alcohol had to cope with a negative self-image. He experienced the world as a dangerous place which threatened his opportunities to have good feelings. To him, it felt as if he barely had a right to live.

By using the model of the neurological levels, you'll understand that this is no longer a case of working with a positive intention at the level of values and beliefs, but that we have to face a profound identity crisis, linked to a self-image of "I, as a person, cannot be accepted in this world."

Somebody once said that communication could be reduced to two types: one is an expression of love, the other a cry for help. Which categories do you think some of your behaviors and emotions fall into?

Further studies show that most early-childhood conditionings are related to negative self-experiences. Once you take the time to re-establish the link between the emotion and its source, you create space for a new, more "grown-up," self-image: the "upgrading" happens by itself. To further support and bolster this new self-image, you can add supporting beliefs, capabilities and behaviors as we showed in the previous lesson.

---

[10]   Neuro-Semantics brings together NLP and General Semantics to study and work on the way we construct meaning, evaluate events and experiences and assign significances.

[11]   L. Michael Hall has written many books, several of them with this publisher. His discovery of Meta-States is revolutionizing the field of neurolinguistics. The book in which he first presented his new model is called: *Meta-States: a Domain of Logical Levels. Self-Reflexiveness in Human States of Consciousness,* Empowerment Technologies, Grand Junction, Co, 1996.

If you need to tackle persistent conditionings, we recommend you operate from a broad field of parallel actions, not just the area where the problem manifests, taking a long-term perspective wherever required and acknowledging the full spectrum of your personality. After all, we are systemic beings and, although a work-related concern may not appear connected to personal or health-related issues, it often has reflections or counterparts in these other areas. Focusing solely on one such area may appear to work in the short term, but the concern may remain in existence in other areas, from which it could transfer back onto the initial problem area. So, in order to really resolve an embodied conditioning, you will need to take a multi-dimensional integrated approach over an extended period of time, especially if you work on your own. An alternative may be to find somebody you trust to work with you, or a professional therapist who specializes in neurolinguistics, as they ideally should know how to operate with such concerns.

Conclusion:
Some Tips for Emotional Development

Given what we have already covered in this first part of the book, we'd like to give you an overview of the ingredients required for effective emotional changework. You need to be able to:

1. Distinguish between emotions, thoughts, behavior, skills and context. Look at your emotions from a distance and re-establish the link between the emotion and a sensory-specific experience.[12]

2. Find the meaning of the emotion.

3. Discover the specific role of the emotion in the process of conditioning.

4. State what other emotional reaction you'd like to experience in a given context.

---

[12] The further chapters of this book will give you further additional techniques for achieving this goal. At this point, it is sufficient to know that "sensory-specific" means that you describe the experience in terms of what you *see, hear, feel, smell and taste*. Further discussion of question-asking techniques, representational systems, submodalities and perceptual positions will deepen your awareness of this topic.

5. Find a reference experience where you fully experienced this desired emotion. Apply the anchoring technique to transfer this emotion as presented in Lesson 1.

6. Take a long-term perspective in relationship to your change process. Give the old pattern time to be replaced by a new one you're generating for yourself.

As people become older, you'll notice some of them start talking more and more about things they could have done, or should have done, but didn't do. Yet, they also have the choice to discuss things they did and things they are going to do. To us, the latter seems more fun! Choose to do the things you want to do!

Application 1: Sharing Goals with Others

Now that you are able to study an effective way of setting goals for yourself and of realizing these goals, a drawback might be that you would want to limit yourself to goals which are within your own control. We are systemic beings, having systems within us and forming part of systems which themselves operate in a social and cultural context. As Emotional Intelligence therefore makes sense only in such a context, we need to address the remaining question, namely: "How can you increase the likelihood of success of *common goals*? Wouldn't it be nice to identify and generate goals which will contribute to the common welfare?" Some people are rather selfish in the goals they pursue. Behaving unecologically, they neglect this possible way of contributing to the greater well-being of their society or culture. Take, for instance, the manager who tries to manipulate his employees using fear and doubt, so that he gets the results he wants. And was Harry Truman correct to state that the core skill of leadership consists in making people do the things they don't like to do in such a way that they enjoy it?

Cicero said that the fallacy of believing that you could gain personally by cheating others was one of the biggest mistakes of mankind. In this section we'd like to assert a difference between plans which are realized at a cost (paid by others) and actual, sincere efforts of collaboration to generate commonly agreed goals.

Yes, of course, one can be successful by accomplishing goals set by others. However, if one realizes such goals at personal cost, sooner or later the books will have to be balanced in some way. In such circumstances, a manager may consider personal costs and think: "Well, if a person doesn't perform sufficiently well any longer, we simply need to replace them." When they consider that the person has become incompetent they treat an individual like an empty can to be thrown away. The 18th-century French philosopher Voltaire, who had been invited to reside with Frederick II of Prussia, experienced a similar behavior at the hands of this so-called enlightened monarch, ended up leaving Prussia feeling very disabused. In his memoirs, Voltaire expressed his disillusion-ment and resentment by comparing himself to an orange which, having been squeezed to have all its juices extracted, is left with only the skin and is then thrown away. This rancor may have been one of the origins of the French Revolution, 30 years later. So, unecological behavior may be sustainable in the short term but something will have to give in the long term. A company that treats their employees like disposable beer cans incurs not only higher running costs but will acquire a poor reputation. Such auto-cratic behavior may prove expensive to remedy in the long run.

Think about it for a moment. When a member of your team oper-ates below par or makes a significant mistake, the easy option is often to dismiss them and recruit a replacement. However, have you ever pondered on the hidden costs of such a course of action? After all, in addition to the purely financial considerations of redundancy and recruitment costs, much valuable time is lost in the process of finding a replacement and in bringing this person up to speed. In the meantime, the team has to cover the duties of the missing member, often with the additional burden of stress this generates. Above and beyond this, departing staff often take away with them a wealth of accumulated expertise, intelligence, networking, and even clients, none of which may be easily quan-tified or even replaced. How many people would you need to fire before considering this a problem? What price are you paying for such unecological behavior? Surely a better and cheaper alterna-tive must exist.

Indeed it does: for a fraction of such costs and far greater benefits, forward-looking companies across the world now employ the services of professional coaches to bring their staff up to speed again and to keep improving their motivation and productivity. Their absenteeism levels drop and, as a bonus, the companies even get to retain performing staff longer. By adopting more flexible approaches which respect and value their staff, a company can enable them to participate fully in the well-being of the company and, therefore, of their own. This, in turn, can reduce the brain drain and generate a good reputation which will precede the company when it sets up new initiatives. In this game, nobody loses and everybody wins.

Of course, when making a common goal, one should strive to satisfy the five well-formedness conditions we presented earlier, while leaving enough room for feedback. This leads to the following checklist:

- ❑ Do all parties fully agree what goal has to be reached? Do they agree with the way the current situation is described? What presuppositions are you operating from? If you want a common goal, this implies that the standpoint of each person is taken into account. The ecological question becomes: "Is what is good for me also good for the others (and vice versa)?" If in doubt, revise the goal!
- ❑ Has the goal been formulated in positive terms? Do some elements remain unclear?
  (**Hint**: the question-asking model we present in Lesson 6 will be helpful to clarify a goal.)
- ❑ Does each person know what part they are expected to play?
- ❑ Do the planned actions fall within the control of the person who is expected to reach this particular (sub)goal?
- ❑ Can the person to whom the task is assigned really do it?[13]
- ❑ How will you measure progress towards the goal, and the result obtained?
- ❑ Does the plan allow for necessary feedback points? Is there time to agree on these feedback points and to discuss the actual situation, without apportioning blame to anybody?

---

[13] It is not because a person is really enthusiastic and really wants to do all they can to reach a goal, that they have the necessary skills to do so. Other limiting factors may be time availability (other obligations get in the way) or underestimating a task's complexities or requirements.

> After all, mistakes are learning opportunities and, given the opportunity, you learn far more from a mistake than from something you did well![14]
> ❑ Timing: When are what results due? When will one measure the intermediate results?

In addition to this checklist, we present several other skills relevant to achieving common goals in this book. We especially recommend combining this checklist with the Walt Disney Creativity Strategy (see Lesson 1) and the discussion on the meta-mirror (see Lesson 5).

Finally we'd like to add a last recommendation: getting what you want may seem a major goal in life. Make sure you can enjoy it too. How much fun is a goal if you have to work like dogs to reach it? All three of us remember occasions when we fell into this trap. So remember to listen to your emotions while working at reaching a goal and use them to motivate you.

Application 2: Expectations and the Structure of Happiness

There is often a wide gap between what one expects from life and what one actually gets from it. As our expectations affect our happiness, such gaps can be a major source of unhappiness. "Being in love" is one of those areas in life where such "ideal and extreme" examples of this process occur. Being in love causes our fantasy to break out and run unbridled.

What's going on when one is in love? Or when one is enthusiastic about a new job? Or when you get this new car you wanted for so long? Or when you were finally able to afford that exotic holiday you yearned for? Notice how, to some extent, all these experiences share a similar structure: the reality gets distorted and there is usually an exaggerated expectation of the new possibilities this situation will bring us. Combined with the effort required to compensate for the missing elements of the dream, disappointment

---

[14] Contrary to expectation, blaming people and punishing them for mistakes doesn't bring you much further towards your goal. On the contrary, if they know this will happen, people will begin to cover up their mistakes, which results in getting an incomplete picture of the real situation, instead of owning up to them and learning from what they have to teach us. This may then result in actions which are no longer appropriate.

and burn-out are often consequences of such exaggerated expectations. For instance, the romantic notion of living as a couple is often very different from the day-to-day life one will lead in reality.

Drawing on the work of General Semanticist Alfred Korzybski, L. Michael Hall suggests that our emotions are the result of a differential comparison between the expectations which arise out of our Model of the World and the Experience of what actually occurred.[15]

So, when our experience exactly matches our expectations we do not experience any emotions: everything is exactly as it should be and nothing stands out which would be worth noticing.

However, if our experience differs in any way from our expectations we perceive this difference and ascribe an emotional meaning to it. The deeper the difference, the more intense the emotion. Thus, if our experience was not as good as we had anticipated and expected, we feel disappointed, unhappy or downright miserable. On the other hand, if our experience is better than we anticipated, we feel contented, elated, delighted, delirious, or even ecstatic.

---

[15]   L. Michael Hall: *NLP & General Semantics: The Merging of the Models.* Course commissioned by Post-Graduate Professional Education, London, 1998–1999

We cannot help comparing our experience of reality with our construct of what this reality is about, including other people. We thus compare our perceptual mapping with our conceptual mapping, and our expectations, hopes, aspirations, demands, memories, etc. with ongoing everyday experiences. In that an emotion reflects the state of our model of the world at a given point in time, any emotion we experience is, paradoxically, always appropriate. So if we go through a situation and experience a negative emotional evaluation of it, this is a sign that we need to change our mapping tools and update our maps, so that they are truer to our experience of reality. The ability to modify our maps so that they become more true to the experience is therefore a sign of our Emotional Intelligence.

On the other hand if we live in a state where expectations do not occur, anything which happens is a treat. Such an attitude is encouraged by many Eastern philosophies: it generates a state which is both of benign detachment and, at the same time, of deep association and belonging to the world. The lifestyle we live, however, where all sorts of schedules and timescales are imposed upon us by our environment, is not conducive to cultivating such states, and we do not suggest you should adopt such an approach full-time! After all, you need to set goals for yourself and to meet other people's goals as well. Nevertheless, you may choose to give yourself some "treats" at some point in the day, the week, the year, where you can set aside your expectations and just *BE*. Such oases of "beingness" need not even take long, but you will emerge from them refreshed and revitalized every time.

We recommend three rules to bring reality and expectation closer to each other.

---

1. Add a sense of reality to your expectations.
2. Go for a long-term expectation, rather than expecting too much from a short-term perspective.
3. Find a way to be happy, even if the circumstances aren't as perfect as you'd like them to be.

Let's discuss each of these suggestions in detail.

1. High expectations may end in deep disappointments. After being in love for a time, you may suddenly discover some negative elements in your partner's attitude, your new job may prove more stressful than you thought it would be and, during your holiday, the exotic food made you ill. As discussed when we presented the Walt Disney Creativity Strategy, adding some sense of realism to your dreams will help.

2. To sustain your happiness longer, extend your motivation to reach your goal over a longer period, if appropriate. When a new manager gets hired, they will begin with full energy, firing on all cylinders, hoping to achieve some major accomplishments in a limited time span. By pushing too hard, they may encounter resistance and, in the end, the expected results may end up even further off than anticipated. Demanding too much of yourself has similar consequences. Do you expect to reach full and total emotional mastery by doing just a limited set of exercises, or do you consider this a long-term project worthy of spending more time and perhaps money on? There are plenty of good courses around which can enable you to do this. (See the end of this book.)

   Burn-out syndrome research shows that employees often have a positive attitude towards work, but that their frustration tolerance is rather low. Big companies often have a culture which is rigid and resistant to change. Although they may want to, a newly appointed manager cannot expect to reach a major culture change in a few months' time on their own. Others in the organization need to change also so that they may support each other. Habits and procedures may require a major overhaul. Pushing the organization to change as a result of unbridled enthusiasm can backfire, as apathy and inertia prevails. Many new employees get fired in such a situation because too many people feel undermined, affronted or attacked. The answer lies in finding the right balance between push and pull, between diplomacy and taking the lead, between respect and confrontation. In such a situation we recommend you look for the positive intention behind the resistance people manifest, looking at the situation from their perspective, and integrating all these perspectives in the final resolution.

3. The rut of everyday life and the imperfection which comes with it are only one interpretation of what is happening. Change your attitude! What seems a routine can be fun as well; it depends only on your state. This may involve some creativity. For instance, how about comparing washing dishes with skiing down a snowy mountainside? Opening up your perceptions may help as well. For example, when you are outside, getting ready to get into your parked car, how about listening to the song of the bird on a nearby roof, or what about being curious of the way the rain touches your coat or your hair? Being aware of such simple things, such treats that life hands us out all the time, and appreciating them opens you to a whole new set of experiences. Although you may not remember, once upon a time, when you were a child, you went through life like that: everything was an opportunity to wonder.

The "superficialization" of life occurs when we ignore or neglect the information we receive from our senses. For instance, do you just put food in your mouth, or can you fully enjoy the experience? How do you perceive members of your family, your partner, your children—is there something to be curious of, with a childlike attitude, in anything they do or do you consider it part of an everyday rut?

Develop your senses! And especially develop your awareness. By attending to everything that is happening around you and inside you, you may be surprised each day how wonderful life is. The Buddhist philosophy, taking other aspects as the result of one's karma and just accepting them, is a clear example of the way one can steer one's experiences to such pleasing aspects of life. But, by conscious observation of what's going on, you may find happiness even in the more unpleasant aspects of life. Buddhist teachings will tell you that happiness can be found in cultivating a meditative awareness towards your way of walking, eating, working, etc. According to Zen, Enlightenment can be found in everyday work. So why couldn't doing the dishes or making up the bed be a blessed activity? If we may give you some advice, you can exercise this principle by choosing to carry out a certain activity without setting yourself an outcome. For instance, take a "goal-less" walk through a park or a part of your town. One option could be that, each time you come to a junction of streets or paths, you take some time to look around and choose the direction which seems the most appealing. And, maybe, at this moment, that's the direction you just came from. Or you could do the same walk selecting the direction that's the *least* appealing, and discover how even that choice may enrich your awareness in unexpected ways.

Exercises for this Lesson

Exercise 3.1: Making goals well-formed

Each of the sentences of this exercise clearly violates one of the criteria we taught you for well-formed outcomes. In each case, identify the underlying criterion and rewrite the sentence in accordance with a correct formulation of this criterion.

Example:

"I want to be like Jack Welch, the famous CEO of General Electric."—*violates Specificity criterion*

Suggestion: "I want to surround myself with formidable executives, in the same way that Jack Welch had Gary Wendt at GE Capital."

GOAL TO RE-FORMULATE	VIOLATED CRITERION	YOUR NEW SENTENCE
1. I want to be able to relax.		
2. I want to improve my communication skills.		
3. My colleagues should take my point of view more into account.		
4. I'd like to get rid of this headache.		
5. I want to be assertive.		
6. I want to be happier.		
7. I want to be President/Prime Minister.		
8. I'd like the others to tell me the truth.		
9. I want to stop smoking.		
10. I should have more money.		
11. I'm going to move to the California desert.		
12. I want to follow a class in Emotional Intelligence.		

Exercise 3.2: TOTE questionnaire

1. GOAL: What is the outcome (goal, target or objective) that you want to reach?

    a. Make sure the outcome is well-formed; describe the goal in positive terms (say what you want, instead of what you don't want); make sure the goal is within your control.

    b. Write down your outcome in specific language. (Make the *movie*: what happens, what will you see, hear, feel?)

    c. Give some concrete examples of your goal.

2. TEST of EVIDENCE: How do you know when you reach your goal? How do you know you're getting closer to your goal? How would others know? What intermediate results have you in mind? What is your timing?

3. ACTIONS: What steps will you take to reach your goal? What activities have you planned to achieve that? If you notice you are deviating from the target, what steps/actions will you take to put you back on target? (What possible problems might arise and how will you take care of those?)

4. EFFECTS:
   a. What do you get from reaching the target? (What is it worth to you, what's the added value, what are your secondary gains?)
   b. What negative "effect" might arise (for you personally)? What stops you from doing it?
   c. What could be the effect on others? (Who is involved? How will they react?)

Exercise 3.3: Contrastive analysis

What is the difference that makes a difference?

Choose an example in which you proved successful. Fill out the TOTE questionnaire (see the previous exercise) for this successful example—use the table below for your answers.

Now take a case where you didn't reach your target. Again, write down the answers to the TOTE questionnaire (again, use the table).

Compare the two columns of the table. What are the main differences? What do you learn from this?

	Goal Failed	*Goal Reached*
GOAL		
TEST		
ACTIONS		
EFFECTS		

Exercise 3.4: When does something become a problem?

List three things that you experienced as "a problem." Now list three other changes you went through recently, but which you didn't consider as "a problem." Compare both kinds of experiences. What's similar? What's different?

Exercise 3.5: Well-formedness self-evaluation

What goals have you set for yourself for the next six months? Check whether these goals are well-formed.

Lesson 4:
Learn How You Perceive the World and Be in Charge of What Makes You Tick

"Experience is not what happens to you;
It is what you do with what happens to you."
Aldous Huxley

Goals
In this chapter you will achieve the following four goals:
- Differentiating between the content of an experience and its structural representation.
- Enriching and modifying the structural representation of an experience, using all sensory channels and their underlying qualities.
- Finding patterns in your emotional abilities, including the sequencing of sensory information and the filters in your thoughts.
- Knowing how to enrich your emotional competencies.

Neurolinguistic Assumptions
In this chapter we will apply the following four assumptions:
- *We continuously process information through our five or more senses.*
- *We operate from our internal maps, rather than from the external reality.*
- *If somebody can do something, anybody can.*
- *Changing the process by which we experience reality is more valuable than changing the content of our experience of reality.*

Why this lesson?
- Emotions lead to competencies. They drive behavior, lead us to filter information and structure our experience. Insight into these processes is required for Emotional Intelligence.

- There are patterns underneath emotions. The more you understand these patterns, the more flexibility you can develop for yourself and the more easily you can understand others. This way, Emotional Intelligence becomes a fascinating road to wisdom.
- By fully exploring the possibilities of your senses you will create a richer experience of living for yourself and find out how to enrich the experience of others.

Introduction

What's your emotional state while you're reading this book? Are you curious or fascinated? Are you surprised or astonished? To answer such questions, you need to be able to distinguish between these emotions. What's the difference between being curious and being fascinated? Between surprise and astonishment? In our introduction to this book we explained that emotions have a bodily and a cognitive component. You may not be aware of the meaning you assign to a strong emotion, even if such a meaning is present. Meaning operates as bodily presuppositions.[1] Being embedded in experience, emotions, like our behavior, thinking and context, have an **internal structure**. We call all such internal building blocks of our emotions "emotional operators." The model of representation channels and the Meta-Programs which we are going to introduce you to below form tools to map out the patterns of our emotional functioning.

Before we do that, let's go back to clarifying what we mean by the internal structure of emotions. Do you know the difference between fear and anxiety? Do you know the similarity between frustration and disillusionment? What's the connection between power and anger? To describe these connections you need a minimum of vocabulary. After all, being afraid may not be as precise as being anxious. Being frustrated is more active than being disappointed. Power is as proactive as anger, but has less direction.

---

[1] Wyatt Woodsmall has been pointing out this difference between linguistic and bodily presuppositions.

In her book *The Emotional Hostage*,[2] Leslie Cameron-Bandler describes the difference between hope and anticipation. She demonstrates how such emotions are related, but have a different structure. On the one hand, anticipation is directed towards the future and has an active component. On the other hand, hope is also directed to the future, but it is more a passive waiting. Or take the difference between frustration and disappointment. While disappointment is passive, taking stock of the past without really hoping to change anything in the future, frustration is active, leaving an exit possibility, serving as a driver for action.

How is all this linked to Emotional Intelligence, you may ask? Well, our experience has taught us that people with high Emotional Intelligence have such a degree of emotional awareness that they are able to recognize and discriminate between the building blocks of their emotions. In our terminology: emotionally intelligent people do not think in terms of emotions, but in terms of emotional patterns, or the building blocks which form the emotions.

Representation systems or channels are a model which will increase your knowledge of your own emotional building blocks.

Representation Systems:
How Do People Construct Their Internal World?

We receive input through our senses on a continuing basis. Until we mention it, you may not have been directly conscious of the typeface we're using, or the weight of the book in your hands, or the quality of the light on the page, or the smell of the paper and glue, etc. And yet, all such items of information come in all the time, through our eyes, ears, skin, nose, mouth, etc., but we're only aware of a minute fraction or selection of them at any one time. We all process them in a number of different ways depending on our personality, as they go through a series of filters which ultimately delete, generalize and distort our experience of reality in order to manage in everyday life, otherwise we'd be overwhelmed. From

---

[2]   That emotions have a structure is one of the basic premises of Leslie Cameron-Bandler and Michael Lebeau in their book *The Emotional Hostage* (Real People Press, 1986). This book was far ahead of its time, and gave a theory of emotions about 10 years before Goleman made the term "Emotional Intelligence" famous.

what remains of that information we create our view of the world. So what we're aware of at a conscious level in the end is, at best, a re-presentation of reality once it has gone through our filters.

These filters are acquired throughout life, but especially in childhood and, for better or worse, they "color" our perspective of the world. You can map out the subjective experience you are conscious of at any one time and are already well-versed in doing so at the (traditional) level of content, e.g. "I see a tree and hear the wind playing with the leaves of the tree. I smell the flower." To make sense of this experience you need to represent it internally in some way.

Since our filters appear to exist and operate regardless of personal desires, all these processes are free of content. In the following pages we show you how to do this and offer you a model to describe your experience at the deeper level of structure, as opposed to content. You will be able to see how two experiences may have a very different content, and yet share a similar structure.

As a provocative example carry out the two following instructions: (1) "Think of a picture of your favourite pet or animal," (2) "Think of a picture of your loved one." To answer these two questions, you've had to carry out a similar process at a structural level. Likewise, two people can go through the same experience and ascribe completely different meanings to them, because they will have structured this experience differently. So, whoever you are, you will engage in the same processes, although where you end up is as varied as the number of people that exist.

Throughout our life we experience reality mediated through our sensory inputs or **modalities**. Broadly fitting in five categories— see figure next page—these consist of: Seeing (V), Hearing (A), Smelling (O), Tasting (G) and Feeling (K). There are two broad kinds of feelings: *External (tactile)* sensations and *Internal (Vestibular or balance, Proprioceptive or posture/movement and Visceral) sensations.*[3]

---

[3]   Most neurolinguistic literature does not differentiate between the various kinesthetic modalities even though we have found this worthwhile. However, this space is too limited to give a detailed exploration of these modalities and their properties.

Note here how, contrary to popular belief, a feeling is not an emotion. A feeling is descriptive, whereas an emotion is evaluative. Most usually an emotion is a (usually visceral) feeling + a label. Thus many people can experience feelings very differently, depending on the label they give it: one person's "stage fright" can be another's "trepidation," another's "anxiety" and yet another's "excitement." Physiologically they will "feel" the same thing, but they will encode it differently from one another. This labeling will depend on the type of formative experience where the feeling was first experienced. Learning to distinguish feeling from label is one of the main steps towards Emotional Intelligence, as it will enable you to recode and relabel experiences on the basis of what you want to get out of them.

So, our five senses, which we call the VAKOG representation channels, also describe the structure of an experience. We will use this VAKOG model to describe what exactly happens when we obey an instruction such as "Think of a loved one," or describe whatever other thinking process goes on.

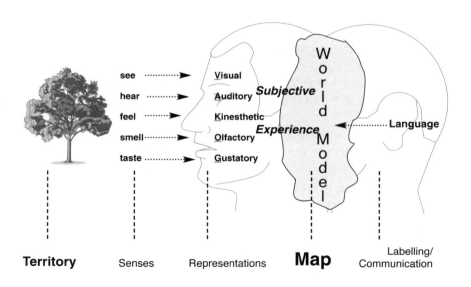

Figure 4.1: Relationship between map and territory

All the time, even in our sleep, our senses are "tuned" to information coming from outside, consisting of these visual, auditory, olfactory, gustatory and kinesthetic sensations. Filtered through our neurology, they are coded to form representations and memories. So, whenever we remember an event, we remember it filtered and coded through our neurology, and re-presented in sensory-specific terms, in sights, sounds, feelings, smells and tastes. Hence, the first distinction we want to make is between the external word and the internal world. Depending on your state of mental health, this is not as obvious as people may think.

1. Sensory-specific information coming from the outside (External)

As Figure 4.1 shows, our senses are continuously stimulated by information coming from the outside. Depending on which channel gets stimulated, we call this:

Visual, **A**uditory, **K**inesthetic (and tactile), **O**lfactory, **G**ustatory
coding: **VAKOG** $_e$ (external)

2. Internal Representations

The information which gets stored in your head (internal representation) can also be sorted according to the different senses. For instance, answer the following question: "Remember the last time you saw the sea?" What does this question elicit? Write it down!

When you read this description back to yourself, you may notice that you have written mainly about things you *saw* when *looking* at the sea, such as the waves and perhaps some boats on it. Or maybe you were rather thinking of the *sounds* you heard, such as the sound of the waves. Or maybe it was the *movements* that caught your attention, such as the movements of the waves going back and forth. Or maybe it was the *feeling* you had inside you on the ferry. Or maybe it was the *smell* of the salt or the *smell* of the sea … Even if you didn't think of all those things when you wrote your text, you had to do that in order to make sense of the sentences you have just read. This proves that you are capable of processing, storing and remembering information from your different senses.

coding: **VAKOG** $_i$ (internal)

In the description of what goes on inside your head, we want to distinguish between the primary system and the lead system: these are two different ways of using representational systems inside us.

The Primary System

Each and every one of us has a representational system we favour and reveal in the words we use when we talk. The discipline of linguistics calls **Predicates** the words we employ to describe, namely: verbs, adverbs and adjectives. These describe visual, auditory, kinesthetic, olfactory/gustatory or non-specific internal processing.

Thus, if your speech reveals many visual predicates in preference to others, this will indicate you operate primarily using the visual system. Similarly with auditory, kinesthetic, olfactory/gustatory and non-specific predicates. Of course, your choice of words will depend on the context in which you employ them; nevertheless we have found that people apply the same primary systems, across a range of contexts, as if you were tuned to the same radio station all the time. This does not mean that you do not use other representational systems as and when, simply that one comes more easily to you than the others.

Identifying someone's primary system and responding in the same system will enable you to achieve a deeper level of rapport than hitherto suspected (see Lesson 7). Likewise, identifying your own primary system may invite you to develop your behavioral flexibility and learn to utilize other representational systems, so that you are better able to achieve rapport at the level you desire wherever and whenever you want or need to.

The Lead System

Early NLP developers noticed that while calibrating clients and customers, people's eyes flicked to specific positions depending on which particular representational system the person was accessing at the time. They identified these as the system which a person uses to access a memory or a state and therefore called it the **Lead System.**

For example, when you ask someone about their mother, they might first recall the sound of her voice: their eyes would flick to the auditory tonal remembered position (usually left lateral). On the other hand, they might first seek to see her face and their eyes would flick to the visual remembered position (*typically up and to the left*), etc.

They identified six key eye positions (*see next page*) which people's eyes flick to in order to access a memory, and labelled these **eye-accessing cues**. As such, they form a specific type of calibrating tool (See Lesson 7).

Eye-accessing cues tend to be cross-cultural, although they may differ, depending on a person's left- or right-handedness or the specific culture. Apparently, the Basques' eye-accessing cues are reversed.

Although, taken on their own, they might not therefore be 100% accurate, taken with other calibrating cues, they offer persuasive indications of a person's internal operating. Likewise we will see that various postures and body attitudes also give us clues as to the type of state and memory accessed.

Separating Lead System and Primary System

The person you are operating with will have a favourite or **lead system** to access a given memory, which may be the same as their **primary system**, but may not necessarily be so. You therefore need to distinguish the role of these systems and their function.

- We use our lead system to access a memory.
- We use our primary system to operate in everyday life.

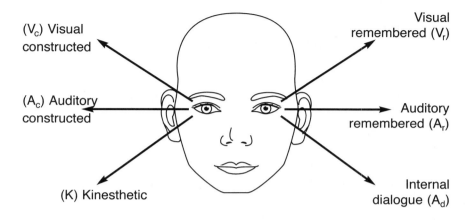

Figure 4.2: Typical eye movements linked to the lead system, for a right-handed person

Lead System Eye-Accessing Cues

We describe below how eye-accessing cues work for a large part of the world's population. The drawing we use is broadly valid for right-handed people. Left-handed people may have reversed eye movements, and some exceptions, such as the Basques, have different eye movements as well. So before drawing conclusions, check the eye movements and their meaning. For instance, you know that if a right-handed person stands in front of you, and you ask them "Imagine the front door of your house repainted in gold," you know that the person is constructing an image, and their eyes will probably go to their upper right (your upper left).

1. **Visual constructed (V_c)**
= internal pictures you make up yourself (imagination)
e.g.: Imagine seeing a flying boat.
    Picture yourself tomorrow morning at 10 am.

2. **Visual remembered (V_r)**
= internal pictures that you remember
e.g.: I remember the first time I saw the house I live in now.

3. **Auditory constructed (A_c)**
= internal sounds that you make ("construct") yourself
e.g.: *Think of someone you could compliment next week. How reso-*
nantly will you say it?
How will it sound if you were to play the guitar tomorrow?

4. **Auditory remembered (A_r)**
e.g.: *What were the first words you said this morning?*

5. **Kinesthetic (K)**
= internal feelings as well as tactile information
e.g.: *Which of your two feet feels the colder?*
What feeling do you get when you are falling in love?

6. **Internal dialogue (A_d, auditory digital)**
= our inner voice: what we say to ourselves; "inner speech"
e.g.: *Tell yourself "It's worth reading this book."*

Although the use of the two other senses can show up in eye movements, they are not generally presented in Anglo-Saxon cultures:[4]

7. **Olfactory (O)** = the smell
e.g.: *The smell of food while cooking.*

8. **Gustatory (G)** = the taste
e.g.: *The taste of marmalade.*
The aftertaste of an old wine.

Note that, in practice, several representation channels may be present in the same sentence. For instance: *"**Looking** out of the plane window, I suddenly **felt** that there was something wrong about that image I saw. Hawaii under the sun, that's very unusual."* Or "I was just silently ***humming** that song **in my thoughts,** and suddenly I **remembered seeing that video-clip** on MTV last night." We code the first sentence as V_e[5] $\Rightarrow$ K/V_{ir} for Visual External $\Rightarrow$ Kinesthetic/Visual Internal Remembered. This means that in the

---

[4]   **Olfactory:** Nose up, eyes straight ahead or slightly crossed forward.
       Gustatory: Head down, eyes straight down or slightly crossed forward.

[5]   We code external perception using the subscript letter *e* and internal representation/access by the subscript letter *i*.

first sentence you expect to see that the eyes first move very fast to their lower right and upper left respectively after the person had been looking outside (in front of them) and up and to the left when referring to "Hawaii under the sun," which supposes they're carrying out a comparison between what they are seeing and a visual memory. We code the second sentence as $A_d \Rightarrow V_{ir}$ for *Auditory Digital* $\Rightarrow$ *Visual Internal Remembered*. Traditionally the eyes will move from lower left to upper left.

Predicates in the Language

Many verbs, nouns, adverbs, adjectives and expressions point directly to a specific representation channel:

e.g.: Suddenly, things became *clear* to me $\Rightarrow$ **visual**

And then a bell started to *ring* $\Rightarrow$ **auditory**

Finally, I got the impression I *grasped* the entire situation $\Rightarrow$ **kinesthetic**

I *said* to *myself* $\Rightarrow$ **auditory digital** (internal dialogue)

Overleaf are a brief sample list of words for each of the five representation channels.

Visual	*Auditory*	*Kinesthetic*	*Olfactory*	*Gustatory*
See, watch, illustrate, show, observe, blush	Hear, say, talk, sound, listen, cheer, attune	Feel, touch, hold, run, batter, wrestle, sway	Smell, breathe in, sniff, inhale	Taste, lick, embitter
Image, perspective, focus, insight	Sound, silence, music, harmony, word, note	Impact, movement, dance, torment	Smell, stench, nose, perfume	Taste, food, drinks
Colorful, vague, dull, brilliant, red, glitter, transparent, dark, clear	Silent, hoarse, false, melodious, cacophony, noisy, rhythmic, deaf, monotonous	Rough, soft, heavy, fast, cold, smooth, dry, slippery, intense, weak, exciting, hot	Burnt, fresh, Penetrating	Bitter, sweet, spicy, salty, dry, tasteless
Keeping up appearances. I'm beginning to see the light. He is no great light. At first sight. It was black and blue. Try to visualize this.	Tune in to each other. Strike an optimistic note. That sounds fine. It has a familiar ring. To have an open ear for something.	The sore spot. It dawned on him. As slippery as an eel. They exert pressure on. An overheated economy. He didn't budge an inch.	He has a nose for that sort of thing. It stinks. To smell a rat To be in bad odor.	Sweet revenge. They swallow everything. They sell like hot cakes. It makes my mouth water.

You may have noticed that the first three columns in the table were larger than the two last columns. The reason is that, in most Germanic cultures (including Anglo-Saxon), the vocabulary for describing tastes and smells is rather limited. A French or a Lebanese would have a much wider olfactory or gustatory vocabulary. Now try this for yourself: expand the table for each category on a separate sheet. Which category do you find the easiest?

What all this has got to do with your Emotional Intelligence you may wonder. Well, experience has shown that people who have problems in some situations where others do not, may operate out of a representational system which does not serve them best at the time or that clashes with someone else's.

To give you an example, we once saw a couple who had marital problems and who, although they liked and loved each other, were considering divorce. Watching them and listening to their manner of speaking soon explained why: the husband mainly used the visual system, speaking of the way his wife *looked*, while the wife mainly used kinesthetic language, saying how much she liked the way her husband *felt*.

Although this, on the surface, does not appear significant, the consequences of this different type of processing meant that they often found themselves at odds about many things. The husband complained about the wife being "all touchy-feely" and always wanting him to give her a cuddle or to tousle his hair, while she complained that he was always "distant" and liked to "make love with the lights on," which she found very "off-putting!"

We were able to make them identify those different ways they had of operating, suggesting they learn to develop their underused representational system and to find a meeting point in the middle, such as talking about things (A), perhaps over a good meal (O/G), which they did.

During the meal the husband "looked at his wife and sponta-neously 'extended his hand out to her'" and the wife "responding, suddenly 'saw her husband in a different light' and realized they could after all, get on together." And they learnt to laugh together about their different ways of doing things. After the meal they went to the cinema together, which they hadn't done since before they were married, and they enjoyed the film while cuddling in their seats.

As mentioned before, you can derive the primary representation channel a person uses from their predicates. If you want to adapt yourself to a person, use the words which fit their primary channel. If you want to speak to a large audience, you might want to say the key messages several times, using different predicates, and you can enrich your text by adding languages from representation channels other than your own primary system. And of course, the same tips can be applied to written communication. Often our language contains equivalent words to describe the same experience in seve-ral representation languages. Let us give you some examples:

Unspecific	Visual	Auditory	Kinesthetic
Teach	Make something clear	Make understandable	Make graspable
Demonstrate	Depict, show	Explain	Enact
Evaluate	Compare and contrast	Question	Weigh up

> *Tip:* A good thesaurus will enable you to enrich your vocabulary. If you use a word processor, you'll find that the thesaurus can be handy for finding synonyms in other representation channels.

Body Language

Today, cognitive scientists such as Lakoff and Johnson[6] start from the presupposition that mind and body are a systemic whole, even if there is no consensus for universal body language. A statement such as "somebody that leans backward is not interested" is just one interpretation of many for what it might mean to lean backward. According to neurolinguists Robert Dilts and Todd Epstein, another reason why someone might want to lean backward and look up may be that they are constructing a better image in order to understand what you are explaining. In other words, body language can indicate what representation channel someone is using.

e.g.:

much movement	→	kinesthetic
head tilted	→	auditory
midriff breathing	→	kinesthetic
high breathing	→	visual
head downwards	→	kinesthetic
movement with hand	→	indicates placement of object or concept in the mental space

As we will discuss in Lesson 7, body language can teach you a lot about a person. One word of warning: you may incur the risk of reaching a conclusion based on the body language of a person without having first checked your hypothesis. For example, a

---

[6]   Lakoff, G., and Johnson, M. (1999). *Philosophy in the Flesh: The Embodied Mind and its Challenge to Western Thought,* Basic Books.

person may furrow their eyebrows today through being irritated about something, while tomorrow they may furrow their eyebrows while trying to solve a difficult problem. So instead of concluding the second time that the person is angry or irritated, you need to check your hypothesis. When in doubt, ask! For example, "Is something irritating you?" would be a good question at this point. As you learn more about the body language of a person, you begin assembling a "non-verbal dictionary" for that person.

Submodalities:
How You Format Your Own Reality

You may have noticed that some particular memories have qualities which give them significance. Your recollection of, perhaps, falling in love may be in glorious Technicolor and Dolby stereo; perhaps the birds were singing with great sweetness that day, and your steps were more springy. Change the qualities of the experience, adjust the various parameters, the brightness, the sweetness of sound, the springiness, and you change the meaning of the whole experience.

These are examples of representational distinctions which give meaning and significance to our internal representation, in the same way that a document looks terrible in one format and font and superb in another, or a film looks very different watched on the big screen or on the television. So, depending on their formatting, memories likewise have different meanings and implications.

A Quick Exploration of Some Submodalities of an Experience
Try it: close your eyes and think of a situation when you had a good time, re-accessing it as suggested in Lesson 1 from the Mind End.

- See what you saw
- Hear what you heard
- Feel what you felt

Keep enjoying this experience, so that you can identify the way it is encoded in your mind.

As you look at the visual representation, play with the brightness: make it dimmer. What does that do to the good feeling you are experiencing? Make it brighter: what does that do to the good feeling? Leave the brightness at the level which gives you the best feeling.

Now, if you see the picture from within, step out of it, so that you can see yourself in it. Or, if you see yourself in the picture, step into it, so that you can experience it through your own eyes. What does that do to the feeling? Keep the picture in the format which gives you the best feeling.

How did these changes affect the meaning this experience has for you?

Use a similar type of questioning for other submodalities, using the kinesthetic coding to check the feeling.

Each representational system or modality thus has specific distinctions within which we encode our experiences and which, all together, give MEANING to these experiences. Changing them, or maybe even a single one, changes the meaning of an experience. Each in turn, they define *"the difference which makes the difference."* They appear, at the current level of our knowledge, the smallest component of subjective experience which has, so far, been identified.

By neurolinguistic convention, we call these qualities **Submodalities**,[7] because they are in themselves components or subfilters of the modalities or representational systems, VAKOG.

Identified from the field of holography, submodalities were first described by neurolinguists Richard Bandler and Todd Epstein in the late 1970s and presented in *Using Your Brain for a Change*,[8] as well as in *An Insider's Guide to Submodalities*.[9] They provide a very useful tool for helping people to change themselves. We can use

---

[7] Some, such as L. Michael Hall, argue that the term "submodality" is an unfortunate choice, since the term implies they are "underlying" (or sub) to the modalities, while in fact it they are qualities of the modalities or representation systems. See *The Structure Of Excellence*, by L. Michael Hall and Bobby G. Bodenhamer, Empowerment Technologies, Grand Junction, CO., 1999

[8] Bandler, R. (1985). *Using Your Brain for a Change*, Moab, Utah, Real People Press.

[9] Bandler, R. and MacDonald, W. (1988). *An Insider's Guide to Submodalities*, Cupertino, Calif., Meta Publications.

them, among other things, for resolving unwanted habits and limiting beliefs—the notions we may have about ourselves, others and the world which limit our outlook and prevent us from achieving our goals.

We need to distinguish Submodalities from the *content* of the internal representation. They form part of the *structure* of experience and of the way an individual encodes his or her experiences. This level is deeper than that of content and therefore has leverage upon it. Neurolinguistics, as a discipline, deals with the structure of subjective experience and actually needs to make very little use of the content of your memories. This makes it an ideal discipline to use wherever confidentiality is at a premium. In addition, since exploring content can be very time-consuming, neurolinguistics, operating on structure, usually enables you to save a large amount of time: this makes it extremely cost-effective. However, we are used to operating at the level of content (storytelling, etc.) from an early age. So, unless you operate in the world of design or the arts, which are essentially process-based, you may not be aware how quickly you can modify an emotion associated with an experience, just by playing with the format of this experience.

As an example, take the submodality of "location." Suppose someone is criticized and replies "I couldn't care less," while making a movement with their hand over their shoulder, towards the back. It's probably an effective way for that person not to be touched by something unpleasant. Notice the body language: the person throws something behind their back, thus removing it from their attention. There is something to learn from this example. When we generalize it, we notice that people who often have difficulties in, say, forgetting an experience or in getting over a loss, have located the image that goes with the memory in front of them. An image that is located in front of you remains in your field of attention: it is "unfinished business." It is easier to "digest" the experience when one moves the image to the side, or even to the back. One word of caution: one can also suppress the image by putting it too far out of the visual field. The conclusion of this brief example is that the applications of submodalities are vast. So they deserve exploring at some length, in addition to which doing so is usually great fun!

Still, you'll notice that you can derive more submodalities from an average conversation than you would think. Movements of hands, used to stress elements during a conversation, often indicate the size and location of certain images a person is talking about. The direction their eyes look and the level of focus they apply will corroborate this location and give you an idea of the distance of an internal picture. Auditory submodalities are often key in understanding the meaning of a sentence. Take, for instance, the three following sentences: read them aloud. (1) It is a car. (2) It is a car? (3) It is a car! The only difference in written language comes from the punctuation marks (full stop, question mark, exclamation mark). In spoken language, the punctuation is replaced by changes in tonality, rhythm and stress.

There are broadly two types of submodalities:
Analog: These can be changed quickly or slowly along a continuum, like a volume control, or a dimmer switch, etc.
Digital: These are mutually exclusive, like on/off, in/out, associated/dissociated, external/internal, etc.

The following table lists the most important submodalities, together with some questions we suggest to elicit them. You can ask those questions about whatever experience a person is recounting. Note how not all submodalities have readily identifiable questions associated to them (especially in relation to olfactory and gustatory channels), so use your common sense.

---

[10] *Envelope, attack* and other submodalities, such as *timbre,* are more technical terms.

ANALOG SUBMODALITIES

VISUAL	AUDITORY
NUMBER (1 picture—many pictures) *How many pictures are you seeing?*	**NUMBER** (1 sound—many sounds) *How many sounds?* *Is it continuous or intermittent?*
LOCATION AND PERSPECTIVE *Where is it positioned?* *From what perspective do you see it?*	**LOCATION** *From what direction does it come?*
DISTANCE (near—far) *At what distance do you see it?*	**DISTANCE** (close—far) *How far away is the sound source?*
SIZE (small—large) *Is the image small or big? How small or big?*	**VOLUME** (loud—soft) *How loud is the sound you're hearing?*
SHAPE *What shape does it have?*	**ENVELOPE**[10]
EDGE *Is it bordered or borderless?* *If bordered, describe the border.*	**ATTACK**
COLOR (black and white—color) *Is it black-and-white or colored?* *What's the dominant color?*	**PITCH** (low—high) *How low or high is the pitch?*
BRIGHTNESS (dim—bright) *How dark or bright is the picture?*	**TONE** (bass—treble) *How deep or high is the sound?*
CONTRAST *How contrasted is it?*	**BALANCE** *Is the sound more in one ear than the other or even?*
DEPTH (flat—3D) *Is it flat or three-dimensional?*	**DEPTH** (mono—stereo—surround) *Is the sound mono, stereo or surround?*
FOCUS (fuzzy—clear) *How fuzzy or clear is the picture?*	**RHYTHM** (rhythmic—non rhythmic) *What rhythm does it have?*
MOVEMENT (still—slow—fast) *Is it moving? Slower or faster than normal?*	**TEMPO** (slow—fast) *How slow or fast is the sound?*
FIELD OF VISION (narrow—wide—surround) *Is it more tunnel-vision or panoramic?*	**FIELD OF HEARING** (narrow—wide) *Is it muffled or echoey?*

KINESTHETIC	OLFACTORY/GUSTATORY
INTENSITY (strong—weak) *How intense is the feeling?*	*Is there a smell? What smell ?* *How intense is it? Is it fresh or stale?*
AREA (LARGE—small) *What area does it cover?* *What form does it have?*	
TEXTURE (rough—smooth/ tight—loose) *What is its texture (structure)?*	Aroma
DURATION (constant— intermittent) *How long does it last, is it continuous?*	Fragrance
TEMPERATURE (cold—hot) *What temperature does it have?*	Essence
WEIGHT (heavy—light) *What weight does it have?* *How much pressure does it exercise?*	Pungence
LOCATION—DIRECTION— MOVEMENT *Where is it located? What movement does it have?* *What direction does it come from?*	**TASTE** (Sweet/Sour/Salty/Bitter/ Meaty/Creamy) *Is there a taste? What taste? How intense is it?*

DIGITAL SUBMODALITIES or META-SUBMODALITIES	EMOTIONAL—TACTILE WORDS—TONES ASSOCIATED—DISSOCIATED ON—OFF INTERNAL—EXTERNAL

Note here how digital submodalities are of a deeper order than analog ones and entail them. For example, no sound is no sound: when sound is present, all the range of auditory submodalities become available, in the same way that you can't play with the volume or the left-right balance of sounds in your sound system when it is set on mute. Although there are exceptions, a picture one is associated in will tend to be panoramic, 3-D, moving, borderless, etc. Sounds, feelings, smells and tastes also become more available. By contrast, a picture which is dissociated will usually have a location in space, a size, an edge/border, a distance, etc.

The quality of one's voice (or its submodalities) can be so distinctive that you'll often recognize a person just by their voice, especially over the telephone. Once you get to know somebody, you can even tell what emotional state they are in, even if you misinterpret from time to time. The range of use of one's voice also varies from person to person. What kind of differences are there between stressing a point of view during a discussion, and getting angry when talking about something that happened to you? You'll also notice cultural differences: submodalities such as intonation, rhythm and tonality used by an English newsreader on the BBC differs strongly from the range of submodalities used by an American newsreader on CNN, and even more from the range of submodalities you'll hear in a sitcom series such as "Friends." Experiments have shown that it takes only a few seconds to hear (without looking at the picture) whether you are watching a documentary, a movie or a soap.

Many people are not aware that they can change their submodalities. As a result they may not recode their experiences as often as they might like. In many ways, they operate like people who buy a TV or hi-fi and use only the default factory settings, whether they like them or not. After all, if watching a horror movie on television becomes too scary, try switching the volume off for a few seconds or putting the main lights on and notice what happens to your emotional state.

Learning to change the submodalities of an experience will greatly enhance your Emotional Intelligence, as it will enable you to recode them so that they serve you instead of you serving them. If the picture on your TV is too glaring, you'll adjust the brightness and contrast, and play with the volume to get the level you want. Do that with your internal picture, sounds and feelings and the world will become a very different place for you.

If you want to experiment with changing submodalities and don't know how, try playing with a modern TV. Change the contrast, the brightness, the colors, ... Change the picture to widescreen (9/16th) from small (3/4th). De-adjust the frequency a bit, and the picture will become fuzzy. Put the sound on mono, stereo or surround sound. Now touch the screen. Is it loaded with static electricity, does it feel warm or cold, ...? And you can change the submodalities of your own internal pictures, sounds and feelings in exactly the same manner.

EQ and the Application of the Structure of Subjective Experience

People do use all the information we have been describing up till now, but mostly unconsciously and in an incomplete way. The better use you can make of it, the more Emotional Intelligence you will be able to develop. We differentiate between three main applications of representation systems and submodalities:

1. **Calibration**: Deriving in what state a person is, through observing the representation channels and submodalities they are using at a certain moment in time.

2. **State Management**: Using representation systems and submodalities to find out the functioning of an emotional state, putting yourself (or someone else) in a resourceful state or enhancing a state.

3. **Rapport Skills**: Adapting yourself during communication, learning how to take into account the primary system of your public.

Further in the book (Lesson 7) you'll find a complete section on calibration and rapport-building skills. In what follows, we go further into how you can enhance a state using submodalities.

Enhancing a state with submodalities

You can elicit the submodalities of the internal representation of a memory, a state, a belief, an attitude, a skill or a habit. Change the submodalities of each of these and you will find that the significance or import of each one will change subtly but significantly: this gives you a different internal representation and, in fact, a different state, belief, attitude, skill or habit. Submodalities, for that reason, prove an extremely useful, powerful and effective manner of channeling your Emotional Intelligence.

Which Submodalities you should change

Certain submodalities hold particular significance for an individual. With some this may be the brightness or dullness of a memory. For others it may be the location within the internal field of vision, the size or distance. With yet others it may be the quality of the sounds or of the physical sensations which make a difference. We call these the critical submodalities or **driver** submodalities, as they have most leverage, and changing them has a cascading effect on all the others. Since their change will, in and by itself, make the most difference to a person's internal representation, identifying them during the course of an intervention will prove of particular use. For example, a young man falling in love may recall the event in Technicolor and remembers the birds' tuneful song. If he remembers instead the first day of his secondary school examinations he may perhaps find that the picture was in black and white and the birds were singing intrusively and out of tune that June! In this case, the critical submodalities or *drivers* are colorfulness and tunefulness.

Drivers and Contrastive Analysis

In order to discover the critical submodalities or drivers, you need to compare the submodalities of contrasting internal representations, such as taking an exam and falling in love. Make a list of the submodalities of each and identify which ones make the difference. These will prove the drivers. They form the distinctions which make the difference in the representation of these two situations.

Contrastive analysis thus means eliciting the submodalities of various situations in order to ascertain which are the ones which effect a difference. In the above case of the young man, he may find that the position of the picture in his internal field of vision is the same whether he is thinking of his falling in love or his taking his 'A' level exams, and so is the brightness of the two pictures. In these cases brightness and position are not drivers, although, by contrast, colorfulness and tunefulness are.

Associated and Dissociated

As you earlier saw, in Lesson 1, this particular pair of submodalities has a special importance in neurolinguistics. When a picture is dissociated, you can usually see yourself in the picture. You look at it from the perspective of a detached observer. If a picture is associated you are looking at the picture from the inside. You will not see yourself in it because you are part of it. Associated and dissociated can also refer to auditory and kinesthetic modalities of the representation. As, when associated, you are in your body. When dissociated, people experience fewer or no body sensations.

Associated and dissociated are usually important drivers. As such, they have many uses in neurolinguistics, some of which you have already seen and others you will learn about by the end of this book. Associated/dissociated are closely connected with feelings. Many people who have been raped describe how, at some stage, they felt as if they detached themselves from their body and observed the action from a distance as if it were happening to somebody else. It may be closely related to near-death experiences, where something similar also occurs. The manner in which people dissociate is also significant. In the rape cases and the near-death experiences, people dissociated by floating *upwards* out of their body. People describe a more ordinary way of dissociating as "taking a step back." Experiment with the way you dissociate and associate and explore what it does for you.

Switching submodalities process: from disliking to sympathy

The following is an example of changing submodalities: how you can have sympathy for people you dislike.

Step 1:   Think of a person that you dislike. How do you represent this person? What representation channel is the most present? Describe the submodalities of that representation channel.

Step 2:   Now think about a person for whom you feel sympathy. How do you represent this person? What representation channel is the most present? Describe the submodalities of that representation channel.

Step 3:   Do a contrastive analysis. What's the difference that makes a difference between both representations in terms of submodalities?[11]

Step 4:   Change the submodalities of the person you dislike into the submodalities of a person for whom you feel sympathy. What happens?

Belief change using Submodalities[12]

You may be surprised to realize that you can have a sensory-specific representation of *anything*, even abstract concepts, such as beliefs. However, this is the case. When we think of something, anything, we represent it in some way, most often projecting it somewhere about us, like a hologram. This explains the gestures people make when they speak, as they are actually manipulating their internally generated constructs, or "mind-objects." We

---

[11]   Did you choose the same representational system in both steps? If not, complete both descriptions by also listing the submodalities of the other channel for both cases.

[12]   An early version of this process was presented by Richard Bandler and Will MacDonald in *An Insider's Guide to Sub-Modalities*, Meta Publications, Cupertino, Calif, 1988.

described earlier how a person moved an image in their field of attention, throwing it over their shoulder, and how they were able to resolve the issue in their mind. This exercise applies similar rules, using submodalities to achieve belief change in a way which requires hardly any content information.

So when eliciting the beliefs of somebody, take care to sit or stand beside the person you're working with, otherwise you may sit or stand in their pictures or mind-objects. While this doesn't matter when their eyes are closed, it does when their eyes are open. How do you feel when somebody steps in front of your visual field when you are watching a movie? Well, that's about the same thing here, only more so, as they may be looking at their own internally generated "hologram."

Key submodalities to notice: location in space, distance, size, shape.

Tip: Be larger than life. Make it as much fun as possible, even if it's a serious issue. You cannot overact too much. Go to town with your tonality.

Find a partner (A) to do this with.
1. Ask A to identify a limiting belief, which we call [1], noting the above submodalities. Ask them: *"If you could see it as a picture, where would it be located?"* Notice their gestures, as they will probably show you the size, distance and shape of the picture without your having to ask them.

2. Ask A to identify a belief they no longer have, which we call [2] which, when thinking about it, they find a bit ludicrous or silly, has been "archived" or is simply "past its sell-by date." Note its submodalities.

3. Invite A to detach [1] from its location and to fix it in the location of [2], and giving it the submodalities of [2]. Use all your play-acting skills. Invite A to imagine they have stretchable arms, like Mr. Fantastic in Marvel Comics Group's "Fantastic Four" series. Make them stretch their real arms to pick the picture and move it as if it was a real object, as it gives the

experience even more reality. Ask them to make sound effects synchronized to accompany their gesture. Ask them for the best possible sound effects for unsticking the picture, moving it, and locking it in place.

4. When this is done, ask A how they perceive [1] in its new location.

5. Ask A to create a new, empowering belief which they would like to have but do not have yet, which we call [3]. It could be a mirror image of the above or, preferably, a more generative one which fulfills the positive intention of the old one and more, *"I can achieve whatever I determine to do."* Note its submodalities. Check the ecology of the new belief to make sure it will serve them and the people they interact with.

6. When A has identified [3], ask them to identify a belief that they have, which we call [4], one which has no emotional content, good or bad, noting the submodalities. It will provide a half-way location, where the belief will be real but unimportant.

7. Invite A to place [3] in the location of [4].

8. When this is done, ask A how they perceive [3] in this half-way location.

9. Invite A to identify a belief held absolutely, which we call [5], a strong, universal belief, such as *"The sun will rise tomorrow,"* noting its submodalities.

10. Invite A to take [3] from its half-way location and to fix it in the location of [5], giving it the submodalities of [5].

11. When this is done, ask A how they perceive [3] in this new location.

12. *Future Pace:* Ask A to imagine a time when the new belief is tested. How does it go in their mind? How do they feel as a result?

Note: Steps 6–8 are optional but recommended to make a new belief real before making it universal.

Conclusion: Realizing the Structure of Your Subjective Experience

By now, you will have noticed how operating at the level of structure instead of content greatly simplifies and shortens working with issues.

You will have realized the difference between descriptive and evaluative language.

You will have learned how to find out more about the way people, yourself included, structure their thinking using sensory-specific language. Attuning yourself to the predicates people employ to express themselves, you will have learnt how to identify their *primary system* of operating. Developing your sensory acuity, you will have found how the directions people flick their eyes suggest the way they access a memory, their *lead systems.*

You will have begun to learn shorthand ways to notate the sequence of sensory information, external and internal, which makes up people's experience.

You will have realized that your perceptions of reality are not only stranger than you thought, but perhaps even stranger than you could think, and yet you will have enjoyed the ways in which you can work with your perceptions.

Realizing the structure of your subjective experience gives you a wide range of new tools to develop your Emotional Intelligence, making your emotions work with you and for you, as opposed to against you. After all, if you don't like them, you can change them and now, you know how to do that! You may even become curious about the formatting which gave them the negative meaning they had. We know of many people who have become aware of this new power over the structure of their experience and have systematically re-explored past unresourceful experiences to recode them in a way which serves them better. They have also found much useful material within them which they had not anticipated and they even had fun doing it. And isn't that what Emotional Intelligence is about?

Meta-Programs: The Filters in Your Thoughts

As mentioned many times above, our thought processing is the result of a series of successive and interacting filters, both "on the way in and on the way out." Emotions, among others, are a consequence of such filtering. To describe the structural foundations of emotions, a powerful instrument like the Meta-Programs model is therefore invaluable, as it enables you to discern and discriminate the filters which are operating in your mind at any given time, and to change them if you need to do so.

The Meta-Programs model was developed in the beginning of the 1980s.[13] It was inspired by the archetypes of Carl Jung and the most widely employed personality factor questionnaire of the day, namely the Myers-Briggs Type Indicator (MBTI), itself derived from Carl Jung's model by his own daughter.[14] Together with a number of similar models Meta-Programs have since evolved into an important instrument in the field of cognitive psychology. You may have heard of them as "cognitive styles" or "patterns of influence." A cognitive style describes a common way to filter and structure information and experience. This includes skills and competencies as well as the values which underlie them.

Like the model of the neurological levels this model helps you to identify a structure in the content of communication. Once you have studied the Meta-Programs and begun using them, you'll become aware that the way people use Meta-Programs can differ completely from one to another, and that a conversation at any level, professional or personal, can end in a complete disaster because of such individual variances.

For example: some people are interested in the *big picture* and do not pay much attention to *details*, while an explanation cannot have enough details for others. If someone is summing up the details of an issue and you're not interested in them, you are each on a different wavelength: you'll probably feel bored by their enumeration and pernickety approach while, on the other hand, they may feel confused by your vague and "woolly" language.

---

[13] Although authorship cannot be firmly established and many people claim the honor of doing so, they were probably developed by Leslie Cameron-Bandler.

[14] She was called Isobel Briggs-Myers.

> ## Definition
> Meta-Programs are unconscious sorting filters which
> determine our ways of behaving, thinking and feeling. These
> filters determine what we are able to perceive at any given
> time and how we interact with ourselves, others and the
> world. They construct and ratify our model of the world.
> Although Meta-Programs are universally shared, the way we
> apply them varies from person to person.

Meta-Programs can be recognized in expressions, behavior and
answers to questions. Indeed, by asking a number of simple questions, we can gain profound insight into the structure of someone's
personality, such as in the way they motivate themselves and how
they tackle problems.

By studying Meta-Programs we can do the following:
1. Increase our self-knowledge by discovering how our emotions
   are linked to specific patterns.
2. Enhance our own flexibility and emotional competence, as well
   as accompanying values, by developing the Meta-Programs
   complementary to those we habitually run.
3. Screen others for suitability by using Meta-Programs.
4. Build rapport with other people by identifying their running
   Meta-Programs and using them to achieve outcomes which
   will satisfy all parties.

When you have discovered a Meta-Program, you can ask at least
two questions:
1. What is so important about using this specific Meta-Program?
   What is the positive intention behind this use? What is the
   underlying *value* which motivates this use?

Example: Person A is an *Away From* person. The positive intention
has to do with being in control of their own **safety.**
Person B doubts a lot, cannot concentrate and is extremely *Option-
oriented*. The positive intention has to do with keeping open
choices and possibilities in order to retain a sense of **freedom.**

2. Where would it be useful to complement your Meta-Program
   with its opposite?

Example: *Away From* people avoid problems. Everything is under control. There are hardly any risks. However, putting too much emphasis on this can have negative consequences. A possible solution, e.g. in a relationship or in a team, will come from complementing your skills with those of another person who is more a *Towards*. Another solution would be to develop the skills of defining goals for yourself, and then of planning actions which move you towards those goals.

The person who keeps options open in order to feel freedom may never be able to decide or to proceed to action. They can acquire the skill to elaborate on one particular option and to evaluate it afterwards. Or else somebody will end up deciding in their place!

A person who often identifies with a particular Meta-Program does this because they treasure and cherish it: it is very precious to them, even "invaluable." For instance, you may say: "I am an *'Options* person,' I am creative and free." However, this kind of attitude may have undesirable effects on the way you operate. Sometimes you may find it more appropriate to behave according to your complementary polarity (in this case: following *procedures*, as when you get checked in at the airport; making decisions and sticking with your choice, as when choosing a new job). This means you'd be well advised to develop the complementary Meta-Program and keep it available for such eventualities.

There are many Meta-Programs, some of which are shared by all and some which we develop ourselves for our own needs. You have already learnt about one of the former, Representational Systems, earlier in this chapter, and about one of the latter, the Disney Model, which sorts people into Dreamers, Realists and Critics, in an earlier chapter. In this book we choose to limit ourselves to the most distinct Meta-Programs,[15] which can be used in the selection of staff and which also allow the mapping out of relationship problems and personal growth.

---

[15] In an NLP training course between 15 and 26 patterns of Meta-Programs are discussed, which is much more than you can remember when you take into account that you can keep, consciously, only 7±2 pieces of knowledge at a time in your mind. For a more complete discussion we refer to the books *Words that Change Minds* by Shelle Rose Charvet, Kendall/Hunt Publishing Company, Dubuque, Io., 1995, and *Figuring Out People*, by L. Michael Hall and Bob Bodenhamer, Crown House Publishing, Carmarthen, 1997.

In order to present Meta-Programs to you we will introduce them as pairs of polarities (which most of them are), in a professional context and as if we are dealing with extremes. Of course real life is much more subtle than that. Our experience shows that the Meta-Programs you apply in one context can strongly differ from those you use in other contexts. In your professional life, for example, you may act in a very proactive way, but at home you may prefer to leave everything to its own devices. We experience extremes of Meta-Programs only in extreme contexts. Although it may be appropriate to be very strongly *Away From* when avoiding being eaten by a lion, and very strongly *Towards* when proposing to a loved one or applying for a pay rise, in most contexts our Meta-Programs are usually somewhere along the continuum.

Motivational characteristics

Our first series of Meta-Programs demonstrates the structure of motivation. By learning about your own motivational characteristics and how to find out about other people's, you can considerably increase the effectiveness of your communication and learn how to influence another person by using their motivational characteristics in a respectful manner.

We will begin by discussing the **degree of action** you can expect from someone. Next we will deal with the **direction** of this motivation, the **criteria** that underlie the motivation, the **reason** for the motivation, the **source** of the motivation and the **factors which govern the decision**.

1. Degree of initiative, energy level: reactive or proactive?

Do you take the initiative or do you wait for others to do so?
How do you reach the customer? How do you know what to do?

- Think about something you did.
  Question: Did you do it in response to an issue or because you
  wanted to? Is that your typical way of operating?

	REACTIVE	*PROACTIVE*
DEFINITION	*Either other people decide what should happen or they think the situation over very well.*	*People who do not wait until the occasion presents itself, but who jump in.*
EXAMPLES AND INDICATIONS IN LANGUAGE	• Are you sure about that? • Think before you start • The market is not ready • First let's consider the risks • "Waiting for Godot" • The wolf scares the little pigs	• What are we waiting for? • Act first, think later • We will stimulate the demand • Everything under control • Dynamic or dynamite • The little pigs build houses to protect themselves
ADVANTAGES	• Good at analyzing jobs • Helpdesk staff: waiting for a call • Research and analysis oriented jobs	• Good for taking initiatives and doing things • Hard-selling, independent

Reactive people refuse to believe they can control their own life.
They cannot do much about it: the organization is stopping them
or the market is not ready. Well begun is half done and not many
new chances will present themselves ... They tend to be fatalists.
Reactive language: passive verbs, subjects left out, uses objects, convoluted sentences.

Reactivity can be stimulated by questions like "Did you check all
the possibilities?" "Do you know the risks and what would you do
if this happens?" At a specific moment you will have to turn to
action.

Proactive people assume that their motivation and action are the
most important source of their success. They take their life in their

own hands and find it difficult to wait for the vagaries of bureaucracy. Life continues and standing still is going backwards ...

Proactive *language: Active verbs, specific subjects, short sentences.*
A manager stimulates **proactivity** by questions like "What will you do now specifically?" "When will I see the result?" ... Sometimes it is useful to guide proactivity in order to keep the person on the right track.

The majority of people are both proactive and reactive. Only few of them will show extreme patterns. In a job interview you should therefore assume that both proactive and reactive factors are operating. Decide for yourself at the end of the interview whether one of the patterns is clearly dominating, or whether the other pattern was almost completely absent.

2. Motivation Direction: Towards or Away From

A couple enters a travel agency. "Where are you going?" the friendly assistant asks. She gets two replies. One answers: "I want to go to Patagonia," while the other says: "I want to get away from here." What will happen?

What is inciting you to action? What direction will you follow? Are you moving **towards** your goal or **away from** your problems?

- Think of something you have chosen deliberately (object, car, house, job, area of living, partner, …)
  Question: Why did you choose this particular item?

- Think of something you deliberately left behind (job, partner, …)
  Question: What made you leave it?

	AWAY FROM	*TOWARDS*
DEFINITION	*People who easily recognize what should be avoided and who are motivated to avoid a number of consequences.*	*People who are motivated by focusing on their goals.*
EXAMPLES AND INDICATIONS IN LANGUAGE	• Solving problems • Quitting smoking because you do not want to get lung cancer • Running away from home, and choosing the wrong partner • Health = "le silence des organes" (the silence of the organs) • Being motivated by deadlines • Saving money because you do not want to be poor • Avoiding pain	• Visualizing, positive thinking • Buying a car because of its status • Helping people because of the satisfaction it gives • Who am I? • Educational goals
ADVANTAGES	• Strong motivation, wanting to change something • Detecting barriers • Steering clear of differences	• Clear direction • Activation of the desired neuro-physiology • Putting first things first

Some managers are moving towards their goals to such an extent that they create many problems. Their colleagues know a thing or two about that because they have to find solutions when their bosses blunder.

Other managers are too much *Away From*. The results of the company stagnate because they want only to avoid risks.

A number of emotions are clearly *Away From*. Fear and shyness are some typical examples. These emotions prevent you from ending up in an unpleasant situation.

Criteria and their connection with Away From/Towards

The three questions below allow an individual to express their "Away From-Towards" Meta-Programs:

> "What do you expect from your job?"

The answer to this question will express the underlying criteria of what is important to the person.

> "Why is it important to you?"

When we make decisions, we are using hierarchical criteria. The content of this question indicates the criteria while its structure gives you the hierarchy of importance between the criteria.

Some possible answers:
- Responsibility
- Respect/honest work
- Training opportunities
- Being able to believe in it
- Freedom/space for initiative
- Being appreciated (and paid accordingly)
- Let myself go, having fun/a good feeling
- Challenges (giving kicks)/ competitive environment

> "When you are able to realize criterion X (elicited above), what will it lead to, which is even more important to you?"

Possible replies to these questions:
>   To question 1: "a challenging job to which I can apply my
>   knowledge"
>   To question 2: "responsibility"
>   To question 3: "being appreciated"

In a person's hierarchy of values, the response to question 3 is the most important value. You can continue to ask the question until the person indicates that nothing is more important or until they begin repeating the same value.

Management

If you know a person's criteria, you can "translate" the assignments you are giving them according to these criteria. The person will be more motivated to achieve their goal, especially when practice has shown that values are important to reach any goal.

Example:
- I really respect you, therefore I give you this assignment.
  (value = respect)
- I am sure you will learn a lot from this assignment.
  (value = learning)

Sales

A client wants to buy your product because it satisfies certain needs, and/or because it meets their criteria.

Example:
- This product will work for you and it will give you more opportunities to do what matters for you.
  (value = freedom)
- We really believe in this product's potential and that it can satisfy the needs of clients like yourself.
  (value = believe in)

3. The Motivation Reason: Options Person or Procedure Person

How do you think (literally)?

Are you constantly seeking to find a better solution or do you prefer to walk well-trodden paths, with a detailed procedure or the solutions which have proven to be reliable?

Do you believe in "the best solution"?

• Choose a field (i.e. relationship, job, home, holiday, ...)
Question: why did you choose it?

• What does your typical working day look like?
Question: why did you choose this job?

	PROCEDURES	OPTIONS
DEFINITION	*People who like to follow a certain path in order to reach their goal.*	*People who usually see different options, and choose one of them after appraising them.*
EXAMPLES AND INDICATIONS IN LANGUAGE	• There is a correct way for doing that • Be determined to finish something • Meticulously plan and follow the schedule • If someone asks them how they got to a specific point, the story will be told in a chronological order, the order in which the events occurred. • Pilots, teachers, nurses, ... • First we do this, then this, later on that, ...	• People who love to create procedures but who never follow them • Even though the person is successful, they will look for other ways • Architects, programmers • 'You have the following options to choose from: ...' • Even if it is clear which option is the best, they will still search for another one.
ADVANTAGES	• Safety, versatility • Methodology	• Possibilities • Choice, ...

This Meta-Program often plays an important role when recruiting staff. Ask yourself: "Is this a job where procedures will need to be followed, or is it one in which procedures are to be devised, or where new methods, products or systems will need to be invented?"

The difference between *Options* and *Procedures* people can often end up in a cultural clash. For example, most computer scientists are rather *Options* people and they are constantly looking for better ways to deal with things. Take, for example, the number of software upgrades and new versions which have been appearing on the market in the past few years. Marketing and sales people despair, the former because they usually develop a schedule about how to sell a product in the best possible way, and the latter since they are not able to adapt their sales strategies to the latest features of the packages. Will it come as a surprise to hear that some of the best salespeople are those who strictly follow a fixed sales procedure? This is not an "eternal truth," however: some companies, especially at the cutting-edge of technology, emphasize the creativity of their salespeople. It may therefore be possible that their salesmen are more Option-oriented. So, instead of fixating on preconceptions regarding people's occupations, the best way to use Meta-Programs is therefore as an analysis tool for determining which, according to the needs of a specific organization, are the most effective and relevant, and to tailor posts only after determining these and not before.

Blindly following procedures might have some strange effects. In December 1998, the *Observer* printed an article about a German driver who absolutely trusted his built-in BMW navigation system. When crossing the Hasel River in eastern Germany, he ignored warning traffic signs and people yelling to him that the ferry was not there. As the "procedure" had not mentioned a ferry at all, his drive ended four meters deep in the river, as he thought he had to cross a bridge. Fortunately he only got drenched. Do you think he will know now that the map is not always the territory?

Let's take another look at our traveling couple. The *Procedures* person has made up an itinerary, which is to be followed. Along the way the *Options* person gets an idea and wants to change the final destination. What will happen?

4. Motivation Source: Internally or Externally Referred
For this pair of Meta-Programs we will broaden out the context to relate it to personal issues as well. Now, how *internally* or *externally* are you motivated in your decisions? When buying a car, are you influenced by what friends or family think about good cars or do you have your own preference, apart from what your surroundings tell you or what the press thinks about cars?

So, what motivates you? The outside world, because of what people you respect tell you, or your own beliefs and standards?

Question: How do you know you did the right thing?
How do you know your decision is the right one?

	INTERNAL REFERENCE	*EXTERNAL REFERENCE*
DEFINITION	*People who evaluate themselves and whose decisions are made according to their own criteria.*	*People who evaluate themselves and whose decisions are made according to other people's criteria.*
EXAMPLES AND INDICATIONS IN LANGUAGE	• They do not take feedback for granted • Appreciation hardly influences them • Generate many ideas • Strong feeling of "I," "Self" • Want to feel they make decisions based on their own experience, not on what others might say	• They need feedback to know how they are doing • Need appreciation • They often think they did something wrong • Try to be nice and good • Cannot cope with arguments or depreciation • Feel personally hurt by criticism
ADVANTAGES	• Self-determination • You know where you stand with these people • Self-confident, self-assured	• Conflicts are avoided • Relationships are preserved

Externally motivated people tend to be easily influenced. A salesman, however, cannot take too much advantage of this. After all, ask yourself how the external person selects the person by whom they will be influenced. Besides, there is still a chance that another person, coming after the salesman, will neutralize their influence.

Internally referred people can easily become dogmatic and set in their ideas, unless they manage to change their mind through a process of internal reflection, a retreat or a sabbatical.

Internally motivated people tend to experience more problems with authoritative or patronizing management. They function optimally in self-employment, in situations with low supervision or where they're given free rein.

External people, however, need this kind of management. They function best when they are under strict management or when good role models are present. Sometimes good contact with colleagues is sufficient to meet this need for external reference. Self-employment or working from home, which the information revolution is now encouraging, will only be a viable option for them if they manage to sustain a network which will provide them with the external reference they require.

External reference forms the basic structure of emotions such as caution, expectantly taking others into account.

Watch our inexperienced couple, now traveling in India. The taxi driver takes them to a hotel other than the one they asked for. The couple are surprised: "This is not our hotel!" "That's right," says the driver, "but your hotel is temporarily closed. This is a magnificent hotel as well." What will happen?

5. Decision Factors: Motivated Decisions based on "Similarity" or "Difference"

What is your reaction to changes and how often do you want to change things? Are you motivated by discovering in new things similarity with something you already know, or do you prefer radically new things? Do you opt for continuous improvement or do you prefer a rather different business process design?

Question 1: Is there a relationship between what you were doing this time last year and what you are doing now?
In your relationships (love relationships, brother/sister relationship), are you drawn to people like you or to people different from you? Sum up a few examples.

Question 2: What is the relationship between the figures of the drawing opposite?

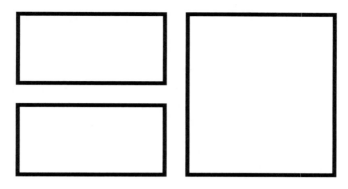

	SIMILARITY	*DIFFERENCE*
DEFINITION	*People who notice common elements in things.*	*People who notice differences between things.*
EXAMPLES AND INDICATIONS IN LANGUAGE	• Do not like changes • Aim for permanent jobs • Like rituals • Can be motivated by showing them the similarities with something they have already done	• Search and find differences • Are discouraged when things do not change • Do not understand the word "relationship" • Like to change interior
ADVANTAGES	• Safety, stability	• Creativity, innovation

People use similarity and difference in many ways throughout their lives. If you are looking for a new job, you'll check to what extent the job suits your competence and your desires. The moment you want to change your job, suddenly you begin to notice all the differences between what you have and what you want to have. Or when you are tired of your house or apartment, you suddenly become aware of how much your home differs from what you really want.

Adolf Hitler was an expert at utilizing similarity and difference to nefarious ends, as you can see in the following quote from *Mein Kampf* (1925): "The art of truly great popular leaders has consisted chiefly in not distracting the attention of the people, but concentrating always on a single adversary. It is part of a great leader's genius to make even widely separated adversaries appear as if they belonged to one category." This style of operating is also used by other authoritative regimes. Libya, Iran, Iraq and Cuba do not need to show much creativity: they can group all their adversaries under the "imperialistic influence of the United States of America," "the great Satan." The *Similarity* Meta-Program has a way of turning variations on a spectrum into extremes or absolutes. Something becomes either Good or Bad. The US themselves have a way of perceiving people in a very polarized manner: "Either you're our ally or you're our enemy." Thus in the 1970s Iran under the Shah was an ally and so was Iraq. Under the Ayatollahs, Iran became an enemy and Iraq was heavily supported in armaments when they fought their very dirty war against Iran. Then Iraq became an Enemy when they invaded Kuwait. Such extremes of polarization do not allow much leeway for diplomacy.

On the other hand, perceiving only differences without being able to regroup them into similarities can also make life very awkward. Communication itself is based on finding similarities between people so that they can share ideas and opinions and, ideally, find common ground on which to build. How easy do you find it to decide what to eat in a Chinese restaurant or take-away, when presented with hundreds of different dishes? If you are strongly *Difference* motivated, you'll probably want to investigate each and every dish and coming to a decision may take a long time.

The very concept of sorting depends on finding similarities and differences: This/Not That. The progress of science is based on this interplay between similarity and difference. This is the well-known analysis/synthesis method of operating. First you notice something(s) nobody else had noticed before—a difference, then you begin to regroup these new findings—a similarity, by developing a theory which explains it, often by comparing and contrasting with existing data.

Another example: when beginning a new relationship you will notice a lot of similarities, which draw you together. After some time you will especially notice differences, some of which might even be sufficient to want to break this relationship. Does that mean they were not there before? Not at all: all this data was present from the start and only your perception has changed. You may therefore find it useful to engage your similarity filter again in difficult periods such as this. Then you will be able to realize that there are actually as many reasons to stick together as there are to separate. As before, context is key. Deliberately using both filters will render a much more complete description, as in the saying: "The real Wisdom is seeing similarity in differences and differences in similarity."

Let's return to our traveling couple. One of them wants something different this year. They have been to the Algarve for several years and one has had it with Portuguese beaches. Moreover, this traveler would like to eat something exotic, you know, something you hardly ever find here. The other—the procedure person?—would prefer to go to the same destination as before. In addition, our traveler wants to take food with them: "You can't really want to eat all this strange food, can you?" How will they solve this problem?

Operating Characteristics

Our second series of Meta-Programs demonstrates the structure of your operating, how you work, in what operating environment you feel comfortable, and what kinds of roles and duties suit you best.

6. The Direction of your Attention: On Yourself or On Others

Do you pay attention to the non-verbal behavior of other people or do you prefer to keep your emotions to yourself and think others should do so as well?

Question: How do you behave in the presence of other people?
On whom is your attention directed?

Note: Instead of asking the question, you may learn more about a person by observing them in a discussion.

	SELF PERSON – INTROVERT	*OTHER PERSON – EXTROVERT*
DEFINITION	*People who focus their attention on themselves.*	*People who show attention to and are conscious about the presence of other people.*
EXAMPLES AND INDICATIONS IN LANGUAGE	• Show few emotions • Hardly show non-verbal contact • Concentrate on content. • Do not get hints or do not feel how they should behave • A person is fully concentrated on a book they are reading and doesn't hear what someone is saying	• Show contact in attitude and facial expression • Become more lively when others are present • Seek eye contact • Are attentive to the needs of other people, often even anticipating them
ADVANTAGES	• You know what is going on inside you	• Good understanding, co-operation, team-working

A *Self* person will select a product based on the criteria they consider important. If you're a salesperson, your language and focus on the preferences of your interlocutor will have hardly any influence on their decision. However, if your interlocutor is an *Other* person, your adapting to them will be of major importance, as your understanding of their need will stimulate their decision.

While an *Other* person considers important the way the message is presented, a *Self* person sets great store on the content of a message itself.

The direction of your attention indicates your ability to be by yourself or your interest in being around other people. How do you recharge your emotional batteries? By being with others or by being on your own?

Many people confuse this pair of Meta-Programs with that of Motivation Source (Internal-External). In actual fact many *Self* people, especially preoccupied with themselves, are often externally referenced: this means that they take high account of what they think other people expect from them. In so doing, they live according to an image of social desirability, hoping to be a sympathetic leader or an ideal wife. They will avoid entering into a conflict because they fear not being appreciated. Paradoxically, people who take into account other people's opinion are worried about their own ego.

Internal reference, however, is a skill you can acquire, which does not at all mean you have to stop directing your attention to what others think and feel. After all, in order to receive enough attention from your fellow people and to become a competent leader, you need, first of all, to be an external person who pays enough attention to other people and their needs, otherwise at best they'll ignore you, or, at worst, you'll alienate them.

If you get in an extreme situation, your Meta-Program can change drastically from your habitual pattern. Consider what happens when a person gets to hear: "You are fired!" At that moment, people often go into a trance where they focus completely on themselves, and have no attention for the world around them. While coping with such a situation, or when losing a relative, it may take a while to "recover" and one could stay in this pattern for some time.

So what are our traveling couple up to? One goes to do a lot of sight-seeing, to visit cities and museums, to encounter other people and cultures. For example, walking round a local market is really nice, because you meet all these people and see how they live. And when you have dinner, say, in the Club Med restaurant, it is really nice to be in the company of other people. The other prefers to stay at the campsite or resort and goes to the beach every day. By the way, they say cooking is something you should do yourself, since others are not that good at it. Moreover, there is nothing more annoying than sharing your table with other people. So, how will they go about this?

7. Sense of Time: In-Time or Through-Time

While you are at work, do you constantly keep an eye on the clock, do you know your daily schedule by heart and are you punctual? Or do you get absorbed by what you do and lose track of time?

Question: How important is it for you to know the time? What is more important, finishing a job you are doing or going to a meeting you have to attend?

	IN-TIME	*THROUGH-TIME*
DEFINITION	*Being absorbed by your work and losing track of time.*	*Although you are working on something, you keep track of time and of the things which are going to happen.*
EXAMPLES AND INDICATIONS IN LANGUAGE	• Not worried about deadlines • Remembers past events by association with other events • Can tell you at the end of the day what they have been doing, but not how long they have been working on specific things • Asks questions which sometimes seem irrelevant to other people: these originate in their own individual thinking process • Creativity, doing things is more important than the actual result • Acts without thinking	• Able to place life events in time (organize chronologically) • Remembers passed events in the order they happened • Can tell you exactly how long something took • Are systematic, knowing exactly where they are in relation to their target • While they are in a meeting they will already start thinking about the next one • They need a lot of background information to reach a conclusion
ADVANTAGES	• When they do something which needs concentration, time is nothing but a distraction	• When planning, they think of a specific period of time

Everybody knows the expression "Time is money," but is this really the case? In some cultures, for example in Bali, people have a completely different experience of time than in our hectic

Western way of life. Studies show that these people are not less happy than the average man in the West, quite the opposite. Or to use an Indian's words: "Waiting is the illness of those who do not live." When you are continuously worrying about what you should be doing later, you cannot possibly concentrate on what you are doing right now.

This pattern is related to the associated/dissociated submodality pattern we looked at in Lesson 1: if you really associate with an event, then you are "In-Time" and live in the moment. To be "Through-Time" and see the inexorable progression of time requires a certain degree of dissociating from what you are doing, so that you become aware of a time continuum.

The anthropologist Edward T. Hall has investigated the way cultures perceive time around the world. He has identified two types of cultures which exactly match the above model: the so-called Western culture, where people are very aware of the passing of time, which he calls "Monochronic," and the rest of the world, including Mediterranean countries, who go with the moment, which he calls "Polychronic."[16]

Every three months you, a medical sales representative, get 10 minutes of a doctor's time. Do you manage to start a conversation in which the doctor loses track of time, or do you get the "sorry, time's up" reaction? And do you think about your schedule for the rest of the day or about something else, or do you also lose track of time?

The most striking story we heard in this context is as follows: a man was angry with his wife because she paid attention to him in bed for only one hour. How could the man concentrate on what he was doing when he kept an eye on his watch?

Ouch, this one will be something for our couple! They have arrived in India and reached the railway station well on time. However, the train they have booked on hasn't and they have to wait for hours ... Frustration and boredom are typically Western reactions. One casts it off and gets fascinated by everything which

---

16   Hall, Edward T. (1976). *Beyond Culture,* New York, Anchor Books/Doubleday.

is going on in the station. The other one is constantly looking at the clock and swears: "I'll never come back to India again." What will happen when the train arrives?

The next two sets of Meta-Programs are also polarities but, as well as the extremes, we present the middle ground.

8. Reaction under Stress: Emphasis on Feelings, Choices or Thinking

How do you react when you are under pressure? Do you get emotional or do you start to think? Or does it depend on the cause of the stress?

• Think about one specific working situation where you experienced problems.

Question: Tell me more about it. What did you think of the situation?

	FEELING	*CHOICE*	*THINKING*
DEFINITION	*People who react emotionally when confronted with stress situations pressure.*	*People who have the choice to react either emotionally or not.*	*People who keep cool in stress situations and who do not show their emotions.*
EXAMPLES AND INDICATIONS IN LANGUAGE	• Easily show emotions • Combination of changes in voice, body posture and gestures or facial expressions • Artists	• First they react emotionally but they can calm down at least for a moment • Can empathize with other people, but when under pressure they can also calm down	• React very cool— not emotional at all • Pilot or air traffic controller
ADVANTAGES	• Are good at passionate jobs (artist, chef, ...)	• Best in sales jobs: good in empathizing as well as in coping with setbacks	• Are very good in high stress jobs

These Meta-Programs are key to achieving the Emotional Intelligence you sought reading this book. In Lesson 1 we already discussed how to control your emotions and we gave some examples of the way emotions can help you and work for you instead of against you. To be able to do this you need to achieve this balance between the heart and the head, i.e. to operate at the level of *choice* between *feeling* and *reason*, depending on the context and the outcome you set yourself, not at either extreme but able to navigate across the spectrum. This way, you will be neither a robot, blindly carrying out a task irrespective of consequences, nor an animal, slave to irrepressible emotions, but plain and simply human, fully and completely, in just the way that you want it. When you get the hang of the techniques we have been introducing you to, you too will become part of the group of "*Choice* people," which according to a survey[17] carried out in the US, constitutes 70% of the population.

Donald Laird, an American psychologist, distinguishes between five skills which are required for leadership and which can be linked to *Choice*:

- Can you deal with a serious insult without actually exploding?
- Can you get through a bad period without being discouraged?
- Can you laugh together with other people when you are the butt of their laughter?
- Do you have enough energy to keep going when everything goes wrong?
- Can you keep calm in emergency situations?

Remember the neurolinguistic assumption about having more chances to succeed when you have more choices available to you. The essence of assertiveness lies in knowing how to balance your emotions, after calmly thinking everything over and putting all elements together.

What is our traveling couple up to, now? They decide to relax and do nothing for a whole week, just enjoy the beach, take a snack and walk about, hand in hand. At night they go to bed. Before switching off the light, they see a gecko crawling on the wall. One screams in panic. The other says: "Don't worry. It's normal here. It

---

[17]   According to a survey by Rodger Bailey, who elaborated the LAB profile, a kind of psychological test for recruiting based on Meta-Programs.

won't do any harm." But the first won't calm down. The other is trying hard but can't get hold of the animal. The first does not sleep a wink. What happens next?

9. Working Style (Independent/Proximity/Co-Operative)

In what kind of context do you work at your best: independently, with strictly defined responsibilities; with other people around, whom you need to help you to achieve your goals; or in a team, with shared responsibilities? How long can you be alone in the office without calling anybody or talking to someone?

- Think back to a situation where you were successful.

Question: Do you attribute the result to yourself or to the team?

What do you need to be successful again?

	INDEPENDENT	*PROXIMITY*	*CO-OPERATIVE*
DEFINITION	*People who want to do things on their own.*	*People who want to reach a goal together with other people, but who do need defined responsibilities.*	*People who like to work together with other people and who consider team spirit very important.*
EXAMPLES AND INDICATIONS IN LANGUAGE	• Working in own office with closed doors • I have reached my goal • I, my job • Autocratic leader	• Together with other people in an office, consulting, but everybody has their role and responsibilities • Other people co-operated as well, but I did …	• Working in open-plan office • The team achieved the results • We, our assignment • Finds it hard to give orders
ADVANTAGES	• Can concentrate for a long time • Functions best where contact with colleagues is not necessary	• Best attitude for managers of people and projects	• Ideal for assignments which are too complex to split up

When you come across "teamwork is important" in advertisements, what does it actually mean? Is the team really responsible or do the people in the team have their own responsibilities? Is a lot of interaction with colleagues required or not?

When designing an organization, one decides about how many people should co-operate and to what extent. An important factor here is how to allocate the tasks. If one person on their own is capable of doing all the necessary work, the degree of communication is very small. Since most organizations employ more than one person, and since it is quite difficult to combine all the necessary knowledge in one single person, processes are often split up. For example: the salesman visits the customer, the administration takes care of the order and the logistics department takes care of the delivery. In a larger organization the administration can be layered up even more: somebody to carry out the administration, somebody to check the creditworthiness, somebody to plan the deliveries, etc. Nowadays, of course, computers make it easier to combine all the knowledge in one operator, which has been at the origin of much "delayering." The person who deals with various parts of the job is called a "knowledge worker," and doesn't need to communicate very often with their colleagues.

We would like to draw your attention to a key pattern we often come across in changework (whether therapy or coaching), most commonly in an employment situation, in relation to these specific Meta-Programs. A consequence of the delayering process we mentioned above is that many people who find themselves on the employment market decide to become self-employed: there are now more people striking out for self-employment in the world than ever before. However, their likelihood of success is proportional to the level of motivation they can sustain in themselves. People usually want to change something or achieve a particular goal, but most will not have the sufficient strength to go through with the changes if they are on their own, without the support of their environment. Without partner or colleagues to change with them, nothing happens, because they need someone to pull the cart or to support them. They need a promoter, a supporter, or sometimes even a bully, to keep them going.

There are two possible solutions to this kind of situation. One is external: you look for a promoter for the new need. This can be a friend or people you get to know and trust, or a coach you visit who can keep you on track. The other is internal: you begin to change your own Meta-Program and learn to believe in your own capacities to motivate yourself and sustain your energy levels, irrespective of the task. This, too, can be initially achieved with the help of a coach although, ultimately, you will be able to strike out on your own. After all, what is a book such as this one, but a coach in paper form, where we have thought out processes to enable you to do this. For example, you can practice this last step by going to a restaurant on your own and by actually enjoying it. Or by learning to find the way to a new destination by yourself.

As you can see, this is a revolutionary vision, not an evolutionary one. Any fear for the unknown you may have experienced in a process of change is strongly related to the fear of being alone and with lack of support. Everything you have read so far in this book will have given you tools and material to resolve emotions such as this, to apply the energy trapped in them to good effect to achieve what you want, whether you're in company or on your own. How you use it is up to you.

Back to our traveling couple. They began by doing everything together. But after a couple of journeys, they discovered differences in their responses. One doesn't at all like to sit on the beach the whole day or get a tan near the swimming pool. The other would not mind doing nothing else, but the first remains inflexible. What will happen now? Will they decide to travel by themselves next time—and do it their way? Or will one accompany the other to do them a favour or to hold everything together?

10. Emphasis in Working Organizations: People vs Things

How do people organize their work? Do they put more emphasis on thoughts, feelings and people or do they prefer dealing with ideas, means of help, systems, products and tasks?

Question (the same as for working style):
> "Tell me about a work experience which was … (fill out their criterion). What did you like about it?"

Alternative Questions:
"Tell me about your perfect working day. What is going on?"
"You have an important deadline to reach in an hour and you still have some things to do. At that moment a colleague whom you highly appreciate enters the room, looking confused. They ask for your help. What do you do?"

You can deduce a person's working style from where a person puts the emphasis in the organization of his work (the difference between *independent*, *proximity* and *co-operative*).

● *"People":* oriented to feelings and thoughts (either of yourself or of the other person (for example a customer)). This focus can be found in the organization of their work.
● *Things:* the emphasis is placed on objects like products, or assignments that have to be done.

	EMPHASIS ON PEOPLE	*EMPHASIS ON THINGS*
DEFINITION	*People who focus the attention on themselves.*	*People who pay attention to and are aware of things, processes.*
EXAMPLES AND INDICATIONS IN LANGUAGE	● Talk about people, reactions, feelings or emotions ● State people's names ● People are the objects in their sentences	● Talk about processes, systems, assignments, goals, products, … ● Hardly ever mention people, unless in generalizations: the customer, they, you ● People are not mentioned in sentences, or only as parts of processes or assignments
ADVANTAGES	● Jobs in client service and reception, social worker, geriatric assistants ● Good in communicating, dealing with conflicts and making contacts	● Jobs which are focused on results, on action ● Good in reaching deadlines. The assignment comes first

What is our traveling couple up to this time? They are shortly to return home at the end of their holiday and are buying presents for relatives, friends and colleagues. One wants to buy presents adapted to the preferences of each person who will receive them. The other wants to buy knick-knacks they like themselves. What will happen?

11. Scope: Eye for details or the whole

What kind of work do you deal with best: surveying a whole or realizing particular details? The 19th-century American humorist Josh Billings illustrated the effect of this Meta-Program very well: "Love uses a telescope, jealousy a microscope."

Question: Tell me something about an assignment you had to carry out.
Describe the interior of your living room.

	EYE FOR DETAIL (SPECIFIC)	*ATTENTION FOR THE WHOLE (GENERAL)*
DEFINITION	*People who give all the details of an event.*	*People who give you the general outline and details will be provided only when they are asked for.*
EXAMPLES AND INDICATIONS IN LANGUAGE	• Specific trees in the forest • Important: documents should have no mistakes • Difficulties in reconstructing the general image based on given examples • Wants to check all the details • Accountants, proof-readers • Gives very detailed explanations	• Draft level, abstract thinking, vague words • Wants to find the summary in a document • Must understand the whole before considering the parts as useful • Only scant directions are enough • Leaves out the details
ADVANTAGES	• Meticulously finishing an assignment which requires much precision	• Quickly getting a global view of a company to start taking steps or giving directions • Determining priorities

Following your interlocutor in this Meta-Program requires quite some adaptations. When you are dealing with a *General* person, they may not give you enough information to understand what they are talking about. The *Specific* person, on the other hand, might mention so many details that a *General* person, at a particular moment, will be tempted to give the conclusion of the story or to summarize the whole.

When your boss is a *General* person, the best is to give them a short summary of the results and give more details only when they are asked for. The bosses who are the most difficult to deal with, however, are both *General* and *Specific* people (yes, they exist): you can expect both explanations about what should be done and details about how it should be done. Therefore there will be little room for initiative.

In sales you need to sum up the whole list of properties and advantages when you are dealing with a *Specific* person. In other cases, broad images and explanations will be sufficient.

The preference of a person will show clearly from the length of their answer. When they are a *Specific* person, you get a long explanation. In the other case the answer could be concentrated into one sentence. A friend used this strategy in oral exams. When there was a part of the material he knew very well, he gave an extensive answer. As a result, there was not enough time to get to some other questions about the rest of the material.

When you listen to *Specific* people chatting during their coffee break, you will notice that many people use a lot of graphic details to embellish their story. The same can be said of their account of events. They find it hard to delete or omit anything which might have the slightest importance and do not tend to draw general conclusions. *General* people, on the other hand, are past masters at the art of generalizations, often to the detriment of explicitness.

Our traveling couple finally gets back home. People ask them: "How was the trip?" One of them answers: "Good. Terrific, a wonderful experience." But when the other one starts to talk, you'd better take a seat: "Well, our plane arrived at 21.30 and it was already dark. But it was really hot. And I said we'd better take a cab to get to the hotel. But when we got outside there were so many people waiting that I said ..."

Conclusion: Patterns in Your Emotions
The Meta-Programs of an Emotionally Intelligent person
When we take a look at the model of the neurological levels, we can attempt to describe the personality of the emotionally intelligent individual, based on Meta-Programs.

Meta-Programs are translated into both **capabilities** and **values** to be used in personal as well as contextual situations. An emotionally skilled person is *future-oriented, goal-oriented*. The past, however, is a determining factor for them and they want to learn from it. Therefore it is still their personal *choice* and they can deal with the world in the way they want to.

An emotionally skilled person uses their values as a basis to live on and they try to embody these values and **behave** accordingly. By doing this, they use strong *internal* reference. In other words, they are not run by their **environment** or by other people, but they check what they consider important. Nevertheless, they are *externally referred* as well and do take other people into account. They check *other* people's expectations and these are integrated into their own actions. Furthermore, an emotionally capable person has a *proactive* relation with their own emotions. These are related to the life plan they are developing.

And what about the **identity** of an emotionally intelligent person? What is their self-image like? Maybe they call themselves "Manager" of their own internal and external context, the "captain of their ship." They can be characterized in words like "self-assured" or "full of confidence." They back their own arguments with their own actions. As people say, they "walk their talk." Life can produce many undesired situations, but this does not necessarily prevent them from remaining happy. The life of an emotionally competent person is actually the answer to the question: "How do I want to live my life?"

Further Division of the Meta-Programs

In the US the Language and Behavior (LAB) Institute has been carrying out some research into Meta-Programs, more specifically those which people present in a professional context. The schedule opposite is a simplified version of the results. You will notice that the table is more refined than the division we gave when discussing Meta-Programs. For example, in order to indicate that some people show characteristics of both polarities, the category "both" was added.

META-PROGRAM PATTERN	DIFFERENT RANGES AND PERCENTAGES				
Degree of Initiative: proactive–reactive	*Proactive* 20%	*Both* 60%	*Reactive* 20%		
Motivation Direction: towards–away from	*Towards* 40%	*Both* 20%	*Away From* 40%		
Motivation Reason: options–procedures	*Options* 40%	*Both* 20%	*Procedures* 40%		
Motivation Source: internal–external	*Internal* 40%	*Both* 20%	*External* 40%		
Direction of Attention: self–other	*Self* 7%	*Both* 10%	*Other* 83%		
Decision Factors: similarity–difference	*Similarity* 5%	*Similarity w. Exceptions.* 60%	*Both* 13%	*Difference w. Exceptions* 12%	*Difference* 10%
Scope: eye for detail (specific) or the whole (general)	*Specific* 15%	*Both* 25%	*General* 60%		
Working Style: independent–proximity– cooperative	*Independent* 20%	*Both* 60%	*Co-operative* 20%		
Emphasis in Working Organizations: activity in relation to people–things	*People* 15%	*Both* 30%	*Things* 55%		
Reaction under Stress: feeling–thinking	*Feeling* 15%	*Choice* 70%	*Thinking* 15%		

Exercises for this Lesson

Exercise 4.1: Representation channels: "Sensory-specific observation"

Which of the following sentences is sensory-specific? Code the representation channels used.

	Sensory-specific ? Yes/No	VAKOG?
e.g.: He had yelled so loudly that his throat was hurting.	*Yes*	*A/K*
1. She looked really anxious.		
2. She frowned.		
3. It was quite warm.		
4. Her hands were wet with sweat.		
5. He tendered his regrets.		
6. He was relieved.		
7. The tempo of his speech increased.		
8. They are tired of each other.		
9. They didn't say a word for an hour.		
10. Their collaboration works out fine.		
11. This is a clear example of madness.		
12. The hardness of the soil made me say it was freezing.		
13. His vision was very compassionate.		
14. The fact that he says "no" makes me conclude that he doesn't love me.		

Exercise 4.2: Using predicates that fit with eye movements

For a sequence of coded eye movements, construct sentences using predicates of the same representation channel. (see p. 166)

Example: $A_{di} \Rightarrow V_{ir} \Rightarrow K \Rightarrow A_{de}$ = I was telling myself "I have to plan that" $\Rightarrow$ I visualized my agenda $\Rightarrow$ then I took the phone $\Rightarrow$ and I asked him if next Wednesday was OK.

Write sentences to match the following:

- $V_c \Rightarrow A_d \Rightarrow K$
- $K \Rightarrow V_e \Rightarrow A_d$

- $V_r \Rightarrow A_i \Rightarrow K$
- $A_e \Rightarrow V_c \Rightarrow A_d$

Exercise 4.3: Exploring your primary representation system

Be quiet and observe your surroundings for half a minute. Through which channel does the most information come in: are you talking to yourself, are you listening to outside sounds, are you rather paying attention to what you see, etc.?

Carry this out in a range of contexts: walking around on the street, in a shopping mall, in a movie theater while they are showing commercials, ...

Exercise 4.4: Enriching your communication

Narrate or write about a funny experience using all representation channels (VAKOG). You can do the same for other contexts: e.g. suppose you have a product to sell, or you have to teach some course materials, ...

Exercise 4.5: Enhancing an experience

Choose a recent experience which annoyed you. Tell it (or write it down) in a few sentences. Now enrich the story by using at least four submodalities in each of the representation systems.

Exercise 4.6: A compelling future

1. Choose a goal you want to achieve in the future. Make sure this goal is well-formed (see Lesson 3).
2. Now describe this goal using an extended range of submodalities.
3. Start changing the submodalities of your representation of the goal so that it becomes compelling and irresistible.
4. Final question: how does this exercise relate to the presuppositions of the course?

Exercise 4.7: Linking emotions to sensations

Step 1: With a group of people (three or more), choose several emotions (e.g. fear, loneliness, spiritlessness, ...).

Step 2: Each person individually looks for some contexts and the inner, bodily sensations that are linked to this emotion (remember an experience where you had that emotion and examine the kinesthetic submodalities).

Step 3: Compare the links of context-sensation-emotion you make with the links made by other people. What's similar, what's different?

Exercise 4.8: Observing the lead system

Exercise with partner. Ask your exercise partner questions that refer to each representation channel and observe their eye movements.

Options:

    a. As an extension to the exercise you can ask the person what (s)he did to answer the question;

    b. Make your own sentences, instead of using those we suggested.

V_r—Visual remembered:	—What's the color of the walls of your living room? —What does your house (apartment, …) look like?
V_c—Visual constructed:	—How would a car look in the year 2200? —Imagine a flying bed.
A_r—Auditory remembered:	—How do ice cubes sound when they fall in a glass? —What does your mother's voice sound like?
A_c—Auditory constructed:	—How would Frank Sinatra sound if he sang while having a cold? —What's the sound of a saxophone when played under water?
A_d—Auditory digital:	— Count to ten in your head. —Suppose you have to give a speech; prepare silently.
K— Kinesthetic:	—How did it feel in your bed this morning, just before you got out? —How warm do you rate this room, on a scale from 1 to 5 (1 is cold)?

Exercise 4.9: Detecting predicates
Buy a newspaper, or tape the news on TV or on the radio. Read a piece, or listen to a piece, and sort out which predicates are used in the different representation systems.

Exercise 4.10: Presenting yourself metaphorically
Represent yourself metaphorically using an image of an object (e.g. a car, a piece of furniture, a bird, ...) and describe the visual submodalities of the image you chose. Which of the submodalities would you keep, even if you chose another image?

Repeat the previous step with the other four senses, selecting a sound, a feeling, a smell and a taste to represent yourself (metaphorically) each time, describing the submodalities and selecting the important ones.

Exercise 4.11: Recognize the Meta-Programs

BEHAVIORAL STATEMENT	META-PROGRAM
e.g.: "I just finished this report. Do you want to take a look?"	*External reference*
1. Someone is assembling his newly bought stereo equipment without reading the manual.	
2. I want another job. I hate it when my boss keeps checking on me.	
3. Oh no, I really like that work. The day is over before I know it.	
4. Can't you tell me exactly what steps to take so that this project will be successful?	
5. If you don't have any goals, you'll never know what you really want.	
6. No, I want to reach an agreement on the general principles before going into that discussion.	
7. Some people travel to be immersed fully in new and strange cultures. Others prefer to visit countries with a well-organized, comfortable tour.	
8. The visitors didn't understand it was time to go home, even though the host was yawning from fatigue.	
9. I'd need some more information about the second sentence of the footnote to the third appendix of your proposal.	
10. Client asks therapist: "Do you really think I'm too externally referenced?"	
11. I think that we can reach a better result by working together.	
12. I don't want to be bothered by routine issues, material problems and money issues.	
13. She doesn't dare ask for a divorce because she is afraid what people around her will think.	
14. I think that people needing external reference are sissies.	
15. It was hard for him to leave things behind, since he had been involved in the project from the very beginning.	

BEHAVIORAL STATEMENT	META-PROGRAM
16. He had been paying attention to his watch at least once every minute while filling out that form.	
17. I need to think it over. I'll sleep on it.	
18. By the next morning he had found a solution on his own, so that next week's meeting could be cancelled.	

Exercise 4.12: Contrastive analysis using Meta-Programs

Using the Meta-Programs in the table below, compare a situation (work, relationship, etc.) where everything works out fine (successful context) with a situation where things go wrong (difficult context). What does this teach you about your own driving Meta-Programs?

META-PROGRAMS	SUCCESSFUL CONTEXT	DIFFICULT CONTEXT
Motivation Direction		
Motivation Reason		
Motivation Source		
Decision Factors		
Direction of Your Attention		
Sense of Time		
Reaction Under Stress		
Working Style		
Scope		

Exercise 4.13: Meta-Programs within your own professional context

1. Determine your colleagues', boss's and perhaps your subordinates' Meta-Programs.
2. Imagine you are having (individually) a professional discussion. How can you adapt your language to them, now that you know their Meta-Programs? (for colleagues, your boss, ...)
3. Imagine you have to defend a project at a meeting where everybody is present. How will you adapt your explanation to take into account the Meta-Programs they have in common while, at the same time, building in enough variation to take into account the remaining Meta-Programs which are present?

Exercise 4.14: Meta-Programs as filters of an experience

Discuss with one or more people a movie you have seen together. What will the individual people talk about? Who is using what filters?

Exercise 4.15: Growth target

Formulate a target for your personal growth by using Meta-Programs.

Exercise 4.16: Meta-Program identification

Groups of five. The explorer talks about a present situation.

Step 1: Four observers listen to the explorer for three minutes without intervention. Each observer screens a number of pre-agreed Meta-Programs.

Step 2: The observers retire somewhere and they combine their conclusions.

Step 3: The observers ask the explorer the following question to complete the Meta-Programs. "What is the effect of the present situation on the experience?"

Lesson 5:
Emotional Intelligence
in Company

"Man has ever been the greatest puzzle of man."
Alfred Korzybski

Goals

- To develop your empathy by learning the model of the perceptual positions.[1]
- To learn to look at the world through the eyes of the people with whom you want to interact.
- To acquire a complete perspective of a situation by looking at the whole picture from different angles.
- To make use of this perspective to respond to potentially conflictual situations with more information about the structure of the relationship involved.

Neurolinguistic assumptions

In this chapter, the following assumptions apply:

- *The map is not the territory. Everybody looks at the world through their own individual filters, guided by their experience of life.*
- *Any given behavior is the best choice available at any particular moment in time. If a person had been aware of a "better behavior," according to their own standards, they would have chosen it.*
- *Relationships constitute a systemic whole. The meaning of our communication is based on the response it evokes in others. You can only change someone else's behavior by modifying your own behavior first.*
- *The most flexible component of a given system controls the system.*

---

[1] In neurolinguistic terminology we use the terms "First, Second, Third, Fourth and Meta-Position." These terms will be explained further in this lesson.

Why this Lesson?

Why would you seek to acquire such skills?

1. For conflict resolution:

- What annoys you in another person is a reflection of the internal structure of your representation.
- A conflict is the result of a difference between your internal structure and that of the other person(s). Determining the structure of this difference gives you the flexibility to represent it differently in your mind. By enriching your representation of this difference in more ways than you already have, you increase your ability to manage it better. By looking at the content of the conflict from different angles, you change within you the structural frame of mind which gave rise to this difference. You can therefore choose to act differently to resolve the conflict. Cultivating your flexibility of behavior gives you better control of the outcome of an interaction.

2. For Emotional Intelligence in general:

- Gaining insight into the reasoning of your conversation partner, empathizing with their reactions and anticipating them, are essential skills for Emotional Intelligence.

Perceptual Positions: Empathy for Yourself and for Others

In our introduction you became acquainted with neurolinguistic presuppositions. You learned that "The map is not the territory." We can improve our map it by comparing it to the maps of other people and, if appropriate, merging it with theirs. This is what ancient cartographers learnt to do, thereby identifying different ways of going to a particular location on the planet and discovering many new resources to tap on the way. Most successful negotiators are masters at this skill: like chess players, they will try to assess each possible move of the opponent in advance. Even the influence that each position holds at the negotiation table is drawn out beforehand. In this way they achieve an overview of a situation, which enables them, for instance, to break stalemates by looking for an agreement which takes both points of view into account.

If you are negotiating with somebody, there are at least four ways to look upon the situation (while *associated*):[2]

1. through your own eyes,
2. through the eyes of the other person involved,
3. through the eyes of a neutral observer,
4. through double spectacles resulting from merging your map with that of the other person. (This is a more recently identified pattern.)

Similarly, one can study this situation from a *dissociated* perspective: for instance, as observer of yourself, as observer of the other person and as observer of the entire system. Neurolinguistics refers to such dissociated, observing positions as *Meta-Positions*.

In the mid-1980s, Judith DeLozier and John Grinder developed the model of the perceptual positions, based on the above-mentioned distinctions.[3] We explain this model in detail to you below, illustrating it by way of two examples:

(1) In a case where you are up against a boss who (according to you) does not delegate enough,

and

(2) In a case where you lose yourself too much in an intimate relationship, where you end up not paying enough attention to your own values and needs, but live more according to the needs and expectations of the other person.

In Figure 5.1 overleaf, the two connections between the First and Second Position symbolize the interaction between the two people involved in the communication.

---

[2] Originally called a "Triple Description," it refers to self/other/observer positions. The name has not really changed yet, as many people are still unaware of the Fourth or System Position.

[3] The Fourth Position was not present in the initial perceptual positions model as conceived by Grinder and DeLozier. It is a more recent contribution by Robert Dilts. See previous note.

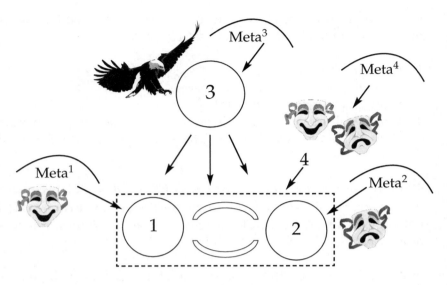

Picture 5.1.: Study of communication: the four observing positions, each with their Meta-Position.

First Position (I-position)

This means looking, listening, feeling, beginning from your own perspective. People with a strong First Position know perfectly well what they want themselves.

To strengthen your First Position, reach a better understanding of yourself by finding out about the structure of your subjective experience. Much of the emphasis of this book is placed on carrying out this process.

Questions   —What DO YOU FEEL NOW?
             —What DO YOU WANT NOW?
             —What are YOUR desires, needs, values?

---

e.g.:

- an employee says: "I do not feel at ease in this job, I want more responsibility."

- a woman says: "I do not feel good in this relationship, I efface myself too much."
- "My idea of an agreeable person," said Hugo Bohm, "is a person who agrees with me."

Benjamin Disraeli[4]

Understanding your motivations and being clear about your outcome and purpose enables you to explore other perceptual positions safely, without losing yourself in them.

An important part of developing your Emotional Intelligence involves being able to shift perspective and looking at a situation from the perspective of another person. This is what we call Second Position. It is best accomplished when you have first investigated the information available in First Position, as you will be able to carry out a "compare and contrast" analysis.

Second Position (You-position)

This means looking, listening, feeling, from the perspective of the other person, as if you were in their shoes.

People with a strong Second Position are able to empathize with the way another person feels and thinks, what another person perceives, etc …

To develop your skills at taking Second Position:
—Associate emotionally; put yourself in someone else's shoes, perhaps even by physically moving into the location of the other person.
—Observe better and decide which observations are relevant from this perspective.

Question :	If you are in someone else's shoes, how do you look at things, at people (including yourself), and what do you feel?

---

4   Quoted in *The Oxford Dictionary of Humorous Quotations.*

The answer enables you to understand the other person and what motivates their behavior. Perhaps, if you were in their shoes, you would do the same thing, and would respond to yourself like that.

e.g.:
- The point of view of the employee's boss: "I hesitate to delegate responsibility to my co-worker because I am scared of losing control."
- The point of view of the woman's partner: "I take the initiative because I want my partner to be happy and because she contributes so little herself."

Notice here how the first two positions we have explored so far are based on an either-or polarity model. This is what is called Digital or Aristotelian Thinking, based on the Laws of Thought devised by the Greek philosopher Aristotle in the 4th century B.C. Aristotle proposed what is essentially an adversarial way of operating,[5] where one person wins and the other loses and the "happy medium" does not exist or is excluded from the range of available options. Such ways of behaving have prevailed for centuries, affecting diplomacy and conflicts as well as parliaments and courts of law throughout the world.

However, our understanding of the world, of people and of the mind has greatly evolved since Aristotle's time. The world is not black and white, but all the grays in between and all the colors of the spectrum, including those below and above our threshold of vision, which we are not aware of. Stepping into other people's shoes can often further heighten the sense of conflict, contradiction or mutual exclusion. Although you have been able to shift your perspective from one tree to another, you still can't see the wood for the trees.

Resolving such conflictual situations requires being able to see BOTH positions at the same time, rising above the fray. Only then can agreement be reached which will not be "either-or," but "both-and," "as well as," which will satisfy both parts. In neurolinguistics, we call this conclusion an ecological one, because it values and respects all parties involved. Great negotiators are able to do

---

5   The Law of the Excluded Middle: "What is is, what is not is not. There is no middle way."
     The Law of Contradiction: "Something cannot at the same time be both A and not-A."

this and generate true *win-win* situations, successfully brokering peace talks between warring factions or pay deals between managers and trades unions. Such skills, essential to the healthy development of Emotional Intelligence, require the ability to take further perceptual positions, which we present below.

Third Position (They-Position, Bird's Eye View)

This means taking the position of a "neutral person," a bystander, for instance a coach or a bird, that *observes* the system from the outside. From this position you can observe yourself, the other person and the interaction going on between both people. You can dispassionately observe the positives and negatives which each party contributes to the situation in order to find ways of resolving the negatives and of bringing the positives together to the satisfaction of both parties. As you can imagine, to learn the Third Position, you must first be familiar with accessing First and Second Positions to find out these resources and discover even more.

People with a strong Third Position can see how they are involved in systems and how, by changing their own behavior, they can create a favourable environment for the other to change as well.

Question: How does the behavior of Person 1 and Person 2 influence each other? What do they do?

This position provides information to break vicious circles, often present in conflicts.

e.g.:
- The first situation as observed by a third person (e.g. the job-coach): "The co-worker is critical towards the boss because he does not delegate any responsibility to him, but the boss does not delegate because the co-worker is so critical."
- The second situation as seen by a third person (e.g. a therapist): "The woman does not feel good because the partner

takes so much initiative, but the man takes a lot of initiative because the woman does not."

A further position was identified more recently, which offers even more insights which none of the others had yet elicited.

Fourth Position (We-Position or Systemic position)

This means the position of "as if" you were the system. When you perceive yourself in *"We"* you relate BOTH to yourself AND to the other. You associate into the global, systemic perspective and  perceive the tensions in the system, feeling the interaction between the different parts of the system, as if they occurred inside you.

Question:	How would it feel to be like Person 1 on the one hand and like Person 2 on the other hand, all at the same time?

To increase your skill in systemic thinking, you can draw out on a piece of paper the different forces and tensions present, and then try to simulate these different forces as if they were present at the same time within you.

This position provides information to understand the forces present in the system.

e.g.:

- The first situation as observed by the system: "If I put delegation and responsibility together I realize that they form the two sides of the same coin, you can't have the one without the other. By explicitly agreeing on the degree of delegation and the level of accountability for this delegating, the tensions will be resolved and I feel confident that the results will be obtained."
- The second situation as seen from the system: "There is so much giving from one side that the other feels pushed into a corner, with nothing left to do. One wonders whether that

side wants to play a more active role and, if so, how to enable it to play it."

Meta-Position (Dissociated Position)

This means being dissociated, observing a person from a distance, while still being the person in that role.

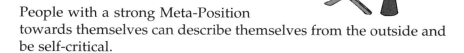

People with a strong Meta-Position towards themselves can describe themselves from the outside and be self-critical.

To exercise Meta-Position, e.g. towards yourself, imagine watching a movie of yourself. You can even choose to use a video camera to record yourself in a particular situation to see how you are doing. This technique is often used in training on topics such as sales, management, handling patients, etc.

Questions:	—How do you look upon yourself?
(for Meta[1])	—Observed from the outside, what is typical about your behavior?

The Meta-Position from the First Position provides interesting information about your external behavior, about how you communicate to the outside world.

e.g.:

- The employee observing himself: "He does not feel good (because he does not get responsibility), and for this reason he cannot be friendly any more with his boss. He has no eye contact and talks in short sentences."
- The woman observing herself: "She effaces herself because her partner takes so much initiative."

Note. Similarly, one can take the dissociated or Meta-Position about any other position we have described. For instance, the question for Meta[2] for the first example could be: "Imagine being the manager, coming home after a conflict with the employee; how would you comment on your own behavior and response earlier on in the day?" We need not consider Meta[3] and Meta[4] in the remainder of this chapter, as these are more theoretical positions used only in some situations.

How to Handle/Control Conflicts

In each relationship you will identify similarities as well as differences. Taken separately, they are no cause of annoyance or conflict in each component. You are going to label something a conflict only when you are annoyed by it. It's not the difference (or the sameness) in and by itself which causes the conflict, but the frame of thinking which leads to your interpretation of this difference.

e.g.:
- Colleagues amongst themselves. One person can deal with the dominant behavior of Person X and the other cannot deal with it at all. When the boss tries "to boss you around," you may for instance "say yes and do no," you might have skills to get your own way, to make the boss think he came up with the solution, etc. If you cannot deal with the behavior of the boss, it may annoy you.

The more tense a conflict is, the more emotions are involved, and the more your personal filters distort your perception of the reality. In such cases you may accuse the other person of being the source of the problem and wish to remove the other person from your life (e.g. dismissal, divorce, or even murder).

By removing the evaluation which this interpretation generates, i.e. reducing it to just stating a fact, you also remove the emotional impact which this evaluation entailed. This thereby reduces the conflict to a level which simply describes differences (or similarities) between the parties involved. Many marriage guidance counsellors carry out such tasks every day. Afterwards the partners can draw up a balance sheet of the relationship together, choosing a way forward from a more dispassionate perspective.

e.g.:

- A couple composed of an extremely sociable woman and an introverted wordless man: after both partners acknowledge each other's individuality (after a lot of communication therapy), there seems to be no desire to go on living with this difference.
- A woman feels misunderstood. She has lost herself in her husband's life, and has lived to take care of his needs, while not taking care of her own. After reinforcing her own sense of self and uniqueness, she has become as strong as her husband and they seem to clash all the time, because she now asks that her needs be taken into account as well. The search for a new form of balance in the relationship begins.

In a conflictual situation, information gets interpreted and ends up being experienced subjectively. To resolve the conflict, you need to reverse this distortion process. To do this, we offer you two skills: One, Asking the Right Questions, in Lesson 6. The other, below, will enable you to complement the available information by successfully taking different perceptual positions, hence enriching your knowledge of the situation by integrating the information uncovered in each position. Thus you will reach a complete view of the conflict which will enable you to create new understandings, leading to forgiveness and change.

A typical characteristic of conflicts is that the amount of information available from the starting position from which you look at the conflict is diminished: this reduces your ability to display empathy for the other person's position, let alone to access an overview of the entire system.

PERCEPTUAL POSITION	FIRST	SECOND	THIRD	FOURTH
Skill Involved	Assertiveness	Empathy	Coaching	Obtaining a win-win

Projection: What Irritation Can Teach You about Yourself

Some joint operations work out better than others. With some persons you achieve a better understanding than with others. What happens if you can't feel good about your relationship with another person?

It is remarkable how some people get entangled in each other's emotions. Sometimes just seeing somebody gets them irritated, expressing dislike and aversion. Or it could be their smell or their tone of voice which annoys them. In such cases, people often describe how bad, dangerous or even evil the other person is. The strength of their emotion of disgust is striking. They cannot stand the other person.

We expect a person matching such a description to be, at that moment in time, associated in their First Position. From First Position, you can state your opinion about a person as being the absolute truth. It *is* like that. But what do you gain by having such an attitude?

In the previous chapters you learned that everybody filters reality in their own way. In Lesson 6 we will study how you filter your experience of reality, leaving out information, generalizing or even changing it in some way. Taking different perceptual positions enables you to partly compensate for your filters. Sometimes you may notice that, starting from First Position, your reaction is very exaggerated, or even caricatural. Irritations have a structure resembling an allergy: it has to do with an overreaction to an environmental stimulus. Even before the other person has become a real psychological or physical threat, you will react in a very emotional way. You may not realize it yet, but your allergic reaction can teach you a lot about yourself, as the way you experience another person is a mirror about the way you think and feel. The involved mechanism is known as "projection" in psychology: what annoys you in others is the part in yourself you seek to suppress.

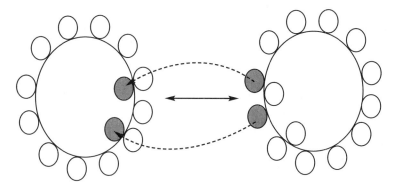

Picture 5.2: Projection in the conflict.

For instance, if somebody's dominant behavior is getting on your nerves, you can ask yourself what your own dominant behavior is about. Maybe you also show dominant behavior, but you consider it bad. Perhaps you are not even aware that you also display dominant behavior (we call this a *blind spot*). Or perhaps you are a very good person and have suppressed all impulses in you to impose your will on others.

Another example: suppose you are annoyed about a person's touchiness. You think they are unable to control themselves and impossible to make appointments with. Of course, this may be the truth, but we do not need to worry about the other person right now. What does the annoyance you are experiencing say about you? What do you mean by touchiness? How come you are annoyed by this? What about your own touchiness? Can you let go or are you rigid? Can there be exceptions to the rule or does everything have to go according to plan?

As guidance, we offer you the following suggestion, which you may find challenging: "What you resent in the other person, is what you need to acknowledge more as part of yourself."

Note
Our experience has taught us that—save in the case of projection in the context of the undeveloped territory of self-development—there may be a further reason why people get annoyed by details of someone's actions. As in the notorious instance of a couple, one member of which got annoyed because their partner squeezed the

tube of toothpaste differently from them, if you begin to take notice of especially trivial details, a deeper source of annoyance could be at work. The trivial annoyance would then be a manifestation of this more deeply-rooted irritation. Many people feel annoyed because they may actually want to have more input into a relationship or because they would like to experience more personal freedom and distance. Whatever may be the case, you need to take your annoyances seriously and to deal and work with them. Conflicts, fights, dismissals, divorces (or even physical injuries) do not result out of differences by themselves, but out of our annoyance about such differences.

A Model for a Qualitative Co-operation

By considering all perceptual positions frequently and discussing their findings with each other, partners may enhance the quality of their relationship and thus increase its likelihood of enduring. If you look at your current or past relationships, you may notice how a certain perceptual position is under-represented. Compensating to redress this

> **BOTH AND**
> instead of
> **EITHER OR**
> instead of
> **NEITHER NOR**
> *Hans-Ulrich Obrist*

balance offers you new opportunities for personal and mutual development!

1. To step forward and maintain your own position

In a number of situations the relationship you have with yourself—the First Position—may get overwhelmed by the attention you pay to the relationship you have with another person, e.g. when you are willing to lose yourself for the other, which results in the other person's priorities becoming more important than yours.

Exaggerated submissiveness often ensues temporarily, as is the case while freshly in love, when you just follow the suggestions of the loved one without rationally thinking about the consequences of the suggestion, but it may also set a pattern for a longer-lasting relationship. If the latter is the case you may "push yourself to the limit" to carry out or undergo what you think the other will approve of.[6] By pleasing the other you may seek acceptance or appreciation in return. In more dramatic cases, you may behave in such a manner as to make the other favourably disposed towards you solely in order to maintain your relationship, no matter how harsh it may be. You may be afraid to express your opinion more openly, for fear of causing unpleasant conflicts or being rejected. You may think: "Better the devil you know ..." In such a continuum, abuse, whether physical, sexual, verbal or mental, or even martyrdom is sometimes not far away. We all know of relationships where something like this occurred.

This is not always negative. Some people are really talented at anticipating expectations. In one course we ran, we taught trainee nurses from the onset to adapt their behavior to expectation, thus ensuring that they got high evaluation grades each time. The best nurse was the one who best anticipated her assessors' expectations of her.

Many people believe that they can sustain even untenable relationships by effacing themselves, and this is often the way in the short term. However, the current high level of divorce and the large turnover of staff in

> **What's in it for me?**

companies are caused by the fact that few people assert themselves from the beginning, setting the scene for burnout, harassment or even abuse. They wait till "the bombshell has been dropped." If they had asserted themselves more from the onset, there would have developed a kind of negotiation model or, at least, a relationship between two full partners, and not between a domineering leader and a subservient subject made to be trampled on. In the negotiation model—based on the model of perceptual positions—the right balance is sought between your self-development and co-operation or socializing. You can enhance your First Position perspective by paying more attention to yourself, actively contributing more to this relationship by being more open about your own needs and wants.

---

[6]   In the language of Transactional Analysis, this is called a "Please Others" Driver. In that of Family Therapy, it is called taking the "Placater" position. In this case the other will most probably assume the "Blamer" position.

Learning to take Second Position more could teach you that many people who have responsibility over you may have no real appreciation for your servile obedience, which they may even despise. Moreover, they might be so self-centered anyway that they don't even notice your process of "devotion." For instance, in a business environment, managers often complain of the low degree of "constructive criticism" and "initiative" displayed by their subordinates.

If servile obedience bothers you, start by changing your beliefs about what constitutes a fully-fledged relationship, about self-respect and about management. Throw your outdated pattern of behavior to the winds and practice getting yourself in a resourceful state (see Lesson 1). Take on power and initiative, take on an attitude of self-confidence, just as we showed you, and notice the difference.

2. To judge yourself objectively and to use this information starting from a Meta-Position towards yourself (Meta¹)

Starting from a Meta-Position you can become aware of what exactly is going on within yourself. Some people too easily go

> When pure sincerity gets its inner space, this is expressed on the outside in the hearts of others.
>
> *Lao Tse, 6th Century B.C.*

into Meta-Position: they judge themselves too much, particularly in a situation where others can assess them. Or they censor themselves because they feel and see themselves acting so clumsily. Nothing is more annoying than judging yourself during a speech, or contemplating first love and intellectualizing about the logistics of making contact and following it up. Your internal dialogue works overtime and gets in the way!

In other cases the Meta-Position is used too little. This happens when you associate with your feelings, but can also occur when you go along with others without realizing you are doing so.

If your ability to take the first Meta-Position hasn't fully developed or is underused, you'd better get yourself described by an outsider to begin with. Ask for criticism or feedback, say from your best friend or a colleague, or perhaps a non-managerial supervisor or coach. Notice how feedback does not have to mean judgment. To begin with, have them tell in detail, using descriptive language, what is so typical about your actions. This way they can describe how you keep your body, what emotions you express with your face, the tone of your voice, etc. They can then continue by using interpretative, evaluative language, perhaps expressing it in a positive fashion. "If I were you, I would not do such and such a thing this way, as this and that might happen. Instead I might do this, this and that … How would that be? What do you think?" Listening to these comments will enable you to acquire an internal dialogue that does not clobber you with judgment about everything at any moment, but will instead act in a resourceful fashion and make constructive suggestions. You will have developed your own internal coach.

However, experience shows that blunt, brute information is often the most relevant or necessary type you need, as only this kind of information will have the required leverage to force you to do something about what is said. It may bring you down to earth with a bump or jolt you out of your self-complacency, bringing you to the all-important state of consciously realizing your incompetence about something. It may smart, but also smarten you up, as this realization state is often the only one when people choose to take action and control over their life. This most often occurs as a result of a crisis. Many clients seek therapy or coaching as a result of such crises. You can often learn most about yourself from people who dislike you as, in their caricatures and cynicism, they will express very striking truths (literally), often articulating what your friends are obviously afraid of telling you. So, for such types of information, go to your enemies!

The well-known phenomenon known as "the bombshell drop" is caused by a lack of Meta-Position. Of course the involved person may sense that something is bothering them, but does not deal with it in an adequate manner, or makes all sorts of excuses to rationalize it. You all know the case of people whose partner is unfaithful and who are the last to realize it. By going into Meta-Position towards yourself, you are able to observe the cumulative effect of many little irritations. You can work with yourself, asking:

"How can I give vent to my little irritations in a constructive/positive way?" or "What's behind all these little irritations that I am not noticing?"

3. To be able to go to Second Position and tune into the other person

If people in a relationship neglect the Second Position, this relationship will deteriorate to a businesslike communal living. You can live perfectly well next to each other without following each other's emotional life. Partners or colleagues often have so many activities that there is no more time for personal intimacy. Always doing, doing, doing. "How long have we known each other?" Jeff asks to Mary at their diamond wedding anniversary. Mary answers: "Do we really know each other?"

Of course, for some a businesslike communal style of living fits them perfectly: perhaps emotional intimacy requires a form or intensity of input you feel unable to deliver, in which case this book should give you more than enough to remedy this.

> If we never want to do things that aren't in our interest, how come we still expect others to do so?

A lack of Second Position is often caused by sensitivity or "thin skin." The more intense your awareness of your own feelings, the harder it gets to dissociate from them and to listen to the other person. In some discussions you'll notice that people get so wrapped up in their own reasoning that they cannot even repeat what the other said. When this occurs you are obviously on different wavelengths.

Extreme sensitivity also deprives a person of the ability of being conscious of their own behavior. No Meta-Position is available. To be able to put yourself in someone else's shoes, you must first be able to go into Meta-Position towards yourself. This requires an awareness of feelings, internal processes, etc. and an ability to work with them. In the next step we will give you some exercises which will enable you to do this.

4. The Third and Fourth Position enable a Co-operation frame

By taking Third Position you achieve a perspective on the relationship and the mutual influences at work. An insufficient use of the Third Position will often result in squabbling or beating about the bush. The Fourth Position results in stability by creating or revising the framework around which the relationship is based.

Such a framework is often broken in a notice period or during divorce. Partners abandon their traditional positions of giving and taking. They are interested in only their own concerns. Reckless emotions during divorces often involve someone being hurt, remaining in First Position. That they may refuse to go into Second Position is understandable: the "ex" or the "boss" or the "system" has hurt them too much. They may perceive themselves as the loser in the equation.

Taking Third Position will make the partners realize that they are immersed in a field of interaction and are equally "responsible" for the way the course is progressing. And, at best, ex-partners are able to assume Fourth Position and to redefine the frame into a broadened pattern of co-operation: for instance, a framework focused on the welfare of the children, or a situation in which conflicts also contribute in a creative kind of way. In the Netherlands a competition was

> You'll get whatever you want from life, if you help enough people to get what they want.
>
> *Zig Ziglar*

drafted for "the best divorce." The winner was the couple doing so well that you wondered why they were splitting up. However, such situations are still an exception for now. In most cases, the side who feels they have most lost out in the divorce experiences difficulty or even impossibility in broadening the framework, and the split-up can become very emotional or even acrimonious.

Look at Your Relationship from a Different Perspective

Now that you know the model of perceptual positions, we'll show you how to apply these different positions to deal with a conflictual situation. In the procedure we describe below, you'll go through the four perceptual positions and the Meta-Positions to First and Second Position. The diagram towards the beginning of this chapter can help you to maintain an overview. By going through all positions, we will gather as much available information as possible about the conflict. Thus everything will become more explicit (*Tip*: if you do the exercise on your own, write down your answers to each of the steps). Once this is done, we will combine all the information. This will enable you to look at the conflict situation from a new angle and should help you to attain a win-win situation.

The Meta-Mirror: a skill for interpersonal conflicts

Step 1: **Preparation:** think about an unresolved conflict or problem you are having with someone else involved. Think back to a discussion you were having with this person. Suppose you had to role-play what happened, in the room where you currently are, where would you place yourself (First Position), and where would you place the other (Second Position)?

Step 2: Go into **First Position.** Tell us about the other person who is annoying you. What is this person's name? What feelings do you experience towards that person?

Step 3: Go into **Meta-Position 1.** If you see this person there (First Position), how do they feel and how did they behave? What suggestions would you have for this person?

*The coach ensures that the explorer is describing from the Meta-Position. A typical description in this position refers to what happens in the First Position "as if it were another person." (**Hint**: asking questions such as "how does HE/SHE feel?" enables the client to assume a better Meta-Position.)*

Step 4: Go into **Second Position.** Step into the other person's shoes and associate in the way the other person (who is annoying you) feels and in the way they look upon the conflict. Why are you behaving this way? What is your purpose? How could you react differently to achieve this purpose in a better way? What advice would you give to (name of the person in First Position)?

As a coach, make sure that the explorer talks in I-terms. The supervisor can stimulate this association by using the other person's name ("Jeff, how do you feel now?") and make sure that they refer to the client out there in First Position by their name.

Step 5: Go into **Meta-Position with regards to Second Position.** If you see the person there (Second Position), what can you say about their behavior and feelings? What advice do you have for that person to make the relationship more constructive?

Step 6: Go into **Third Position.** Suppose you were present while the interaction between both parties is going on. What are your observations as an outsider regarding this system? What advice would you give to the involved sides if you were to coach them?

As a coach, make sure that the explorer talks in I-terms. The supervisor can stimulate this association by making sure that they refer to the client out there in First Position and the other person in Second Position by their names.

Step 7: Go into **Fourth Position.** Stepping between the two people, imagine you are the system made by these two people, being both sides at the same time. Feel the tensions and power lines in you, the giving and the taking, the pushing and the pulling, the energy flow. How do both sides get on the same wavelength? How do you perceive their differences? How could these be minimized? How do you perceive their similarities? How could they be optimized? In what way do both sides contribute to the interaction pattern? How does the behavior of one person affect the other person's behavior? What things should change in this system for it to work?

Step 8: Go into **Meta-Position 1.** Go through all the *information* you have gathered from these positions. Considering all this information, how would you deal with the situation now? Choose a useful state which will enable you to change the pattern of interaction.

Step 9: Associate in **First Position** using this resourceful state. How does your feeling and your behavior change towards the other person? What would you now say to this other person? Empathize completely with the modified situation.

Step 10: Associate in **Second Position** and notice the changes which have taken place, in you as well as in the other (person of First Position) as a result.

Step 11: Finally go back into **First Position** and notice any further changes which have occurred. Imagine how it will be in the future when you meet the other person again. Set actions for the future.

The Meta-Mirror in actual practice: Empathy in Court

 Gerry Spence is a famous American lawyer who never lost a criminal trial. In 1995 he wrote a book[7] showing how to "win" every discussion. If you read the book, filtering it through the model of perceptual positions, you can discover that he proves to be a master of empathy. He takes on the position of other persons involved in a lawsuit, in order to come to a "fair trial." While doing this, he very explicitly takes into account the possible reaction of the opponent (Second Position) and looks for the best solution as regards the system (Third and Fourth Positions).

Some of his techniques, repeated in terms of perceptual positions:

1. *Situation:*   Express your reasoning in a way which takes into account the opponent's situation.

   Go into Second Position with your opponent. What does he want to achieve? What is his positive intention?
   Go into Third Position: as an outside observer, what do you think is going on?
   Go into Fourth Position: how can you obtain a win/win situation? How can you reconcile your positive intention with the positive intention of your opponent?

2. *Word choice:* Choose your words for your argumentation in a way which makes sure you do not alienate your opponent, but which contributes to them as well.

   Go into Second Position with your opponent: how do your words come across from their perspective? Adapt your words accordingly to cause no unnecessary recriminations or discussion.

3. *Tell the truth:* If you lie, you can fool the other for some time, but as soon as they find out, they'll seek redress.

---

7   Spence, Gerry (1995). *How to Argue and to Win Every Time*, New York, St. Martin's Griffin.

Go into Second Position with your opponent, the judge, the jury ... What does each want to hear? How will they know you are sincere? What are their feelings towards you?

Tell the truth in a way which convinces them you are telling the truth. If there are weaker points in your statement, indicate them yourself (if your opponent gets the chance to criticize these weaker points, the result will be worse for you).

Tell them what you think their feelings are (which you were able to gather earlier on from Second Position).

These few points distil Gerry Spence's use of perceptual positions. Apart from these, when you read his book you will easily recognize some other models we have already presented, such as the use of your emotions (see Lesson 1) and building rapport with others (see Lesson 7).

Conclusion:

The key message we invite you to remember from this section is that, in order to know a situation completely, you need to access the four perceptual positions. Part of Gerry Spence's success lies in combining these positions. By using all four positions, you identify new information which, in turn, gives you more options. In Lesson 1 we presented approaches to developing your Emotional Intelligence on the basis of this information and by using creativity. Einstein's work offers another wonderful example of using different perceptual positions. The way Einstein came to his theory of relativity makes extensive use of the First Position and the observer's position.[8]

Interacting Socially: How Do You Bring Emotion into Your Communication?

Whether we like it or not, our non-verbal language often "betrays" our emotional state. Pokerfaced masters are adept at avoiding this,

---

[8] He imagined himself (Meta-Position) sitting on a photon (First Position) traveling at the speed of light, and putting himself in the position of observers (Third Position) looking back at him and experiencing both time and space distortions as this occurred.

but do not always completely succeed. Communication is always much more than the verbal content. Not just what you say, but the way you say it, when you say it (context, timing), to whom you say it, … determines the effect of your communication. As we keep emphasizing in this book: the meaning of communication lies in the effect you achieve!

When we refer to the strict content of communication (the words that are actually uttered), we use the word "message." The other communicated elements determine what we call the "meta-communication.[9]" This meta-communication deeply influences how the receiver of the message will interpret your message.

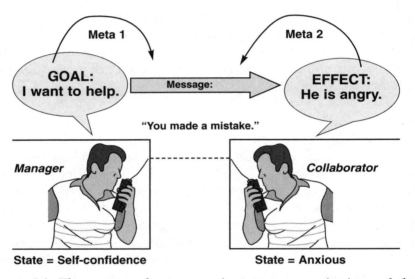

Figure 5.3: The purpose, the message, its meta-communication and the result

No matter how you try to control the meta-communication, you will often notice that the received message (the interpretation) does not entirely correspond to what you intended. This can be due to all kinds of factors, including the receiver's pattern of expectation. The question then arises: "What can you do to make your message require less interpretation?"

---

[9]   Meta-communication has been discussed at large in *Communication: The Social Matrix of Psychiatry* (1951, 1968) by J. Ruesch and G. Bateson and in *Pragmatics of Human Communication* (1967) by Watzlawick, Bavelas and Jackson, W.W. Norton & Company.

First, begin by separating the facts from your own opinion about these facts.

Second, be clear about the way you communicate your feelings about these facts.

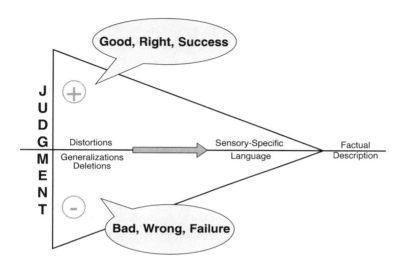

Picture 5.4. Transition from Judgment to Description.[10]

The DESC Concept [11]

When separating facts and opinions you are only halfway. After all, your communication also has a purpose. So, what result are you seeking to achieve by communicating? You must be seeking agreement about this "result" with your conversation partner. So, in addition to the two recommendations above, your communication also contains a problem-solving aspect and a decision component with which you determine together how you will continue. Therefore split up your communication into four parts:

---

[10]   Inspired by the *Communication Envelope* figure found in *Coaching for Performance, Second Edition* (1996) by John Whitmore, Nicholas Brealey Publishing.

[11]   This concept is one of the many variants on the theme of "de-mining communication." The oldest variant we came across is Thomas Gordon's "I Message," as described in his book *Parent Effectiveness Training: the Tested New Way to Raise Responsible Children* (New American Library, 1970). We adapted one of these variants for use in an Emotional Intelligence context.

D: "Describe":	Describe (as precisely as possible) what facts you want to communicate about.
E: "Evaluate":	What is your opinion about these facts? What is the result these facts have on you? How do you feel about it?
S: "Solve":	What is to happen? Either you propose a solution, or you look for a solution together with the involved person. Our experience has taught us that the solution reached with the other is usually more powerful (the possibility for correctly understanding and executing the solution is larger).
C: "Continue":	What is the conclusion of the communication? How do you deal with it further on? If actions were planned in the "solve" phase, agree on when you expect each result. Agree interim evaluation delays if necessary.

We not only split facts and opinions here, but also expect results from this communication. What solutions are possible? What agreements should be made in the future? This kind of communication is as useful for bringing good news (compliments) as for bringing bad news.

Some examples

1. A manager is satisfied with his co-worker.

   D: Ian, I have noticed you composed this presentation from a clear summary, after which you presented very detailed slides about all the important subjects. You had a very specific answer to each question they asked.

   E: To me, this came across as a very professional presentation. I'm really glad I let you do it. I believe we made a good impression on that customer and I think there is a good chance that we'll get the deal.

   S: Perhaps you could apply this approach in other situations as well? What do you think?

2. A manager is dissatisfied with his co-worker.

    D: Tell me, Peter, wasn't it you who did the repair on the filling machine on line 5? Well, one screw was not tightened enough and the vibration of the machine caused it to come off again. As a result the screw got stuck between the cog-wheels of the gearbox and the engine jammed. The total damage amounts to 15,000 euro.

    E: Personally, I am rather frustrated, as this will cause the machine to be down for about five days.

    S: What can you do to avoid such a problem in the future?

    C: OK, and when can I check that you have carried out the agreed actions?

Active listening[12]

Suppose you are on the receiving end of the communication loop and the person sending you a message does not split up the message according to the DESC concept. In such a case you can split up his communication for him while formulating your reply. We consider this approach as "real" active listening. By so doing, you indicate what you think you have understood of the other person's communication, and it gives the other person the opportunity to adjust their communication in a non-violent manner. To interpret the communication as well as possible, we advise you to assess it by going into Second Position: if I put myself in the other person's shoes, what is the intention of this strained statement? What am I trying to communicate?

Some examples

- Person says: "I think it is a stupid idea."

  Reaction :   "If I understand you correctly, you think there are elements that will get in the way of realizing this plan?"
  (ask question to find the facts behind the interpretation)

- A woman says: "I feel abused by him."

  Reaction: "What exactly did he do?"
  (what are the facts for your feeling abused?)

---

[12] This form of active listening also appears in Thomas Gordon's book *Parent Effectiveness Training.*

Exercises for this Lesson

Exercise 5.1: Code the perceptual positions

What perceptual position are the following statements said from?

	Perceptual position
e.g.: "I'm baffled when I consider how you'll feel about this when you come home this evening."	Meta[2]
1. I already see myself dancing there.	
2. You have blinkers on.	
3. You should have a look at yourself.	
4. If I were in your shoes, I would feel lost.	
5. To distance oneself often results in a solution.	
6. Both of you should see how ridiculously you are communicating.	
7. The way you interact with him is not going to solve the problem.	
8. If both of us work together, the sky is the limit!	

Exercise 5.2: Know yourself: your autobiography and some biographies

In this exercise you write your own life story each time: on a separate page, looking at your life from different perspectives.

1. From First Position: your life story as told by yourself. What were the significant events in your life? How did you feel?
2. As neutral observer of yourself (Third Position): if you have heard the life story of this person over there, how would you tell it yourself?
3. From Second Position:
   (a) through the eyes of someone who loves you (your partner, your parents, ...),
   (b) through the eyes of a colleague,
   (c) through the eyes of your worst enemy or critic.

Finally write the summary starting from Fourth Position. If you put all the stories together, what stands out as most important?

Note: If you do this exercise in a group with people who already know you a little, you can do a round with each member first telling your biography, and you finishing by telling a summary yourself. The stories from each of the positions are probably dissociated (meta). If you write the associated story, tell it as if it's going on right now, when you are talking.

Exercise 5.3: Preparation of an important appointment
Think of an appointment you are about to have (subject as desired: a meeting, a sales talk, an encounter with a friend, etc.).

1. Write down what you want to say (from First Position).
2. Consider how the other will react to it (Second Position).
3. How can you deal with the other's feedback as positively as possible (Third Position).

If you do this exercise in a group, do it as a role-play. Use the instructions above as a preparation. After the preparation, you begin the role-play. Then play yourself and give your exercise partner instructions on how they are to react.

Exercise 5.4: Fine feathers make fine birds
In pairs: Person A is dress adviser for Person B. This exercise is most enjoyable if you do not know each other very well.

Step 1:   Person B gives three contexts for which they require clothes (e.g. work, garden, beach, kitchen, city clothes, party, etc.). Describe a very detailed occasion at which you will wear these clothes.

Step 2:   Person A imagines the event when the clothes will be worn, and thinks about what they should wear for this occasion.

Step 3:   Person A empathizes with Person B, and thinks about what they would like to wear.

Step 4:   Person A finally advises Person B, based on the information gathered in previous steps.

Variant: Go a step further, and take Person B to some clothes stores, letting them put on the clothes you suggested, then let them comment.

Exercise 5.5: Reference experiences of the perceptual positions

If you discover that during your life up till now you have developed one perceptual position less than the other positions, you can learn from others who have developed that position well. For instance: suppose your First Position is weak, what can you learn from a person with a lot of assertiveness? Or suppose that your Second Position is weak, what's there to learn from a person with lots of empathy?

In fours. Aim to have in the group people who rely on different perceptual positions.

Take turns. In each round the person asks questions of someone else in order to learn more about the position they want to develop for themselves. (Make the person associate in three experiences and investigate the submodalities, emotions, beliefs, skills, etc. which emerge in this position.)

For example, people who seek to reinforce their First Position model somebody from the group with a strong First Position. For this, they elicit a reference experience.

Continue for the different positions.

Exercise 5.6: Investigating projection

Step 1:   Determine the behavior you find annoying in the other person.
Step 2 :   Find the corresponding part of yourself that thinks and acts just the same as the other person.
Step 3 :   Look for the positive intention in that part.
Step 4 :   Afterwards go to Second Position and check your information. How accurate was it?

Exercise 5.7: Looking for the positive intention of your feeling.

Choose a behavior you find annoying. Go into First Position and describe what you feel. Then seek the positive intention for having this feeling. What made you feel annoyed or influenced your behavior?

Exercise 5.8: The quickened meta-mirror.

Choose a well-defined context when an unsatisfactory interaction occurred. Successively assume First, Second and Third Position. Make the person describe the same situation each time:

—Perceive yourself and the other from this position in see, hear and feel terms.

—Talk aloud to yourself about what happened.

Make the person shift from one position to another faster and faster, until they clearly identify exactly where the hindering filter is situated. What information do you get and what can you do differently in the future now that you know?

Exercise 5.9: Giving feedback by means of Second Position information

Think about someone who annoys you. Describe their behavior. Go to Second Position and consider the positive intention of this behavior. In what way could the other better express this positive intention? Provide feedback in this way:

—When you do ... (describe the behavior)

—Then I think the purpose is to ...

—Is this correct?

—If it is correct, would you be happy to express this meaning differently so that your positive intention emerges better? How will you do that?

Lesson 6:
Asking the Right Questions

**"The limitations of my language
are the boundaries of my world."**
Ludwig Wittgenstein

Goals

In this chapter we aim to enable you to accomplish three objectives:

- To develop awareness of how a person changes their experience by talking about it.
- To learn to question in such a way that the other person begins to explore their own map.
- To learn to examine yourself so that you realize what you really feel and think.

Neurolinguistic Assumptions

Three assumptions in particular apply in this chapter:

- *The map is not the territory. Experience is subjective.*
- *The meaning of communication lies in the effect it elicits.*
- *People do not directly react to the world, but to their map of the world.*

Why this lesson?

Why would you read this chapter?

- By asking the right questions you can help a person to describe their experience in a more precise and detailed manner.
- In addition, you can apply this tool to your own mapping of the world, and rectify the distortions and filters you have applied to this mapping. This will enable you to get in touch with your real emotions, instead of those you may be expected to feel.
- Who knows better than you in what areas you need to increase your Emotional Intelligence? Sayings such as

"Know Thyself" and "Wisdom Begins With Self-Knowledge" may sound pat to begin with, yet one should learn to appreciate their importance. We will enable you to interpret such sayings as meaning "Know your Own Map of the World." After all, as we explained earlier, all emotions are connected with cognitive contents.

- Appropriately questioning a statement someone makes will help you to keep track of their thinking and bring you closer to real understanding. It can also be a very effective way of defusing conflict.

  e.g.: Somebody says: "It's always the same thing with you, you don't respect me." Instead of defending yourself, replying: "That's not true!" you could ask: "How do you know that I don't respect you?" or "What makes you think that I don't respect you?"

- From the language a person uses, you can deduce what values they uphold and track the thought patterns their reasoning follows.

A Counter-example: What NOT to Do

"Do you sleep like you used to? Don't you have more headaches? Don't you show more nervousness or more disinterest? Did some kind of allergic reaction, such as mucous inflammations, breathing problems or skin diseases, cause you trouble lately? More stomach or intestinal problems? More heart complaints? Losing hair? Other pains, such as cramps, etc.?"

If one is to believe a letter from a local doctor that was published in a newspaper in July 1998, your mobile phone could be the cause of all these troubles. Once you have made it through this lesson, you'll understand how this way of questioning tends to make you sick. In fact, the language used by this doctor is rather hypnotic: in order to "understand" the questions quoted above you need to imagine already having each of the described diseases, just to make sure that you haven't got any of them ... If you ask such questions to someone who is easily influenced, the likelihood of getting a "yes" answer to one of these questions is much higher. If all doctors were to use this diagnostic style, half of the population would be on sick leave.

Introduction

Could it be that we tend to ask questions in order to get our own ideas confirmed? What would be preferable, and certainly more constructive, would be to ask questions which increase our own knowledge of the map of the world of other people. Our motto is: "There is no such thing as a stupid question, but there *are* stupid answers!" By asking questions which show that we are interested in the person we are talking to and respect their perspective, we increase the likelihood of getting a significant answer. And building better rapport helps too!

As early as the 4th century B.C., Aristotle, in his book "On Rhetoric," described a technique for asking questions. This collection of questions lives on today as "rhetorical questions." Their purpose was not to find out the map of the discussion partner, but rather to be used as a tool for discussion. In fact, Aristotle's questions were meant as a weapon to win an argument. One particular type of question was used to make the argument of the opponent appear absurd. Another was employed to steal the argument the opponent was going to use, so that you seemed clever, since your question contained the point the other was trying to make. Further questions helped Aristotle to highlight contradictions in a reasoning. In addition, he recommended avoiding the use of any question which could make the opponent look smart, since that would be equivalent to admitting that you had lost the discussion. Given Aristotle's influence on modern Western culture, his approach to "the art of asking questions" can still be found to influence our ways of thinking, especially in the realm of politics, journalism and debate. We aim to show you an entirely different way of asking questions which will be far more constructive and beneficial in the long run.

One of the social skills linked to Emotional Intelligence is the ability to identify solutions which correspond to something your partners can agree upon. A first step to this end is finding out how they think, as well as what their needs and plans are. Using the presupposition that "The map is not the territory," we can expect other people to reach different conclusions from ours, based on their own map of the world. So, how can we find out their needs and plans if we don't ask them? This could explain why Peter

Senge, author of *The Fifth Discipline*,[1] points to this question-asking skill in two of his five disciplines, namely for obtaining "Shared Mental Models" and reaching "Team Learning."

In order to reach a shared mental model you first have to know your own "map" of the world, which corresponds to Senge's notion of "mental model." Having done this, you go on to elicit the map of the world of the other parties involved. Finally, you build a common model through a "learning conversation" in which the art of asking questions is key.

Senge explains that "dialogue" is the first step to "team learning."[2] Dialogue is derived from the Greek words "dia," meaning "through," and "logos" "speech."[3] Translated, these two words stand for "the free flow of questions and the creation of meaning between humans." This process enables you to make your own presuppositions explicit so that you reach a "thinking together." The best way you will succeed in making these presuppositions explicit will be through mastering the art of asking questions. In addition, consider that 75% of employees are afraid to express their point of view. No wonder there are many misunderstandings and that we often experience a lack of dialogue in our interactions.

We'll give Dale Carnegie the closing words to this introduction by summarizing his advice on building friendship in his book *How to Win Friends and Influence People*.[4] He said: "Have a truthful interest for your fellow man," and "Become a good listener and encourage others to speak about themselves." Needless to say, the tools we offer in this chapter will be of incredible help, otherwise we wouldn't bother …

An example

In the table opposite we illustrate how differently a "pushy" salesperson and an interested salesperson can use questions.

---

[1] Senge, P. (1990) *The Fifth Discipline: The Art and Practice of the Learning Organization,* New York, Doubleday.

[2] Ibid., p. 10.

[3] This term actually came to us via Latin, where *dialogus* meant philosophical conversation.

[4] Carnegie, Dale (1935, 1998). *How to Win Friends & Influence People,* Pocket Books.

The Pushy Salesperson	The Interested Salesperson
Q1: (salesperson) Do you agree that the characteristics of our product comply with the needs of a company like yours? A. (customer) Yes, at first sight this seems true. Q2. How about buying one or two cases to try it out? A. Oh, let's start with one case. I want to make sure it complies to our quality standards. Q3. When can I deliver? How about at the end of the week? A. No, this week is too early. I have to check how I can make this order fit in our purchasing strategy. Q4. But you agreed that we satisfy your needs. You want to profit from this exceptional order, do you? A. Oh, price doesn't really matter, you know. I'd be more interested in the quality of your products and of your organization.	Q1: (salesperson) What's the difference between your organization and your competitors? A. (customer) Well, we try to minimize our stock but link this to volume deals. This is a new approach for this sector. Q2. What would be a good type of contract for you, and how can we make one together? A. Well, it is our policy to start with a test order. Afterwards we negotiate the price for the volume contract. Q3. How do you see this test order? A. Well, let's say we would take one to two cases within a fortnight? Q4. OK, let us start by giving you a good price on two cases. I'm sure we will continue working together in the future! A. Thanks a lot!

The questions asked by the pushy salesperson are "closed," in the sense that they aren't intended to learn more about the customer's map of the world. This type of salesperson believes he'll be able to push his customer towards closing a deal by using his clever arguing techniques, against which the poor customer won't be able to put up much of a defense. Indeed, the first question is already a statement from our salesperson. His second question aims to make the customer choose between only the two options proposed, from the psychological knowledge that it is difficult for a person to suggest a third answer when asked this type of question. But after a few questions the salesperson gets stuck, and concludes he is facing a "difficult customer."

On the other hand, the approach of the interested salesperson consists of looking for a win-win solution. That's why he starts by finding out the point of view of the customer, before attempting to make an offer "that can't be refused." By asking "open questions" he obtains information which allows him to reach a new perspective. What is considered as an "obstacle" by the first salesperson is now perceived as "feedback." And instead of using price as his only argument, he prefers to focus on "service."

Note that there is more to it than simply "asking questions." Asking questions isn't just a mechanical process. Cross-examination is also about asking questions, and some journalists now appear champions in this discipline. Really mastering the art of questioning also means building rapport with your partner: show real respect and real interest for their opinion.

Filters

The way you turn observed "reality" into your own experience, storing this experience in your memory and then talking about your experience, is determined by the transformations you make between different levels. You could compare these "transformations" to a coffee machine: you first pour in water and ground coffee beans, and out comes a black liquid. In between you'll find a filter, which "trans-  forms" the blend of water and ground coffee beans into the coffee you drink. Similarly you use a series of filters which distort, delete or generalize information from your sensory experience.

An example: the blind spot

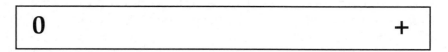

Look at the cross with your left eye and with your right eye closed, or at the zero with your right eye and with your left eye closed. Move the page towards you or away from you. At a certain point, you will not see the other figure.

Types of filters

We distinguish between three types of filters. While the first type works in a similar way for nearly everybody, other filters are so specific to each individual that they make us unique. However, everyone has some filters of each type, even if we are often unaware we operate from them.

1. Neurological filters

These filters are inbuilt into our brains and are determined genetically.

- Absolute threshold to our senses: to be actually able to perceive or not.

  e.g.:

  ▲ We cannot perceive infrared or ultraviolet waves.

  ▲ Our ears cannot hear sounds above 26 Khz (up to only 20Khz at a conscious level).

  ▲ Deafness, shortsightedness, color-blindness, anosmia, etc.

  ▲ Differential barriers: perceiving minimal differences.

  e.g.:

  Since our eyes work by detecting differences, if your eyes were to be immobilized while you look at a fixed object, you would not see anything. When looking at an object, this difference comes from moving your eyes (saccades).

2. Socio-cultural filters

These filters are typical of a certain social standard or culture. Education, religion, media, arts or literature, all these influence us to use these filters.

e.g.:

- Not saying "good morning" = having no respect.
- Disputes and conflicts are unpleasant.
- An illness can be cured mechanically.
- You should be on time for appointments; being more than 15 minutes late is unacceptable.
- To please another person is a sign of love.

3. Personal filters

This third set of filters makes us really unique. They result from the way we interact with the environment, both during our education and later on.

e.g.:

- I must be perfect, otherwise …
- My parents have taught me to be good and obedient.
- I have experienced that I cannot go out late.
- By following my husband, I demonstrate love.
- If I say "yes," I avoid conflicts.

The consequence of filtering is that a person cannot but incompletely express what they have experienced. The way we use our filters indicates the way we give meaning to what is happening around us. So, ask yourself:

- What do I pay attention to?
- What do I emphasize?
- What have I forgotten?

We cannot say that filtering is good or bad: it just exists. Sometimes it may enable us to function resourcefully, sorting out the relevant from the irrelevant, or finding useful connections between apparently disparate facts. At other times it may limit us, especially when problems arise, for example, if we filter information in such a way that it results in an undesired interpretation, or if it restricts our range of responses to some issues.

Filters are only partially under our own control. When we analyze the way our interlocutor speaks, we can often notice which kind of filter is in operation at any one time. This enables us to ask questions which will, to some extent, rectify the filters' effects.

The Basic Model: Three Traffic Rules for "Good Questions"

Containing about 15 language patterns, each with a typical question, the initial model that neurolinguists developed for asking questions was known for its complexity. In this part of the chapter, we present a simplified model, which we have used since John

Grinder suggested it in June 1997. In the next part of this chapter, we will present the full model which offers you greater precision, so visit it when you have mastered this simplified model.

Three types of language patterns

It could be said that reconstructing the details of an experience from what a person tells you resembles a film director's task when they make a movie from a script. So pretend you are a director and ask yourself:

—"What is the starting point of this and where does it end?"
—"What action do you want to show the public?"
—"Why do you put the boundaries there, and what will be left out?"

You will end up with a sequence of images you want to show and then you start working it out: "So, what are the important details?" The simplified questioning model below shares many similarities with this process. Let's begin by presenting you with the three types of language patterns and questions we will consider.

1. Getting the picture: unspecific nouns

In order to describe an image, we use a set of words. Much of the time, these words aren't specific enough to capture all the elements in the picture. No wonder somebody once said: "A picture is worth a thousand words," as this may be what you would need to describe it. Lewis Carroll taught us: "Words mean more than we mean to say when we use them; so a whole book ought to mean more than the writer means." In addition, all words are not equal. Some are quite precise, allowing only limited room for interpretation, while others are more fuzzy or abstract.

e.g.: When somebody talks about an "apple," you can create a clear picture of this, once you know the person is talking about a fruit or a computer. But even then you won't know the exact size, shape, color, smell and taste of this apple. Compare this with a word such as "respect." This abstract word is even more difficult to understand. How does one recognize respect? You'd need a complete movie scene to describe what the person meant with the word, and even this might not suffice.

The rule of thumb is: "If you are not sure, ask a question." Continue asking questions until you end up with elements that can be measured or "put in a wheelbarrow." (Of course if the object described is too heavy, your wheelbarrow might collapse, but the wheelbarrow is only a metaphor for reminding you that you should end up with material things only. So, for the sake of argument, we accept that even a car or a boat can be put in a wheelbarrow.)

Please note that adjectives as well as nouns can be fuzzy or clear. So feel free to extend the rule to include adjectives you want to question.

Some examples:
- Organization, company, accounting, control, imagination, …
- Respectable, honest, friendly, adventurous, incredible, arrogant, …
- "Marriage isn't a word, it's a sentence!"

How do you ask questions?
Ask questions beginning with: What, Who, How, Where, When, Which, etc.

Avoid asking "Why?" questions: this type of question will provide you with only a justification, rather than the more specific description you are looking for.

In general, there are several possible questions for each sentence. The question you will want to ask will depend on what you seek to achieve. What can you derive from the context? What question will give you the information you are looking for?

We presuppose that you are interested in what the other person has to say. Also, remember that it is impossible to have *"no influence."* Each question you ask will lead the thinking of your conversation partner in a particular direction. Some questions aren't really questions but just guesswork, such as the ones which begin with: "Could it be possible that …," "Ain't it so that …," "Do you mean to say that …," "Are you thinking that …," etc. Notice how a person could respond to these by saying only "Yes" or "No." So, the *least* influence will be achieved by asking open questions (neither closed, nor rhetorical, nor suggestive).

In the examples that follow we show you how to do it. We use *italics* to mark the words which trigger the question.

Examples

- He bought a very popular *sports car* ➔ Q: What make is it?
  A: Well, it's *American* ➔ Q: Anything more specific?
  A: It's a *Ford Mustang* ➔ Q: What year was it built?
  A: It's a '68 Convertible.
- It was really *heavy* ➔ Q: How much did it weigh?
  A: I've no idea, but it sure was *heavy*! ➔
  Q: When do you call something heavy?
  A: Oh, anything weighing more than 10 tons.
- This is an *organizational* problem ➔ Q: What kind of problems did you encounter?
  A: Well, they didn't expect this *situation* ➔ Q: What should have been expected?
- I'll ask the *administration* ➔ Q: Who do you have in mind?
  A: Well, *those guys* working on the fourth floor ➔
  Q: Somebody in particular?
  A: Maybe John, or Jerry, or else Richard.
- I want a *meaningful* answer ➔ Q: Tell me what you want to know?
  A: I want to know your point of view on this note.
- It must satisfy all *needs* ➔ Q: What are the requirements?
  A: Price and *quality* are important ➔ Q: How do you plan to evaluate the quality?

2. Assembling the movie: unspecific verbs

Getting the picture is one thing. A movie has a whole sequence of them. So, what are the most important ones? What sequence of images do you need to describe the complete process? Most verbs are short-hand words which represent a process —the main exception to this is the verb *to be*. So, they indicate how you go from one step or image to the next. As long as the verbs remains vague and unspecific, you have no idea of the way the next step is reached. Some examples of unspecific verbs include: *thinking, doing, treating, processing, solving,* etc.

How do you ask questions?

> Ask a question to transform the verb into a specific process. Get the plan of action, refine the procedure until you can grasp or even reproduce what the person is explaining.

Examples
- Let me *think* about this
  Q: How are you going to find an answer?
  A: Well, first *I pay some closer attention* to the previous file of that customer.
  Q: What are you searching for in that file?
- We have to *do some research* first
  Q: What do you need to find out?
  A: Which customers are involved.
- I want to *reconsider* the organization structure
  Q: What kind of approach did you have in mind?

3. The boundaries: restrictions
Verbs such as "must," "ought," "should," "can't," "need," "may not" all indicate limits to your freedom. So do words such as "always," "never," "everybody." Consider statements such as: "*Everybody* does it that way," "You *cannot* steal," "You *must* speak with only two words," "I *can't* do that," etc.

Such restrictions indicate the boundaries someone puts on their behavior and the driving forces behind their actions (or lack thereof). Of course, restraints such as "You shall not kill," may often be useful. On other occasions it may be useful to challenge the restrictions. Ever the provocateur, Richard Bandler once said that he considered the Catechism, which specifically seeks to restrict the behavior of Roman Catholics, as a collection of suggestions of things he could start doing the moment he felt bored.

"Want to" versus "have to"

In his book *A Guide to Personal Happiness*[5] Albert Ellis writes that people often confuse an obligation (absolute must) with having no choice. They feel compelled to do something, but if they were to only examine the situation, they might find an alternative. As you read above, something is a restriction when you say *"I have to."* Ask yourself: "What changes about my film if I replace obligation (having to) with wanting to?"

e.g.: "They **have to** treat me correctly (and they do not always do that)."
Consequence: You are to deal with an administration that treats you impolitely (e.g. a problem with your telephone bill, troubles with your train season ticket, etc.). You feel unhappy because you are not treated well.
Solution: Replace obligation with wanting.
Consequence: Unfortunately the administration indeed did not treat you very well. In fact they should know better, but you can decide not to have your day ruined by it.

Perfectionism also fits within this category of restrictions: we set ourselves a goal we *have to* reach. If we score less, we consider it a failure and we have an excuse to be unhappy. Ask yourself: "Can it be a little bit less?"

e.g.: "I **have to** mow the lawn each week from March till the end of October (and I do not like doing it)."
Consequence: You become a slave to your garden.
Solution: Ask yourself who it would bother if you were to skip mowing the lawn for a week. Or what if you were to change a corner of your lawn into a "natural lawn," such as those you see next to motorways, which you would mow only once a year?

---

5   Ellis, Albert, and Becker, Irving (1986). *A Guide to Personal Happiness*, USA, Wilshire Book Company.

How do you ask questions?

There are two types of questions you can ask, both of which help to challenge the boundaries of a person's map of the world:

- *The Historic Question* (Q1):
    the purpose of this question is to find out where the boundary comes from
- *The Consequence Question* (Q2):
    this question helps to find out what would happen if the person were to trespass this boundary

---

Note how both questions refer to time. The first one is oriented towards the past: where does the boundary come from, why is it there, what problems are present as a result of its being there? The second one is oriented towards the future: what would be the consequence of crossing this boundary, what possibilities would this create? Unless you really enjoy digging into the past (a hint for some therapeutic work?) we'd like to suggest that the consequence question would be more constructive. On this subject, you may like to know that Cicero called the will to keep one's mind busy with things one cannot change or improve "one of the biggest mistakes of mankind."

Examples

- You *have* to be polite.
    Q1—Who told you that? (Why?)
    Q2—What happens if I'm not?
- I *can't* master those damn mathematics.
    Q1—How come you can't? (Why?)
    Q2—What would you gain if you could?
- We *need* some extra government intervention.
    Q1—What makes you think so? (Why?)
    Q2—What risks do you expect?
- It's *against the law.*
    Q1—What is stopping you?
    Q2—What is there to gain if we ignore that for a moment?
- The same things are *always* happening.
    Q1—Always? Has nothing else ever been happening?
    Q2—What would be other possibilities?

Using the patterns: three traffic rules

Now we combine the three patterns into a model. Follow the rules below for deciding which question to ask:

---

1. Whenever you encounter a restriction, ask the consequence question.
2. Pin down the nouns by making them specific.
3. Once you have the specific nouns, go for specific verbs: ground them as well.

Go back to the nouns if you get a noun in response to a verb. At the end, backtrack.

We recommend that you respect the order of these rules. For a specific sentence, first consider the first rule, then the second and finally the third.

Examples

- We *should* start by thinking out a new organizational structure.
    Q—What would happen if we don't? (rule 1—restriction)
    A—Everything will become an enormous *mess.*
    Q—What would go wrong?   (rule 2—unspecific noun)
    A—We won't make the *deadlines.*
    Q—Which deadlines are the most at risk?
                      (rule 2—unspecific noun)

- Everything is going according to *plan.*
    Q—What is the plan?   (rule 2— unspecific noun)
    A—First we finish *moving* into the new headquarters.
    Q—How are you going to handle that?
                      (rule 3— unspecific verb)

- I *need* money; can I borrow some?
    Q—What would you do if I don't lend you some?
                      (rule 1—restriction)
    A—Well, that would certainly cause me some *budget troubles.*
    Q—Can you be a bit more specific? What did you budget?
                      (rule 2—unspecific noun)
    A—I wanted to buy a new car, but the bank refused my loan.

Conclusions

The advantage of generating your own questions in order to find out about unspecific elements or restrictions is that these questions remain more spontaneous than if you had begun by asking standard questions or adhering to strict rules.

A catch-all question you can use if you lack inspiration is: "What do you mean specifically by...?" Our experience shows that this question generally helps you to obtain the answer, with the disadvantage that the question itself may sound "odd" to the listener. It may trigger suspicion in your conversation partner, who may end up asking you in turn: "How come you keep asking such odd questions?" especially when there is a lack of rapport. This is therefore a plea to cultivate your communication skills so that other people will either never notice your questioning style or simply accept it as non-threatening.

Remember also that your questioning directs the conversation. So, ask questions only if you are interested in the answer. A tip to help you: for each question you ask, you first need to know for yourself what you want to find out, what outcome you seek to achieve by asking. Also, consider whether this is a "real question," or rather just a way to get your point of view confirmed —a rhetorical question. Finally, remember that the wording of your question and the way you ask it will influence the answer your interlocutor will give you. So learn to develop your word power.

The Meta-Model: Questions for Dealing with Emotions

Once you have started to master the basic three-rule model you learned about in the previous part of this lesson, you may begin asking yourself: "What questions could I ask specifically to get even better results?" or "What could be the best way of asking about this?" This part of the chapter aims to provide you with further answers. As a starting point we take the work Bandler and Grinder carried out during the 1970s, itself based on previous results from linguistic research. What we present below offers you more precision than we have taught you in the first part of this chapter, but it comes at the price of a higher complexity. One could call this model the next rung on the ladder. If you are reading this book for the first time, you can easily skip over this section of the chapter till next time. It will be there for you when you need it.

The Meta-Model patterns: specific questions for particular language patterns

We give you below a list of the main Meta-Model patterns, which we have grouped in seven categories. Each time we'll begin with a description of the pattern and then show you what question to ask in relation to it.

1. Deletions and unspecific language

People have to leave out information when talking about an experience. Otherwise there would never be enough hours in the day to get beyond the stage of saying plain "Hello!" If you have read Tolkien's *Lord of the Rings,* you will remember one particular category of beings, namely the Ents, who speak like this. Naturally they call ordinary humans "hasty"! The more emotional a person is, the more information (not related to this emotion) they will tend to omit. A good listener will recognize such "deletions" and, where relevant, ask for information to fill the gaps. Where irrelevant, you'll leave the gaps. As you will notice in the table overleaf in the column "pattern," we recognize, within the category of deletions and unspecific language, a range of categories of information which can be left out in a message. If you were to attempt to reconstruct the original experience, you will notice that information is missing, therefore preventing you from doing so.

An untrained listener tends to fill in the missing pieces by themselves by guessing: "Oh, they probably mean this." Depending on the situation they may be right or totally wrong about it, with all the consequences this may entail. If in doubt, ask for this missing information: it's easier in the long run.

Example	Pattern	Question
You make me angry.(…)	Deletion	What are you angry about?
I don't care anymore.(…)	Deletion	What do you not care any more about?
I eat *too many* sweets.	Deletion of comparison	In comparison to what do you eat too many sweets?
Grandmother is better off in an old people's home.	Deletion of comparison	She is better off than where?
They are gossiping about me.	Deletion of referential index	Who is gossiping about you?
Help me to get over it.	Unspecific verb	What do you mean by helping?
People are so selfish nowadays.	Unspecific noun	What people do you mean?

2. "Labels"

When we talk about an experience or process, we often summarize a whole event by reducing it to one single word. Such words are called concepts, "labels" or nominalizations. So, when we hear a statement containing such a word, we tend to spontaneously fill out the concept or label with a personal experience of our own to fit our understanding of the label. Again we may be right, but then again we may be way off track. For example, the words "achievement" or "love" may have a totally different meaning from person to person. If you want to know more about the background of your conversation partner, you can ask questions to get more information about what exactly they have experienced or what they mean by that word. *"When I use a word,"* Humpty Dumpty told Alice in a rather scornful tone, *"it means just what I choose it to mean – neither more nor less."*[6] So, Mr. Humpty Dumpty, what did you mean when you used this particular word?

---

[6]   Carroll, Lewis (1998) *Alice's Adventures in Wonderland* and *Through the Looking-Glass (Centenary Edition),* London, Macmillan.

Example	Question
I'm working on my self-development.	How do you develop yourself?
I want to save our marriage.	What do you want to save?
Education is obligatory till the age of 18.	What do these children have to do then?
I am depressed.	What exactly do you feel?

3. Exaggerations ("quantifiers")

Sometimes people tend to exaggerate. This happens in particular when they are emotionally involved in the experience they are referring to. In these cases we need to question the exaggeration, to redress, as it were, the caricature of the experience we're being offered. When asking the question, a small dose of humor often helps a person to revise their initial statement.

Example	Question
He never touches me.	Has he never ever really touched you?
It is always the same thing here.	Always?
Nobody loves me.	Nobody?
Nothing is good about it.	Nothing?

"*Eternal*" and "*forever*" are some other examples of such language. Note how exaggerations in the other direction have a similar effect, such as in: "He notices me *only* when I've done something wrong." Sometimes people emphasize this further by saying: "This happens *only ever* when we're together."

4. Generalizations

When people generalize, this may be interpreted as if they are proclaiming the "Universal Truth," but in actual fact, they are just talking about their own individual experience. When this occurs, you may want to ask the proclaimer: "Who says that?" or ask them on what facts their conclusion is based. You will sometimes discover that a statement originally presented as a definitive, and general conclusion may be based on only one or two observations or that, even though it sounded as if everybody was agreeing with it, the only person actually backing the statement was the person who initially made it.

Example	Question
People are so selfish nowadays.	Says who?
Scientific research proves that people forget when aging.	Says who? In what book or article did you read that?
John is a difficult boy.	Says who? From what do you gather that?
Practice makes perfect.	Says who?

Pay attention in this context to words and expressions such as: *absolute/definite, proved, really, sure, it cannot be denied that, is it not so that, ...*

5. Freedom restrictions

In the previous part of this chapter we reflected on how people restrain their own freedom and possibilities of learning about the way they express themselves. We showed you how you could question both the origins of this restriction and the consequence of breaking the freedom restriction. A third possibility is to reflect the statement back and see how your partner will react.

Example	Question	
I have to tell him.	What makes you tell him?	*(origin)*
	What would happen if you did not tell him?	*(consequence)*
	What do you have to tell him?	*(reflection)*
I am not allowed to cry.	What/who stops you from crying? What would happen if you were to cry? Are you not allowed to cry?	
I cannot sing.	What prevents you from singing? What would singing do for you? Can't you sing?	

6. Mindreading

When people are mindreading, they are talking about other people as if they are inside the head of another person and know how that person is and how they think or feel, whereas in actual fact they may have little explicit information about the person. By asking specific questions, we find out how they have come to their conclusion. Again it may be accurate or erroneous. The reply to this question is usually expressed as a Connection (see below).

Example	Question
She did it to hurt me.	How do you know she did it to hurt you?
He does not love me.	How do you know he does not love you?

7. Connections.

People connect pieces of their experience as if it relates to a particular truth. According to Edward T. Hall, a famous American anthropologist, this is typical of our Western culture. In his book *The Silent Language*[7] (1959) he says:

> *The Americans, as so many other cultures, use time as a way to connect events.... The fact that one event succeeds another causes attempts to connect the second event to the first and to find the causal connection between both incidents.*

Such a connection or relationship between cause and effect is a personal construct. It is often very useful to enable us to predict what will happen if a given event occurs. In other cases the relationship indicates what is needed to make something possible. Many events in the world of physics or mathematics are based on such connections.

You may sometimes find the connection within a single sentence. In other cases you notice the connection in the way a person puts sentences one after another. In everyday language you can recognize connections in words such as: *as, because, caused, determines, demands, makes it possible to, connects, creates the possibility to, ...*

---

[7]   Re-published in 1990 by Anchor Books, a division of Doubleday.

Sometimes the connection or causality principle is incorrect, in which case you can ask questions as to its validity or spuriousness for this particular case, or for other situations.

People often interpret events or behavior, for example: "Who does not speak in two words, is impolite." We often need to know what interpretation will be given to a particular behavior in order to identify what kind of behavior is socially acceptable (or not). However, many of these statements express cultural or even familial influence and may not apply in other parts of the world.

Example	Question
If the Augusta helicopters are better armed, we can use them for peace missions.[8]	What makes them unavailable for peace missions unless they are better armed?
If the weather is cloudy, it will rain.	Have you not experienced it being cloudy a whole day long without starting to rain?
He does not love me, because he does not cuddle me.	Why do you think the fact he does not cuddle you means that he does not love you?

Note here how a connection a person makes between two elements is a belief. Such a connection may reflect their values. For instance, if someone makes the statement "This meeting was a waste of time," we may deduce that *time* is a very important value to them, probably more important than the human aspect of the meeting. Another person may clearly make a different connection between the same event and the time value, e.g.: "That meeting was great, it was about time we got to know each other." A sentence, such as "That was an informative meeting" shows the value accorded to *learning*, and so on. In addition, expressions which technically present a cause-effect relationship, such as "If it is profitable, we go on" often indicate a hidden value, in this case *money*. The values and beliefs of a person can be strong incentives to achieve certain results, but can also turn into freedom restrictions. In Lesson 2, we dealt with the subject of "values and beliefs/convictions."

---

8   We found this remarkable statement in the Belgian newspaper *De Standaard* on April 30, 1998.

Questioning beliefs

Because beliefs and presuppositions belong to the category of "connections," we revisit this subject below. In the previous part of this chapter, we showed you how, by questioning beliefs, you can move your own and other people's limits of the world. People keep changing their opinion. Now we will show how it occurs and how you can analyze a belief (and possibly help it change) in three steps.[9]

1 Identify a belief by the value judgment somebody pronounces/expresses.
   e.g.: It is hard to find a residence in London.
2 When asking: "How do you know?" the person will begin to give proof for this statement. After the first answer, you may probe further by using: "How else?" as a question.
   e.g.: I have tried for a fortnight. The places I saw were expensive. In the end, I actually did not find out where best to live in London.
3 Now you can unravel the decision procedure by asking: "When did you first decide that?" or "How did you decide that based on this evidence? (How else?)"
   e.g.: It was in April. Actually, I have not looked since. I think my conclusion was really a good excuse to stop looking.

From this last sentence you can conclude that the person will be prepared to change their belief if, after being questioned, they perceive it as unnecessarily restricting. Detecting which values matter to the person (some of which can be derived from the answers given to the questions), and suggesting another solution which takes these values into account, may help the person to break through the limit imposed by the belief.

Reasoning in circles and other paradoxes

When a person is "inventing" a series of connections, this sometimes results in a vicious circle form of reasoning. When reasoning in circles, you use as evidence for your statement the other statement, a 2-point loop. This principle is splendidly illustrated in the book *Catch-22*[10] about World War II:

---

9   This pattern was presented by John McWhirter at the ANLP Conference in June 1999.
10 Heller, Joseph (1961). *Catch-22*, New York, Simon & Schuster.

You can only be fired as a pilot of a B-25 bomber if you become crazy. If you want to get fired, because you understand that flying above Germany is too dangerous, you are not crazy. So, we cannot dismiss you.

Or even:

The commanding officers of the 27th army tell you to fly 40 missions before you can go home. But nobody tells you to go home. So if you do not want to fly any more after your 40 missions if you are ordered to do so, you are refusing an order. So, you have to go on flying.

In the case of a paradox a pronouncement proves to be both true and false. Example of a paradox: "Be spontaneous!" or when a teacher announces: "Next week there will be an unexpected test." The person making the statement does not seem to notice this paradox. Indeed, you can break such reasoning only from outside the reasoning pattern. You have to make different connections to break or display the existing reasoning.

Questions as application of presuppositions—making sense out of nonsense

Given the presupposition that "the map is not the territory," we'd like to attract your attention to some "mapping errors" and language problems you'll find in everyday language. For instance, many sentences can be interpreted in different ways depending on the emphasis. A well-known example in linguistics is the question: "Did you give the money to John?" Try putting the stress on different words of this question, and see how that would change your interpretation. How does "Did **YOU** give the money to John?" differ from "Did you **GIVE** the money to John?" or "Did you give the **MONEY** to John?" or "Did you give the money to **JOHN**?"

Some types of sentences lend themselves especially to misinterpretations. Different ways of saying the same thing may lead to different interpretations, as the following examples demonstrate.

Who did it?

Compare the sentences *"The big bad wolf scared the three little pigs"* with *"The three little pigs were scared of the big bad wolf."*

In both cases, we end up with three scared little pigs. However, in the first sentence the little pigs have to "suffer," are the "victim" of some behavior of the wolf. In the second sentence, the little pigs seem to be in control. They have the choice of how they feel and act. And as the story goes, depending on how hard they want to work, you'll find them building houses in the next part of the tale.

Studying this from a grammatical perspective, you can see that the wolf is the subject of the first sentence: he plays a direct active role in the state of the little pigs, whereas the little pigs take that role in the second one. In the first sentence, the little pigs are "direct object," however, in the second sentence, expressed in the passive voice, the wolf is only an "indirect object," introduced by the word "of."

As a rule, a sentence where some actors play a passive role is a more incomplete description or map of the territory than one expressed in the active voice. When a sentence is expressed in the passive voice, you might want to examine the exact role the actors are playing.

True, false or maybe?

What's the difference between *"The elephant isn't pink"* and *"The elephant is grey"*?

When considering the first sentence, you have to think of a pink elephant, and then draw an imaginary cross over that elephant, telling yourself: "No, it wasn't that." It is clear that the second map is a "better" map of reality, which gives you more information. At least, now you know what the color is.

In general, our brains have difficulty processing negatives, because it involves constructing a map which may be very distant from the territory you're after.

You may also want to consider the presupposition: "The meaning of communicating is the response that it elicits." If the purpose of communicating is to be understood, then unless you want to mislead them, why make it difficult for people to understand you? Unless you have a good reason to do so, you may wish to favor using a positive formulation. After all, how many of us appreciate the government building a three-lane highway in a place where there is virtually no traffic, only to add road signs indicating "30 miles per hour"? Unless the police carry out frequent speed controls, you know what the effect will be ... So, by analogy, build a highway to the territory you want the listener to reach.

What do you mean?

How about the sentences *"The decision was to take action"* and *"Two bank robbers got out of the car"*?

Again we have two sentences which lead to the same territory. But the first sentence also leads to several other territories, which are cut off by the second one. For instance, if the territory you imagined after the first sentence was a group of friends sitting in a pub, deciding to finish their beers and order the next one, you might have been "too creative." And that group of union workers going on strike isn't relevant neither. So the first message wasn't specific enough. Be warned, however, that the second sentence remains less specific than you might wish. After all, if I were to tell you that, after getting out of their car, the bank robbers entered a jeweler's store to buy some jewelry, that might have been a territory you didn't consider.

Conclusion

This section showed how we can make use of presuppositions as a way to analyze what we say. In fact, each time you notice that a sentence seems to "violate" one of the presuppositions, you have a "clue" that you could benefit by questioning the person who said it.

Use of the Meta-Model
1. To deal with other people's emotions
When you look at the previous list of patterns for which you can ask questions, you may be wondering: "So what? How can I use this?" Well, this kind of question is the right reflection. Each time you ask somebody a question you also have to ask yourself a question, namely: "What goal do I aim to achieve by asking this question? What do I actually want to know? What result do I want to achieve with the other person by asking this question?"

Phrasing is perfect to help somebody to express themselves more realistically about their experience. However, they need to be willing to follow your questioning. Dramatic emotions can prevent this.

Experience has taught us that such a line of questioning is not recommended for calming down people with a strongly emotional response, and that the opposite result may occur instead. If, for instance, you were angry and said to another person: "I can't stand it here any more, everything you do means we have nothing to say to each other," and they were to ask you: "How do you know you can't stand it here any more?" how do you think you would respond?

If somebody has strong emotions, you may be better advised to combine this line of questioning with other techniques, such as those from Lessons 5 and 7. Your voice tone as well as other non-verbal signals, such as body posture, may make all the difference. A soft, deep voice and an understanding attitude will influence the way in which you succeed in calming somebody down.

To help you, we will go through all the points once again. What can you do with these Meta-Model questions?

1. Question the transformation. By this questioning you can:

    a. Retrieve the distorted or deleted information.

    b. Discover the model of the world and the typical filters a person uses frequently. The correcting of these filters can induce a person to access other values. Applying these filters yourself, by pacing a person, will improve your relationship with this person.

e.g.:

- By avoiding putting yourself in a "freedom restriction situation," you can experience more freedom in relation to what you do (more choices).
- By questioning nominalizations you can get closer to the experience and the feelings.
- You can learn a lot from mindreading and relating it to differences between people.

  c. (Re)move the limits that seem fixed in the language use of the person.

  d. Bring the person in touch with their full experience.

Once you know the kind of transformations (deletions, generalizations or distortions) somebody typically uses, you'll be better able to elicit the underlying event they are actually referring to when talking about their experience (surface structure).

2. To deal with your own emotions

The Meta-Model patterns offer many possibilities to relate to yourself in a better manner, by analyzing the way you talk about your own experience. If, for example, someone annoys you, and you catch yourself thinking or even saying to them: "It is always the same with you: you never help me when I need you," you'll immediately be able to recognize a number of Meta-Model patterns in your own speech. *Always* and *never* are generalizations, *help* and *need* are unspecific verbs.

Of course, as mentioned before, we already know the origin of these exaggerations and transformations, namely: your physical emotions. The more emotional you are at a certain moment, the more transformations will show up in your reasoning. This means that, by using the Meta-Model, you can remove or redress your filters to handle your own experiences in a way which brings you closer to the way the event actually happened. Thus, simple thinking will enable you to manage your emotions better.

Reasoning and speaking correctly are a first way to deal with your internal cooking. The question is, of course: "Who do you allow to rule your life: your emotions or your reason?"

Note: Socially desirable answers

The answer you'll get to a question you ask is influenced by a number of factors:

- How was the question understood?
- What does the person do to come to a reply (e.g. looking in their memories for the answer or inventing one by using their memory ...)?
- What is the conclusion of this mental process?
- How does the person formulate the reply in the end?

Typically, this process gets completed in less than a second ... People who design surveys have a wealth of experience in facing the complexity and unpredictability of the ongoing mental process between the moment a question is asked and when it receives an answer.[11] Even the inquirer influences this process (as in Heisenberg's Uncertainty Principle). You can include the relationship between the questioner and the questioned, and the interpretation of the inquirer's intention, amongst the elements which play a role in this answering process (see also meta-communication, presented in Lesson 5).

When responding to some questions many people act in a restrained manner, preferring to answer in a socially desirable way or saying what they think you expect them to say: this is known as compliance. Upon asking other questions, people do not even think about the real answer. For instance, take the question "How are you?" The answer we usually expect is probably "All right" or "Okay" or "Not bad," followed in turn by the question: "And how are you?" If we were to get an answer such as: "Today I am not really well, my father passed away last week," we would probably feel quite uncomfortable. The reason for this is that, despite the actual meaning of the question, it is not at all the reply we expect to receive for what actually is a rhetorical question. In practice,

---

[11] The book *Thinking About Answers: The Application of Cognitive Processes to Survey Methodology* by Sudman, Bradburn, Schwarz, and Bradburn (1996) treats this subject in detail.

you will get such an answer only from neighbors or your friends. You would never reply this way to a stranger in a business environment, for instance.

What's the message behind all this? If you really want to know the answer to the question that you are asking, check it out. If necessary, ask a further question, or you'll be none the wiser. After all, if you didn't really want to know the answer, why did you ask the question anyway? Know your outcome.

An example of a conversation using the seven Meta-Model patterns:

We draw out an example of a short conversation between a company employee and his coach. A coach's role is to seek to enable clients to come up with alternatives as far as possible (e.g. by having them search for solutions or resources in their own experience), instead of telling them how we would deal with that situation. In the case of a coaching session you aim to help a person to improve by enabling them to reflect upon past events, and by finding out together with them the different approaches they could take. *You'll find in italics what patterns each statement contains and the coach's purpose behind his questioning.*

1. ***He thinks*** I am a lousy co-worker.   *(mindreading)*
C. ***How do you know*** he finds you a lousy co-worker?
                                        (gather more information)
2. ***Because*** he gave me a telling off just now for not having called back that client.   *(belief)*
C. So because he gives you a telling off ***you think*** he finds you worthless?   *(challenging the statement)*
3. Yes, in fact he was right to give me ***a telling off.***
                          (to give a telling off: unspecific)
C. ***What exactly*** did he say to you?
                          (questioning of unspecificity)
4. It is ***a sign of little respect*** if I did not call the customer.
                                        (belief)
C. And not calling would be ***a sign of little respect?***
                                        (challenging the belief)
5. In this case it was rather a matter of ***priorities.***
                                        (unclear priorities)
C. ***What*** were your priorities?   *(gathering more information)*

6. Well, I *had to* make a contract with another client *very urgently.*　　　　*(freedom restriction + urgent = unspecific)*
C. *Could* the contract not wait longer than the customer?
　　　　　　　　　　　　　(questioning indistinctness + fr)
7. No, as a matter of fact, the contract *had to be* OK because of the budgeting of that customer.　　*(freedom restriction)*
C. *What else could you have done* to make your boss see the light in this situation?　　　　*(challenging the fr)*
8. *I should* have informed him in advance, so *he would* not be presented with a *fait accompli.*

There are many possible variations to this imagined example in everyday use. As an alternative you could choose to analyze the conversation for the pattern which arises most frequently. Once you identify the pattern you can use it as a starting point for asking questions in order to create a change in the reasoning of your client or interlocutor.

The theory behind the Meta-Model of language

Lewis Carroll once said "One of the hardest things in the world is to convey a meaning accurately from one mind to another." Language expresses your experiences and your thoughts. So, how do you do that? Many linguists, on inquiring about this subject, ask: "What are the rules according to which we combine words to build sentences?" After 10 years of research at MIT, the linguist Noam Chomsky presented his standard theory of Transformational Grammar[12] in 1965. Transformational Grammar is a model which explains how every sentence you utter is a summary or an abbreviation of your thinking: you unconsciously select words and combine them in order to communicate your thoughts as compactly as possible to other people. To quote Chomsky:

To understand a sentence, you need to (but it is not sufficient to) rebuild its representation on each level, the transformational level included, in which we consider the underlying core sentences of the

---

[12]　John Lyons wrote a readable introduction to Transformational Grammar titled *Chomsky* which appeared in the series **Fontana Modern Masters** (Third edition in 1991).

given sentence to a certain extent as the composing elements of the sentence.[13]

In plain English this means that whenever someone utters a sentence that we want to understand properly, we need to unravel this sentence until we come to its basic components in sensory-specific terms: what you can see, hear or feel. As Ilya Prigogine succinctly put it:

The world is richer than what you are able to express in any language.

The language which comes out of your mouth in everyday conversation (at surface level) is a transformation of the way you recall an experience or formed an idea (deep structure). Your memories are again different from what you experienced with all your senses when the initial experience you recall actually took place.[14] As you recall from Lesson 4, we encode this mainly using sensory-specific language (VAKOG).

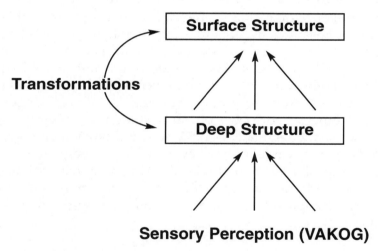

Figure 6.1: Transformation from experience to words

---

[13] The difference between surface structure and deep structure was first described by Chomsky in 1965 in his book *Aspects of The Theory of Syntax*, MIT Press.
[14] Chomsky, ibid.

Surface Structure	= the set of words you hear or read.

e.g.:
- I had to say "yes."
- Marlene broke her leg.

Deep Structure = meanings internally experienced which give a complete linguistic representation of the experience.

e.g.:
- I feel you can say only "yes," otherwise he will get angry.
- Marlene fell down the stairs and broke her leg.

Perception = our input channels of sensory information.

e.g.:
- He *looks* at me (Visual) and *asks* me (Auditory) "Come with me" and I *feel a* tension in my body (Kinesthetic).

Transformation = the process in which an event is transformed into a memory (deep structure) and the deep structure is itself transformed into spoken or written sentences. We presented earlier the three universal transformation patterns, namely: omitting, transforming and generalizing.

e.g.:
- You reduce your options to "not being able to do anything else than ..."
- You connect the consequence with the wrong cause.

Chronologically, the process goes as follows:

1. Once a person has lived through an experience they file it as a recollection in their memory after an initial transformation.
2. This recollection is used as the deep structure from which the person recalls their experience or talks about it.
3. What you hear as an observer is the surface structure, which is in its turn a transformation of the deep structure.

Exercises for this Lesson

Exercise 6.1: Some "homework"

Some tasks for the coming week: carry out one a day.

1. Buy a newspaper and read the opinion sections. Applying the three-rule model, consider the questions the articles arouse in you.
2. What kind of memos are circulating in your work environment? Select one that stands out and analyze it.
3. Take a look at some text you have written yourself. What language patterns can you discern using the three-rule model? How could you change the text so that it becomes more specific and contains fewer restrictions?
4. Watch the news on TV (record it if need be). How specific is the language used by the different people appearing on the news? Do they use freedom restriction patterns? What questions would you like to ask them?
5. Use the three-rule model as soon as you disagree with someone: instead of arguing, ask questions for clarification.

Exercise 6.2: An interview

This exercise is designed for three persons: Person B asks the questions, Person A answers them and Person C observes. The three participants take turns for the three roles. Continue for about 10 minutes per round.

- Person B chooses a subject which Person A said he is good at. Person B asks questions for about 8 minutes following the three-rule model.
- Person A keeps his replies as succinct as possible!
- Person C is a "guardian angel": they check that Person B asks questions within the rules of the model and make Person A "shut up" if A begins to talk too much.

2 minutes feedback:
- Person C suggests other questions Person B could have asked.
- Person A indicates the effect of being asked such questions.
- Person B explains what he has learned about asking questions.

Note: this exercise can also be done on your own: choose someone you want to learn something from, and start applying the three-rule model.

Exercise 6.3: Inventing questions

A. For each of the statements below, find out which questions you could ask by applying the three-rule model. As you can see in the example, a few statements invite more than one possible question.

Statement	Question
We have to start	*What would happen if we don't start?* *What do we have to do specifically?* *More questions applying the three rules, please.* *Rule 1:* *Rule 2:* *Rule 3:*
1. I'm really impatient.	
2. I have to succeed in this exercise.	
3. The others understand it.	
4. He gives me a lot of distress.	
5. If you want to, you can.	
6. He can't stand me, I know it.	
7. It couldn't be worse.	
8. She doesn't like me, she doesn't even smile.	
9. I keep making the same mistake.	
10. It's in the interest of everybody.	
11. They told me this would be enough.	

B. You can redo this exercise using the Meta-Model patterns. Which Meta-Model patterns do these sentences present? What kind of questions would each generate?

Exercise 6.4: Survey for restrictions: having to versus wanting to

A. Identify your limitations

Go through all your daily activities. Note them down in the table beneath in the left column. Judge each activity: how much time do you spend on each activity? How much did you like to do it? Did you do it because you really wanted to or because you had to?

Activity	Satisfaction	Time spent	Have to vs Want to
E.g. 1. To set the table	Reasonably	10 minutes	⑤ 4 3 2 1 0
2. To read the newspaper	Yes	25 minutes	5 4 3 ② 1 0
3. To go shopping	No	45 minutes	5 ④ 3 2 1 0
4. To wash the baby	No	35 minutes	5 ④ 3 2 1 0
1............................	....	....	5 4 3 2 1 0
2............................	....	....	5 4 3 2 1 0
3............................	....	....	5 4 3 2 1 0
4............................	....	....	5 4 3 2 1 0
5............................	....	....	5 4 3 2 1 0
6............................	....	....	5 4 3 2 1 0
7............................	....	....	5 4 3 2 1 0
8............................	....	....	5 4 3 2 1 0
9............................	....	....	5 4 3 2 1 0
10	....	....	5 4 3 2 1 0
11............................	....	....	5 4 3 2 1 0

B. Break through your limitations!

From the table above (or from other activities you did during the rest of the week) choose five activities you did not want to carry out but thought you had to. Write down who made you do them. Imagine what would have happened if you had not carried them out. What would be an alternative solution?

Activity	Who	Consequence of Not Doing	Alternative
3. Shopping 4. Washing baby	I My wife	No food in house Dirty baby	To shop together/to eat out Having babysitter wash baby
....	....	....	....
....	....	....	....
....	....	....	....
....	....	....	....
....	....	....	....

Remark: Of course, you can choose to extend this exercise to all weekdays.

—According to you, what do you spend too little time on and what do you spend too much time on?

—How much more fun would the week be like if you would adjust your agenda?

Exercise 6.5: The difference between presuppositions and mindreading
Decide in the sentences below if the comments are a presupposition or an interpretation. Reminder: a presupposition is a given, a fact that has to be true if the sentence is valid; an interpretation is what the reader "thinks of," based on the information he gets: it is a kind of mindreading.

1. I think I should stop criticising my boss.

	Presupposition	Interpretation
● He has a boss. ● He appreciates his boss. ● He criticizes his boss. ● He deserves a sanction.		

2. I (girl) cannot understand why I am not allowed to do this. My sister can already do it.

	Presupposition	Interpretation
● She thinks she is being unfairly treated. ● She wants her sister to be forbidden to do something. ● Her sister does something she does not. ● Her sister is older.		

3. I should dream more.

	Presupposition	Interpretation
● This person is bored. ● This person has expectations. ● This person is able to dream still more. ● This person is already dreaming.		

4. If she does not learn to communicate better, she is out of here.

	Presupposition	Interpretation
● She does not know how to communicate better. ● She can be dismissed. ● Her possibly being dismissed relates to better communication. ● This person feels powerless.		

Exercise 6.6: Presuppositions and question asking

For the next few days, choose an operational presupposition you want to test in your communication with others. Find out what changes when you use it and when you don't use it.

An example: suppose I tell you "Just believe the world is flat." Starting from the presupposition "there is a positive intention behind every behavior and a context in which every behavior has value," we will set off on a quest to find out the positive intention and the positive value behind the statement. Now suppose the context was that you had the plan of your house lying in front of you. When you live in a flat area like Flanders, for example, architects will often consider the land as flat and discount the fact that the earth is round. If, on the other hand, you had chosen to ignore the presupposition, you might answer my statement with "What's wrong, man? Did you decide the Catholic Church was right after all and that they should have burned Galileo?"

Exercise 6.7: Presupposition Identification
Find the presuppositions in these sentences:

1. In what case can I apply NLP?
....

2. If the cat spits again, I will kick him out.
....

3. Would you like a glass of red or white wine?
....

4. His inappropriate behavior gives the institute a bad reputation.
....

5. Why don't you visit your friends more often?
....

6. Only you can teach this.
....

7. If he had come home in time, the party would not have got so out of hand.
....

8. Your kitchen is as sloppy as mine.
....

9. How did you get depressed?
....

10. What resources do you want to use for that?
....

Exercise 6.8: Defending a point of view

Begin a discussion with someone, where you each defend a mutually incompatible map for at least five minutes. After this first round, switch sides, so that each now starts from the other's point of view. A possible topic could be discussing "the communist system has failed" vs "the current events in Europe prove that the communist system succeeded so well that it is no longer needed," or any other you fancy. Another topic you could consider is taking one of the operational presuppositions shown in the Introduction and defending it for five minutes, or trying to prove it wrong.

Cautionary Note: If you defend a point of view for long enough, you might actually begin to believe in it. This principle was one of the brainwashing techniques used by the North Koreans on captured GIs. An example of this was a daily contest set up with a packet of cigarettes as the main reward. The pack would go to the GI that could make the best speech presenting the advantages of the communist system. Another example of this is "Stockholm Syndrome":[15] after a while the hostage-takers succeed in winning the sympathy of their victims, who then defend the cause fought by their captors. This happened to Patty Hearst in the 1970s, after being abducted by the so-called Symbionese Liberation Army.[16]

Exercise 6.9: Map/Territory Evaluation

Express some beliefs you have about (a) yourself, (b) another person, (c) the world. Answer the following questions in relation to each:

How do you know it is true?
Which elements of this belief are "map" (*interpretation*) and which ones "territory" (*sensory-based evidence*)?
What presuppositions lie behind each belief?

---

[15] The term "Stockholm Syndrome" was coined to describe a certain psychological phenomenon in hostages following a 1974 bank holdup in Sweden. Four employees were held captive by two robbers for 5 ½ days. During the ordeal, some hostages became sympathetic towards the robbers. In fact, one female hostage swiftly and unaccountably fell in love with one of her captors and then publicly berated the Swedish Prime Minister for his failure to understand the criminal's point of view. For a limited period of time after her release, the former hostage continued to express affection for her captor (Ochberg, 1978).

[16] For details of the process, read R.A. Wilson: **Prometheus Rising**, New Falcon Publications, Phoenix, Ariz., 1989.

Exercise 6.10: *Facts versus opinions*

Read the following text carefully.

> *Linda has been absent for a few days.*
>
> *When returning to work on Thursday, Linda told her boss, Ms. Van Laer, that illness in the family had made it impossible for her to come to work.*
>
> *Ms. Van Laer had tried to reach Linda during her absence, but could not contact her. Linda was fully aware that staff members have to inform the department when they are absent.*
>
> *For this reason Linda got a formal warning.*

Compare the statements in the table below to the statements in the text and verify whether or not they transform the information (interpret). Determine the presuppositions in each.

Statement	Is this a fact?	Is this an interp- retation?	If it is an interpretation, what's the presupposition behind the interpretation?
1. Linda was absent three days.			
2. Illness in the family prevented Linda from coming to work.			
3. Ms. Van Laer tried to contact Linda, but she was not at home.			
4. Linda was not aware of the fact that staff members had to call if they were going to be absent.			
5. Ms. Van Laer gave Linda a formal notification.			

Exercise 6.11: Using the Meta-Model patterns to analyze an experience

A. Describe in a few sentences a personal experience which had a strong emotional component.

```



```

B. What Meta-Model patterns do you identify in the sentences above? Write down the questions that come with these patterns.

```



```

C. Answer the questions under B, especially the less trivial ones (those that you didn't consider before doing this exercise).

```



```

(repeat steps B and C as long as relevant)

At the end of the exercise, take some time to review the Meta-Model patterns you have come across during the exercise. What patterns are the most common in the questioning? Which patterns are not present?

This exercise can also be done with a group of two or three persons. In that case the first person tells their experience (step A) and will answer the questions (step C). The second and the third person will discover the Meta-Model patterns, formulate the questions (step B) and observe the process (keep repeating).

Lesson 7:
Successfully Interact with Yourself and Others

**"Hate is a form of suicide.
Forgiving is recovering a lost possession."**

Goals

In this chapter we aim to enable you to accomplish the following objectives:

- Get a complete picture of the structure of someone's subjective experience, considering all the models you have come across in this book.
- Observe the non-verbal language of a person and find out how to use it to achieve better rapport with the person.
- Learn calibration skills, to find out in what emotional state a person is at a given moment.

Neurolinguistic Assumptions

The following assumptions particularly apply in this chapter:

- *We simultaneously communicate at unconscious and conscious levels.*
- *We continuously process information through our senses.*
- *Recognizing responses requires sensory channels which are clean and open.*
- *The most important information about a person is that person's behavior.*
- *Respect for the other person's model of the world is essential for effective communication.*
- *Rapport is about meeting individuals at their map of the world.*
- *The meaning of your communication is the response that you get.*
- *Resistance in a person is a sign of lack of rapport: there are no "resistant" people, only inflexible communicators.*

Why this Lesson?

People who excel at building and sustaining relationships use a range of skills and supporting beliefs to do so. We'll cover these in this chapter and link what we're doing to the previous chapters of the book. You have already learnt many complementary models to help you make the most of emotions in the way you operate. Here you'll see how you can apply all the previous models we have presented to interact with others in the best possible manner, and to achieve what people call "rapport." In so doing, you will realize the crucial importance of body language.

Introduction: Mastery in Building and Maintaining Relationships

Is it one of your dreams to be of importance to others? Are you slightly jealous when someone dies and the whole community goes to their funeral because they liked that person and the relationship they had with this individual? Do you like being honestly appreciated by others for what you have been doing for them?

If your answer is "yes" to any of these questions, you too can choose to become a "loving person." You can also develop your mastery at enhancing the quality of your interpersonal relationships. For a moment, consider the way you say "hello" to other people. Do you consider it purely a formality, or is it meaningful to you? Is your greeting begrudged, mouthed by your lips only, or full of heartiness?

The Meaning of Your Communication Is the Response that You Get

The purpose of communication is for one person to change another, in some way. Communication, therefore, achieves its purpose when the desired change, i.e. the response which was desired, is accomplished. In order to achieve this, people need to communicate with each other through many channels: verbal (language), para-verbal (sounds, intonation), body language (postures, gestures), including many subtle unconscious messages. However, only a few of these pass the threshold to our conscious awareness, as our conscious mind is aware of only 7 ± 2

items of information at any one time.[1] Indeed it would be true to say that most successful communications are unconscious. (*"Some enchanted evening, you will see a stranger ... and, somehow, you'll know ..."*)

A study carried out in 1967[2] identified that:

COMMUNICATION IS:

38%
Tonality/
Para-verbals

7%
Content/
Language

55%
Facial
Expression

Interestingly, the format of the study did not analyze the remainder of the body language used. Had that been the case, the total amount would undoubtedly have increased even further and the proportion of *Content* in the whole matrix of communication might have been reduced accordingly.

---

[1] This rule comes from the article "The Magical Number Seven Plus or Minus Two: Some Limits on Our Capacity for Processing Information," written by George Miller, originally published in *Psychological Review,* March 1956.

[2] The original study on the importance of verbal and nonverbal messages by Dr. Albert Mehrabian, the percentages of which we quote above, focused on communications of feelings and attitudes. The experiments carried out initially sought to ascertain the proportion of verbal to non-verbal communication in situations where these conflicted—i.e. in situations of *incongruence*—and the percentages do not hold in other contexts. Another study carried out by Ray Birdwhistle found that 35% of the communication was verbal (content + vocal) and 65% was non-verbal. Rather than taking such percentages as absolute, considering the limited nature of such studies, we seek to highlight the importance of non-verbal communication (tonal and body language) which, having evolved prior to language *per se*, has the power to confirm or invalidate what is expressed verbally. Therefore one cannot pay too much attention to the non-verbal components of communication which, being indicator-based, express the *meaning* of communication, whereas language, being signal/symbol-based, expresses the *signification* of the communication (Wishart, Trevor (1996). *On Sonic Art,* Amsterdam, Harwood Academic Publishers GmbH). For more information on scientific findings on communication and body language, see Dr. Mehrabian's book *Silent Messages,* a private publication available from the author.

For reasons you will soon realize, a message is never fully expressed AND received consciously by both parties. Sometimes, the expressed message goes out consciously and is received unconsciously. At other times an unconscious communication may be received consciously. At yet other times, unconscious communicates directly to unconscious without any conscious awareness whatsoever. This last form of communication is also the most common.

Neurolinguistics acknowledges the importance of both conscious and unconscious processes as representing the cybernetic quality of the mind/body system. For this reason, it often refers to the unconscious and the conscious minds as if they were distinct entities, albeit with the understanding that this is no more than a useful metaphor. An even better approximation could be to say that consciousness is a property of our unconscious, or that it is the only aspect of our unconscious we are aware of.

As seen before, we live in a world of difference, as the anthropologist Gregory Bateson[3] identified. Below a certain intensity threshold, such differences pass unnoticed. Only those above this threshold may come into our consciousness. Yet even then, if the information which is left passes unnoticed through other filters, such as our beliefs and values, which shape our model of the world, we may miss out some very important clues also, as if we had a "'color-blindness of the mind." You can easily see here how few items will be left of any informational input we receive at any one time: indeed, 7 ± 2 of them. It is this essential filtering process which enables us to operate in everyday life and not be overwhelmed by data overload.

Yet this filtering can work just as much against us as for us, as when we are in a hurry and can't find our keys. It can also cause us to miss vital clues about the behavior of others, as happened in the case, mentioned in a previous chapter, of a person whose partner was unfaithful and who was the last one to realize.

---

[3]   Bateson, Gregory (1972). *Steps to an Ecology of Mind,* New York, Chandler Publishing Company. (reprinted University of Chicago Press, 2000).

The Art of Calibration: What You Can Learn from Body Language

What do you know of what goes on inside somebody else's head? Nothing at all! After all, you aren't in there, are you? But, if this is the case, how do we manage to communicate at all? The answer is: we guess. From babyhood onwards we have been making guesses about what other people think. Sometimes we are right and benefit from this lucky guess, and sometimes we are wrong and suffer the consequences in some way.

How do we guess, then? We make observations, comparing our observation with some reference experiences in our own model of the world and, having evaluated our information, come to a conclusion. Life is a training school where we continuously educate our guesses and, like any other school, there are stars and dunces. Whereas the former appear to learn easily and effortlessly and become experts at communication, the latter find it a struggle or perhaps even give up altogether. However, this is not to say that people can't learn. Maybe the first ones had better models to learn from to begin with and all the latter need is a few tips to educate their guesses. Hence a book like this, a manual to educate our guesses, a Primer on the Art of Living, and of Loving Living. Whether you began reading this book as a star or a dunce, you will enjoy shining in the firmament of your life by the time you finish it, or at least know how to do so when you're ready to make your life as good as you would like it to be.

So, the quality of our guessing or mapping tools will dictate the quality of the results we get. First of all we need to have "clear and open filters": this means that we cannot allow ourselves to interpret anything until we have gathered enough information. Evaluative filters will follow in their turn. If you remember from an earlier chapter we said the same thing about emotions: they are behaviors to which we assign a label. The type of label we assign will dictate the type of emotion we perceive. This is the same with other forms of behavior, including our own. If we engage our evaluative filters too early we may jump to the wrong conclusion.

One of the questions that Darwin never dared answer is: "What value does non-verbal communication have?" During the 19th century, the official answer was probably along the lines of: "God gave mankind facial expressions to express their intimate emotions." The anthropologists Margaret Mead and Gregory Bateson were known to oppose the point of view that non-verbal expression was universal. To some extent, this approach has been adopted into neurolinguistics. Mead and Bateson's thinking strongly influenced the models we now use to understand emotions.

In 1872 Darwin published his book *The Expression of the Emotions in Man and Animals.* It became an instant bestseller in England in the same year, and was forgotten afterwards. About 125 years later, at the beginning of 1998, HarperCollins published the third edition of this book. It contains a new preface, as well as an afterword written by Paul Ekman. By publishing studies which show that people from all over the world will recognize the same spontaneous expressions of anger, fear, disgust, dismay, surprise and happiness, Darwin and Ekman are to be situated amongst the scientists trying to prove that facial expressions are universal.

In her anthropological fieldwork, Margaret Mead, who once was married to Bateson, met several counter-examples of facial expressions which were not in "accordance" with Darwin's theory. For instance, a Chinese may well be smiling when in fact he is angry with you. Mead therefore strongly opposed Darwin's point of view. You may already have thoughts on the matter yourself. We personally think that both opinions are correct, and that the word "spontaneous" is the key. After all, many of our facial expressions are not spontaneous at all, but contrived, whether to express something we seek to communicate or to repress something we do NOT wish to communicate. We all know what it is like to put on a "poker face." Throughout life, we achieve a certain modicum of unconscious competence at controlling our emotions and the way we display them to others, and also at learning to observe the non-verbal behavior of others to find out more about what's happening inside their head. This unconscious competence is what we call Emotional Intelligence.

So, there are patterns of body language which will be universally recognizable wherever you go AND there are patterns which are idiosyncratic to an individual, community or culture. When we work and meet with people, we can to some extent rely on our knowledge of body language, but must seek to identify these idiosyncratic patterns as well, or we may be way off-track in some of our interpretations.

To come to the conclusions he reached in *The Origin of Species*, as well as *The Expression of the Emotions in Man and Animals*, Darwin spent many years sailing round the world, exploring, gathering facts and collating them. Meeting a new person is like exploring a new land hitherto unknown, at least by you. It's as if a person was a volcanic island in the middle of the ocean. When you arrive by boat, you will see only the island, which is in fact the top of a volcano. To discover more, such as the coral reef below the surface of the sea, you would need a submarine. Below the surface, what you find are the sides of the volcano, supporting the visible part of the island. Completely at the bottom, on the sea floor, you'll find out that the volcano is connected to other islands and archipelagos by the continental shelf. By using seismic and fume detectors as well as a range of other sophisticated scientific equipment on the island you can also find out much more about the underlying structure of the volcano. You might find a working core and a magma chamber, and come to some valid conclusions about the level of volcanic activity. You can even observe the behavior of animals on the surface to identify if and when an eruption is impending.

Similarly, all that we know of a person is their external behavior, enacted within the sea of their environment. Human behavior is like the emerged part of the island, and if a person is really angry, they might even resemble an erupting volcano! As you saw in an earlier chapter, a state can be accessed from the Body End or from the Mind End and is made up of their External Behavior and their Internal Representation. So you can learn about the structure of their internal representations and maps just by observing their behavior, as long as you know what there is to observe and how to use the tools you have. Below the surface level, you can detect the supporting structure of this representation. This structure will consist of the skills a person needs in order to do what they do and, at a deeper level, the beliefs and values of this person which motivate them to carry on as they do. If you keep going further, you'll find the person's core or true self and finally realize that, although we are all different from each other, we all partake of human nature and are connected to everyone else around us.

So, we begin our mapping by observing with all our senses, noting all the components of communication which the other person offers us. Contrary to what some people may think, there is an abundance of them, depending on the precision of your observing tools. Somebody once said that "We ooze who we are and what we think through every pore of our skin," and that is probably quite literally true, as lie detectors can tell us. We, too, have lie detectors inside us and you will certainly know a lot more about yours by the end of this chapter.

Calibration and synchronization

Calibration is the first step you need to carry out to pace your conversation partner and achieve rapport. We use this term in neurolinguistics to signify the act of deliberately paying attention to our conversation partner so as to identify when they go into a particular state. By calibrating a person's physiology associated with a state, what it means to them, you are thus able to notice what changes occur when the person changes state. You can then use the information gathered in calibration to synchronize your-self to their own patterns and achieve rapport with them.

Calibration and Synchronization Categories

As we will observe and work on the same categories when engaging in Rapport, we will comment on each category with suggestions pertinent to either process.

Purpose of Calibration
1: To discover the meaning of a specific change to a person.
2: To discover the non-verbal analogs of a particular state.

1. Territorial Position

- Where people sit or stand.
- Where is your partner standing or sitting in relationship to you?
  e.g. standing next to someone in a conflict instead of facing the person, using a round table instead of a square one in negotiations, etc.
- At what distance?
  e.g. in a territory considered as public, social, personal or intimate?

2. Body Language

All the non-verbals you can see, touch, smell or taste. Their eye-accessing cues, which tell you how they access some internal information.

An important pattern to calibrate for is Symmetry: Asymmetry, of whatever type, is usually a tell-tale sign of i n c o n g r u e n c e . Symmetry is associated with beauty and elegance.

- **Posture**
  e.g.: How do they place their shoulders? How do they sit? How balanced are they?

What to observe when calibrating:
THE MINIMAL SIGNS OF MENTAL STATES
For instance, notice changes in body language.
Tip: Use descriptive language instead of evaluative language. Instead of thinking: *"He frowned,"* think: *"His eyebrows tensed and furrowed and his palpebral fissures narrowed."* Instead of thinking: *"She relaxed,"* think: *"She let her shoulders go down and began breathing more deeply and slowly. The muscles in her face loosened and her cheeks became more colored. Her lower lip filled out and became shinier."* Notice also how descriptive language is non-threatening. Every thing you say is factual and not laden with values.

- **Mobility**
  e.g.: How do they move, how do they walk? How do they balance on their feet?
- **Gestures**
  e.g.: What are their typical arm movements? How do they move and use their hands?
- **Breathing**
  e.g.: Is it a deep, belly breathing or a shallow breathing, noticeable in only the upper chest?
- **Facial Expression**
- **Skin**: color, tone, shininess
- **Muscular Tension**: cheeks, brow, lips, jaw e.g. tensing the eyebrow
- **Mouth**: set, tightness, twitch
- **Set of Lower Lip**: size, shape, color, shininess
- **Eye**: movements, pupil dilatation, blinking, color of iris, palpebral fissures (the space between a person's eyelids when their eyes are open), direction of gaze, focus of gaze, moisture
- **Asymmetry**

3. Tonality

All the auditory components of communication, irrespective of content (see below). Tests carried out using oscilloscopes, which give a visual representation of the voice, have shown that, whereas the voice of people in a resourceful state is clearly displayed as a rounded sine wave, the voice of people in unresourceful states is displayed as a saw-tooth shape.

e.g.: ● The speed at which your conversation partner speaks (adapt to the same speed), the tone of voice, …

4. Representation Channel

The sensory-specific language they use, which tells you how they process information.

e.g.: ● A kinesthetic client says "I didn't manage to get a good contact with that customer," instead of replying, "I see what your problem is" (visual); the coach says: "I know how you feel" (kinesthetic).

5. Content

The story they tell you.

e.g.: ● If somebody talks about their education, you reply by asking questions about it.

6. Keywords and Typical Expressions

The words and expressions they keep using.

e.g.: ● Discussing the weather at the hairdresser's.

● Repeating keywords, the jargon someone uses.

7. Values and How They're Expressed in Criteria

What they appear to consider important. This can be identified if they keep going back to a subject or have a hobby-horse, and also by their tonality and the way they emphasize some words when speaking.

e.g.: ● A person who is always formal and principled.

● Another person may consider law and order important.

● Another person may value their freedom and independence and thus avoids taxation.

● A new trend towards being honest in contacts with executives of the company is approaching, and one expects that the management is also honest and doesn't withhold information.

8. The World View: Beliefs, Presuppositions

What they believe is true or false, what has to be true for what they say to make sense.

e.g.: ● Someone considers a political party's points of view as unacceptable.

● A person may have strong beliefs on how to educate kids: "They need spanking, you know!"

● Some persons consider big companies that treat employees as machines as evil.

9. (Neuro)logical Levels

The level at which they pitch the conversation.

e.g.: ● During a discussion you notice that a person is mainly discussing skills. To match this, you can keep the discussion at the same level.

- During a conversation a person talks about how a certain software package can help to solve a problem. Discussing whether another package would be a solution would be remaining at the same level. Discussing whether the problem itself is a symptom that should be solved by re-organizing a department, is a solution on another level.

10. Meta-Programs
The type of sorting filters they preferentially access.

e.g.: • A salesperson notices that their customer is mostly focused *Away From*. The sales-person now stresses the "away from" advantages of the product, such as: "I can assure you this machine is very fault-tolerant."

The latest two categories are more specifically used for synchronization purposes.

11. Similar Experiences/References
Finding commonalities in both parties.

e.g.: • "Funny you should say that: I went through something similar."
- "Isn't that a coincidence! I studied at Harvard as well!"
- "Isn't it amazing? We too went to Saint-Tropez on our last holiday."
- "We have many things in common. I've been working in the insurance sector as well."

12. Contextual Elements
Some aspects which appear to correspond or be expected in a given context.

- Clothing
  e.g. a white shirt and a blue or black suit when meeting bankers, wearing a tie when going to a restaurant, casual dress at a barbecue party, …
- Possessions
  e.g. wanting to have the same kind of car or house as other people in your environment
- Places to go to
  e.g. the jetset meets at the golf course, goes to Aspen, etc.

- Behavior

  e.g. social drinking: if they are having a beer, I can't drink water.

The Dangers of Interpreting

Having calibrated a person, using descriptive terms, you are ready to come out with some conclusions of your own. However, watch out when generalizing the meaning of body language, especially if you're just regurgitating the opinion of others. For example, not everyone leaning backwards is being "uninterested." Nor does someone who crosses their arms suddenly necessarily become "closed." Of course, if you decide to believe these kinds of theories, they will begin to operate as self-fulfilling prophecies. You'll begin to adapt your own non-verbal behavior, and as a result the relation with your conversation partner will change. Virginia Satir, a well-known specialist in Family Therapy, noticed that most misunderstandings between family members were caused by misinterpreting body language.[4]

Achieve Rapport with Yourself

Having learnt how to be more emotionally intelligent and intelligently emotional, you are now ready to interact with others in a resourceful fashion, and with what neurolinguists call "Rapport." The word, of French origin and based on the verb "rapporter," initially means: "to be in contact or in touch with another," or "to take back." "Être en bons rapports" means "to be on good terms with another person." "Bien sous tous rapports" means "good on all accounts." The term "rapport" therefore means "a state of (good) communication with another, in which connections are achieved at a range of levels."

People traditionally think that rapport can be achieved only with other people. However, it is a state you can also engage in with yourself. Achieving good rapport with yourself enables you to easily obtain good rapport with others. Many of us seek to achieve

---

[4]   Virginia Satir was probably the second person modeled explicitly by Bandler and Grinder. The three of them jointly published a book entitled *Changing with Families,* 1976, Science & Behavior Books, Calif, 1976.

rapport with others when we're not even on good terms with ourselves. Is it any wonder, then, that we don't get what we want?

Sometimes we use our body language to make it difficult to reach our goals. Most people who seek to explain their point of view demonstrate in their body language what they expect to get out of the conversation, even if that is a negative outcome for them. For instance, when observing participants in courses who are preparing a meeting with a customer or their boss, their non-verbal behavior will reveal when they expect that they won't succeed. The result is that it becomes even easier for the other party to say no. Talk about self-fulfilling prophecies! Do you think the people who communicated with their tonality or body language that they did not believe in their outcome, are happy with themselves? We don't think so either.

Matching someone's body language

Have you ever noticed how some TV reporters use body language during an interview? Sometimes they seem to be nodding their heads "in agreement" with the person they are interviewing. And afterwards they ask a question which shows they didn't agree at all! The effect of the nodding is to make the guest feel at ease and keep on talking (especially if he didn't plan to avoid this).

Having identified the above calibration categories, now try the following experiment. The next time you are talking to someone, observe this person's non-verbal behavior. Adapt your own body language to theirs, so that it becomes similar to the language shown by your partner. You'll notice that this smooths the conversation. In neurolinguistics we call this "matching." Now change your body language, so that it displays some clear differences. You'll notice that, the larger the difference in body language terms, the more difficult the conversation will become. In fact, most of the time, the person will "think" you're no longer listening, or that you do not understand what he/she is talking about. In neurolinguistics, we call this "mismatching." We have been experimenting with this exercise in groups for years and found that less than 5% of the participants will keep on talking if their partner is clearly mismatching.

You can use this principle during communication. Match your body language to the other person if you want to get your message through. To check if your partner is matching, make small changes to your body language and see if your partner makes these changes themselves.

Getting into Rapport with Someone's Thoughts and Experience

Research shows that people have a natural tendency to adjust their body language to a conversation partner they are in agreement with. If people are in rapport, their behavior and language patterns spontaneously become similar. Remember the movie *When Harry Met Sally*? This film shows some nice illustrations of the observation that a couple who have been married happily for a long time begin to resemble each other. In fact, they get better at matching their body language in a similar fashion. Business partners agreeing on a point will probably show similar body language at that point in the conversation. A spectacular example of a form of rapport was discovered by the American psychologist Martha McClintock. She found that the ovulation cycles of women who live together or work in close collaboration tend to synchronize. An issue of *Nature*, in March 1998, contained an article which proved that our axillary organs (specialized sweat glands inside our armpits) secrete pheromones which enable this synchronization.

Next to such natural, spontaneous forms of synchronization, you can find other ways to consciously achieve better rapport with a conversation partner. For example, pacing someone's body language is very helpful for a salesperson, as well as for a therapist, to gain rapport, as it puts the other side more at ease. If you want to resolve a conflict with someone, pacing may again serve as a useful strategy. Why keep on fighting, if there is more to win by gaining rapport and sorting out the differences?

Rapport with Others: How to Achieve It

Rapport is linked to a feeling that one seems to get along quite well with another, and may contain an underlying assumption of safety: the other can be trusted. So, how do you go about achieving rapport? Anything a person says or does is a good source of information for this purpose. Rapport occurs when you align yourself, consciously or unconsciously, with one (or more) of the calibration categories we have just presented. If there is rapport, this synchronization occurs naturally. A group of interested people listening to a trainer will tend to display very similar non-verbal behavior (typical way of sitting, facial expression, etc.). You could say that the people are "mirroring" the other person's behavior. Maybe that's why we get the impression that a couple who have been together for many years begin to look more and more alike. Similarly, if you observe an audience listening to a good public speaker, you'll notice a lot of similarities in their body language.

We feel most at ease when having others around
who appear similar to ourselves.

We classify eight different ways of applying the synchronization categories mentioned above:

1. Copying

This means doing exactly the same thing as another person you are matching in a synchronization category.

e.g.:
- The person you are with moves their right arm; you move your right arm as well.
- Imitating the rhythm and the pitch of the voice of your conversation partner.
- Adapting your breathing so that it becomes the same kind of breathing of your conversation partner.

One word of caution: when matching a person do it with some discretion. If your imitation is too striking or too obvious, the other person may think you're mimicking them to make fun of them, and completely miss your goal of improving rapport. So build up your matching slowly, changing your own behavior bit by bit before slowly fully matching the person.

2. Mirroring

This means copying as if you were playing the mirror of the other person. It works best when facing each other.

e.g.:
- The person you are with moves their right arm; you move your left arm.
- The person you are with puts their right leg over their left leg, so you put your left leg over your right leg.

This technique is a bit more subtle than fully copying the other's behavior, while you still get a remarkable improvement of rapport.

3. Crossover mirroring

This means mirroring by using another synchronization category.

e.g.:
- The person you are with moves their right arm; you move your right leg.
- When the other crosses his legs, you cross your arms.
- You match the other's breathing with the speed of your speech.

This technique is even subtler than the preceding one, and it requires a bit more imagination and technical skill.

4. Echoing

This means matching, copying, mirroring or crossover mirroring in an attenuated fashion.

e.g.:
- The person you are with moves their right arm; you move your right hand.
- When the other crosses his legs, you cross your feet.

This technique is quite subtle and is also perceived as very respectful.

5. Delayed mirroring or matching

This means using the previous techniques while building in some delay.

e.g.:
- The person you are with moves his right arm, some time later you move your left arm, stressing a similar point in the conversation.

- During a negotiation, you take over the keywords of the other person while explaining your own point of view.
- The other person uses a four-letter word; you use it some time later.

Using this technique you decrease the chance that the other will make a cause-effect link between his behavior and your reaction. Only their unconscious will detect it.

6. Backtracking

This means exactly (literally) repeating verbal and non-verbal language.

Backtracking can be done using words, but also non-verbal elements. For instance, you may want to repeat the keywords of a person, along with the arm movements that accompanied it. While you are backtracking, check how the other responds, and correct your own actions according to their reaction (e.g. when you back-tracked some words or movements incorrectly).

7. Second Position

This means copying the complete body language of the other person, having the same feelings, aiming to have the same thoughts (see also Lesson 5).

Good communicators, whether they be therapists, public speakers or business leaders, will unconsciously or consciously try to figure out in what state the other person is and how they are reasoning. This is a systematic mindreading which, technically, means you associate in the Second Position.

When you display that you take Second Position during a conversation, the other will feel not only understood because you are using similar words, but will sense that you are living the same feelings they are living and sharing the same map of the world.

8. Mismatching

This means breaking the similarity between your behavior and the other person's, perhaps in order to get the other's attention or involvement, or as a rapport-building strategy (agreeing to mismatch, as a way of matching on a different level).

e.g.:
- Content mismatching: you give a person a compliment, and the person will minimize his contribution; you give the person an order, and the person reacts by looking for an alternative approach, etc.

You will meet people who mismatch spontaneously. They tend to be labelled "Polarity Responders." We spoke about mismatching when we referred to the *Similarity/Difference* Meta-Program. People who have a tendency to mismatch will change their behavior as soon as they notice (even unconsciously) that you're matching them. If you know they are mismatchers, match their mismatch! Suggest the opposite of what you think, as the other will mismatch that and reply with what you want. Mind you, this is a high-risk strategy: if they are less of a mismatcher than you think, they may agree with what you suggest, and you'll end up with what you don't want! If in doubt, leave this out; it's not as if we were short of rapport-building patterns.

9. Other forms of rapport building

Even if they appear less obviously related to the synchronization categories, further forms of rapport building exist, such as:

- Displaying honest courtesy and politeness: this tends to disarm even the most aggressive. Somebody once called courtesy the "essential lubricant of society."
- Showing your appreciation for some element of the other's presence (*hint*: all the elements of the synchronization categories come to mind as subjects of your appreciation, as long as your appreciation is sincere). The importance of being earnest, indeed!
- Making a factual statement based on something about them that you can see, hear or smell.
- Paying them an honest compliment based on something about them that you can see or smell, e.g. something they're

wearing: a jewel, a perfume, etc. (*hint*: this works best with people of the opposite sex, unless you're both lesbian or gay).
- Earnestly displaying attentiveness to them, as children naturally do when told a story. This works particularly well with people who are very expressive with their hand movements: track their gestures and hand movements with your gaze, so that you can refer to them later on when backtracking.
- Revealing something about yourself (preferably authentic); this expresses trust.
- Your internal state of congruence and truthfulness.

> When people come into contact, the nine described ways of rapport building will help to build up a relationship of trust.

We suggest you try out the above ways of building rapport, perhaps one at a time, and test out your skills at them. Notice which come more easily to you. If you are better at some than others, practice the ones you are least good at, as you stand to progress most by developing them. Extend your comfort zone!

How Do You Know You've Got Rapport?

Rapport is one of those special states we experience throughout life and knowing when it occurs is as useful as knowing how to reach it. After all, how will you know when you've got there, if you have no idea of what it's like? As it is, the odds that you have never yet experienced rapport in your life are vanishingly small. At worst, you have and can't remember it. We would also like to think that you have calibrated your own state of rapport, let alone other people's. However, you may appreciate a few examples of calibration others have identified, some internal, others external. These are:

- *A feeling inside you.*
  This is usually expressed as a warmth, a feeling of energy, of flow.
- *A flushing of the skin about the face.*
- *Pupils dilating.*

The previous three examples from physiology demonstrate how rapport engages our parasympathetic nervous system, which is part of our autonomous nervous system. This usually occurs when there is no threat present.

- *A verbalization.*
  Other people will comment on their own internal responses in terms like: "We're really working well together," or "You're good at this," "I know I can trust you," "Oooh, this is fun!," "We're on the same wavelength," etc.
- *An ability to lead.*
  The other person will spontaneously want to follow your lead.
- *Creativity.*
  The system you are making with another person is in *synergy*, i.e. the sum total is greater than the sum of the parts. This is one of the many rewards of rapport. "Magic" happens.

When you start practicing, you will observe that people who are in rapport with you will synchronize their body language to yours as well, unless you've just met that mismatching counter-example. We call *pacing* the way you match the behavior your conversation partner is displaying. When the other person matches the behavior you displayed first, you are *leading*. Note here how these expressions presuppose a "dancing" metaphor and, indeed, many people have described rapport as an elaborate dance or courtship rite.

Pacing

This means: when you are synchronizing yourself with the other person, adjusting yourself to them, as when walking or dancing together.

Leading

This means: when you mismatch the (non-)verbal language of your conversation partner, and the other person follows your lead by re-synchronizing and adopting one or more elements of your behavior. This also occurs in dancing.

Coming to a "good understanding" implies building a context in which the other person feels safe enough to follow your lead. The neurolinguistics definition is "they are in rapport." When you get in rapport with several of the non-verbal synchronization channels, you can afford to disagree on one or two other channels, such as content or the way one is dressed, as this will not be perceived as important.

Examples:
- Consider two partners having a conversation while in bed close to one another. They have a matching body language indicating love, while disagreeing on content.
- A boss with a sales representative having problems with a customer says: "That's up to you to solve. You'll learn by doing it." However, she is saying this with a warm voice showing she cares and is compassionate. This way, the sales representative feels supported.

Notice that when people are in rapport with each other the pacing and leading continuously shifts between the participants, unconsciously for the most part.

Example: Meta-Programs and rapport? We don't get married like that!

It may seem rather artificial to go to the marriage bureau and put down the criteria for your Mr. or Mrs. Right. Opposites often attract. However, many people often display aversion to something which we can easily describe as a Meta-Program. Not accepting a specific extreme way of behaving often seems to be the decisive factor in breaking a relationship. This aversion to a particular extreme of Meta-Programs, of course, also plays a role in other situations, for example at work.

For example: an *Options* person emphasizes creativity and freedom, but her partner holds on to *Procedures*. They always argue. Or one person, again and again, associates in his *Feelings*, while the other easily goes into "Meta-Position" (emphasis on *Feelings* vs *Thinking*).

In these differences we also see the real nature of Meta-Programs at work: they are, at the same time, ways of behaving and patterns which are typical of a person. In many cases a person gets stuck in a specific Meta-Program because of the result it gives them. For example, the *Procedures* person becomes rigid because the procedure gives them safety, while the *Options* person holds on to keeping their options open and postponing choices because it gives them a sense of freedom.

From our perspective it is certainly worth the effort to go through the list yourself and to check which polarities you strongly refer to and which ones you are averse to. As you will have guessed already, this list can also be used outside the marriage bureau or the office. For example, draw up a list of the Meta-Programs of your colleagues and check the matches and mismatches with yours, comparing their aversions with yours.

Study your relationships

One might say that a proof that your Emotional Intelligence is developing is when you notice that your skills at building better relationships with others have improved. We offer you some questions for self-reflection, so that you can find out where you stand.

1. Find someone with whom you have a good relationship. Check the different synchronization categories and examine how you are using them, in order to build evidence for the good relationship.

2. Find a context where you try to lead, but the others don't follow you. Find out what you can do in order to build a good relationship first.

3. Find someone with whom you get along quite well. Check out how your rapport-building skills function in this case. Now check how you could mismatch the person. What would happen?

4. Compare the previous person to someone you can't get along with. Find out what makes the difference. What could you do to build up rapport with this person? What can you learn about yourself from this inability to build a good relationship? What does it teach you about being in rapport with yourself?

5. What does "having a good relationship with yourself" mean to you? What does "mismatching yourself" mean to you?

6. Rapport when being in love. What information would you need at a level of structure to get the impression that the other person is in love with you? To answer this question, go through the synchronization categories in a systematic way.

Levels of Rapport

From trying out the above, you will have noticed that rapport is not a digital pattern which is or is not, but rather exists along a continuum, one end of which is hatred, the other is love. In the middle lies indifference. This continuum will parallel that of mismatching/matching.

So the level of rapport you seek to achieve to sell a product will be of a different order of magnitude from that which you will express when you want another person to fall in love with you. Confusing such levels can be embarrassing at best and dangerous at worst. People who have not experienced much rapport in life or are in a state of physical or mental (dis)stress will have a very much poorer representation of this continuum. A simple expression of appreciation may make them fall head over heels for you or they might flip completely at a slight mismatch. However, these are the exception and you will doubtless have calibrated the situation in advance. People in helping professions often encounter situations when a client mistakes their help as a sign of love and seek to bond with them. This is known as "transference." Recognizing the signs and ensuring that the relationship remains strictly professional, while cordial, is another sign of Emotional Intelligence.

The practice of using rapport-building information during a conversation

The more you observe your conversation partners, the better you'll realize how much interesting information there is to gather from this observation. By getting into rapport with others through matching (copying, mirroring, etc.) their synchronization categories, or by going into Second Position, you are able to obtain information about their emotional state or even about a message they might not want to tell you. In fact, few people are bold or brash enough to dare give you their opinion straight to your face, and many people refrain from showing their emotions. Pacing them gives you the clues you need, and the better you get to know a person, the more accurately you'll be able to read the information you get. Still, we want to give you a word of warning here. Consider the information you gather this way as a first guess. The test will come by asking questions based on this information during conversation, but in a careful and considerate manner, and test out your hypothesis this way.

Warning

Most people derive information in a more or less unconscious manner from the non-verbal information they observe. However, in many instances we forget to ask the question to check out our hypothesis and stick with our interpretation of the non-verbal messages. This can lead only to miscommunication. Virginia Satir, one of the communication experts that Bandler and Grinder modeled, really focused on this kind of miscommunication, and she used it as an important tool while doing family therapy. Indeed, much of family therapy consists of disentangling misunderstandings which originate out of misreading non-verbal information.

A negative example

A woman comes home from work full of enthusiasm and says: "Hey, do you want to know what a great idea we've had?"

The husband reacts from his previous knowledge, knowing that once the initial enthusiasm fades away problems will arise. So, with a sententious tone of voice—hoping to protect her from further disappointment, he says: "Yes, that sounds like what you were saying last time."

Guess how the woman feels after this "supportive" statement?

A constructive example

When you meet a friend, you see they're looking depressed. Instead of their usual grin you're met with a wan smile, their shoulders are hunched and they walk in a heavier fashion than usual.

- If you want to pace, you can ask something such as: "What happened? Did the sky fall on your head?"
- If you want to mismatch, putting on a big smile, give a reply such as: "Do you want to know how lucky I have been this time ...!?"

Mind reading exercise

The purpose of this process[5] is to calibrate the inner thoughts, sounds, images and feelings that are occurring in another person at that time. For this exercise we take an easy subject, "mind reading," to figure out what the other person is thinking about.

Step 1: Calibrate

Person A thinks about three figures: a triangle, a square and a circle (without talking). Each time, they indicate what figure they are thinking of. Person A gives Person B time to calibrate by observing their non-verbal behavior (use all clues described in the synchronization categories). Repeat several times, until Person B has figured out some differences between the three figures and you can proceed to the test.

Step 2: Test

Person A now thinks (at random) about one of the three figures, without telling which one it is. Based on their observation of the non-verbal behavior, Person B now "guesses" which figure A is thinking about. Person A answers by saying "correct" or "wrong." Do several guessing rounds.

If there were too many mistakes (less than 66% correct), repeat both steps.

---

[5]   This exercise is based on one which Richard Bandler and John Grinder used to present in the early days of NLP, but which has disappeared from most "modern" NLP workshops.

Depending on the observation skills, it should take Person B less than 15 minutes to "guess" right about 7 times out of 10.

Self-calibration

This process is similar to one we presented in Lesson 1 for accessing a state from the Body End and furthers it. It is particularly useful to rapidly identify an unresourceful state and thus change it.

When you become aware of a particular state you do not want to experience any longer, take mental notes of the way it is represented in body terms and focus on a particular component which stands out in your mind. It could be: the posture, a gesture, a tension inside your body, the way you breathe (or not as the case may be, as many unresourceful states seem to involve holding one's breath), dryness in the mouth, a tonality component, such as whistling in your ears, a loudness, a particularly insistent tune in your mind, or the sound your voice makes. It could also be a recurring keyword or a significant train of thought.

The list is far from exhaustive, as most people have an abundance of ways of representing unresourceful states. Indeed, this is often the only abundance demonstrated in a condition usually encoded in scarcity terms! Tolstoy, in his introduction to *Anna Karenina,* said that: "Happy people seem to be happy in a similar way, but unhappy people are all unhappy in different ways." What matters is that this self-calibration has provided you with a marker, so that next time you notice yourself enacting this marker in your external or internal behavior, you can interrupt the state and get into a resourceful one.

See how noticing this state immediately disrupts it in some way. A good way to quickly build on this disruption is to appreciate the very fact that you noticed, which should immediately give you a good feeling. You're entitled to feel smug, as if you were giving yourself a gold star for noticing. Such an encouraging way of responding generates a virtuous circle inside you and you will probably detect unresourceful states more and more easily as you practice paying yourself compliments.

Rapport with yourself

Take a deep breath in and on the out breath, which you make slow and deep, close your eyes and go down inside yourself. When you have reached a good place to be in, say "Hello!" inside yourself. Remember that the meaning of communication is the response that you elicit, so make this "Hello!" as warm and loving as you can. Notice the response you're getting (there is always a response). It could be a picture, a sound, a small movement, a feeling in you, perhaps of warmth or relaxation. If you are not aware of any response, notice that not responding is, in itself, a response, and say to yourself: "Thank you for the response." Notice what response you receive from the acknowledgment that you have received the response, and that you are appreciating it. It may be a different response or a development of the previous one. Keep doing this a couple more times, until you feel happy with the results. When you are, express your thanks for your happiness and take your leave with courtesy, promising yourself to be back soon.

You can do this last thing at night before drifting off to sleep. When you are inside yourself again, thank yourself for all the good things which have occurred during the day. Notice the response. Thank yourself for the things which didn't necessarily go so well for the learning opportunities they gave you, and invite yourself to learn from the experience so that, should something similar happen another time, the outcome will be more to your satisfaction. Notice the response. Finish by giving yourself an internal hug or cuddle. Nobody will notice.

Applications
Application 1:
Adapting yourself to a client during a sale

Applying all the above techniques as a way to increase your Emotional Intelligence means that you'll be able to observe your customer and apply your findings to adapt yourself to them accordingly. Given the number of synchronization categories we have identified, this means that, pacing the customer in several other categories, you can afford to disagree on the content (such as NOT giving in on the price). One example of the game of pacing and leading is the following description of three cars.[6]

Purchase of a car

If money didn't matter, which of the three luxury automobiles described below would you buy?

The paint of the first car shines as if it were a pearl. This car really has a special appearance. You notice that the available colors, as well as the splendid interior, have had all the attention they deserve from the designers. The dashboard displays all instruments in one easy glance. The window surface of the car has been considered from every angle, so that you get an optimal view of the landscape surrounding the car. Even the engine is a show of brilliance from the designers. This car really appears to have a bright future.

The sound isolation of the second car is well thought out. It can easily keep out the sound of the engine, so that you will be able to hear the birds sing while the V12 engine hums along. Even the sound of the doors as they close resonates with a car with such a name. The interior of the car is harmoniously designed, answering any question and responding to whatever further arguments might have needed addressing. Any specialist would tell you that you must mention this car on your shortlist.

You immediately feel the third car is surrounded by a special atmosphere. It is solidly built and attracts you with all its special characteristics. Its interior catches you with all its comforts and you are immediately drawn into its seat by the desire to feel the nice leather and take the steering wheel in your hands. This car guards you with active safety. Just press on the accelerator, and you'll feel how the engine pulls you to where you want to go. How could you walk away from such luxury? Add this car to your wish list.

---

[6] You'll find similar examples in several NLP books. Both Robert Dilts in *Visionary Leadership Skills* (Meta Publications, Calif. 1996) and Anthony Robbins in *Unlimited Power* (Simon & Schuster, 1988) prefer to give you descriptions of three different houses, but we like cars.

Please decide for yourself which car you'd prefer before reading on.

The main difference between these three descriptions is the representation channel they are described in: if you prefer the first car, *visual* information is more important in your decision strategy. If you'd rather buy the second car, the *auditory* information convinced you. Finally, if you liked the third car, the *kinesthetic* information caught your attention. The similarity between the three descriptions comes from the fact that the cars are actually one and the same model!

When it comes to making a product such as a car as appealing as possible, today's manufacturers are paying great attention to all these elements. Some makes, like Lexus, have even been studying the noise a door should make when it slams shut. They have come a long way from the metallic slam which seemed to be a trademark of Japanese cars. They will also harness the primitive power of smell to sway customers further: second-hand car dealers have been known to spray a "new smell" into old cars.

Now try it out for yourself

a. Write some sentences to describe your current clothes, also indicating why you like to wear them. Start by analyzing these sentences using the different representation channels. How rich is your text? Did you use all five channels? How about adjectives and adverbs? Once you have done this analysis, how could you enrich the text? Write a new version!

b. Write commercial blurbs to sell a product or service. You may choose to take a product or service that the company you're currently working for is "producing." If you don't work for a commercial organization, choose another product you're familiar with, such as your favorite TV program, a book, your favorite movie or even your shoes. To begin with, draft a separate text for each of the channels. Then write a text which blends together all predicates from all five representation channels.

Application 2:
The language of love

During an intensive experience, all representation channels are activated. Traveling to a country far away, your first day at a new job, or a new love, all share the common characteristic of intensity, of vision, hearing, feelings, taste and smelling. Such an experience leaves a deep track in one's memory and this will be self-evident when one is talking about such an experience: what the heart thinks, the mouth speaks.

Once the intensive phase is over, however, the sensory experience also usually becomes duller, and you fall back on your previous habits of observing and communicating. This may happen in a relationship: the love people have for each other is displayed in the synchronization category they prefer. This may mean that the husband thinks he needs to work hard and earn the money needed so that they can own their own house; or instead he thinks it is important to take part in the domestic activities by doing some of the chores, cooking, etc. In the same traditional family, the wife may show her love by listening to her husband and showing tenderness, while primarily being concerned with the education of the kids. In such examples, both keep on loving each other, but their ways of showing this are expressed in completely different ways. And so it may happen that, after a few years, the woman thinks: "He doesn't tell me enough that he loves me" and "He almost never shows his emotions to me." The husband may be thinking: "She doesn't make as much effort as before to look nice, she has lost her broad world-view by primarily focusing on the house." Notice how the woman was using kinesthetic terms, while the man used visual language. This may be reflected in their sexual life: maybe the husband wants to see something, where the wife prefers to feel, and hides under the sheets. This doesn't mean that their relationship is over the hill, but both are expressing it through other synchronization categories.

In their respective representation channels, both may be thinking: "I still look at her as I did/love him as much as before, but her/his love for me has faded/dwindled." They can solve this by asking themselves the question: "What is my way of communicating? How does this differ from my partner's way of communicating? How can I adapt myself to the other (pacing)?" The husband may consider spending more time being nice to his wife, instead of working so hard in order to afford an even bigger house. She might pick up some outdoor activities and enlarge her interests, so that they have new subjects of communication to share.

Application 3:
Customer representatives—enacted friendliness?

This section applies to all the people who are in direct contact with customers. This includes hostesses, telesales representatives, helpdesk staff, cashiers, ... as well as secretaries, nurses and doctors. In short, one could say that most of these professions should consider the contents of this book as "elementary skills" that their profession requires. They could consider exercising the principles explained and acting in harmony with others.

After supermarkets in the US started introducing codes of conduct which included an obligatory smile, some female cashiers found that their male customers began falling in love with them. Apparently, probably due to cultural filtering, smiling and other elements of the body language were interpreted as signals of attraction and seduction. Try it out for yourself: what are the effects of looking someone straight in the eyes, having a real smile on your face, and keeping eye contact for a somewhat extended period? We think you'll be more successful at this than you think, especially if you keep in mind that in our current society lots of people don't get the attention they deserve. Take care, however, to keep it in proportion if you don't want to break hearts or be pursued by stalkers!

Professional training for hostesses, where a lot of attention is paid to friendliness and customer care, may also teach us something in this area. It's not because one appears friendly on the outside that the customer will "buy;" it's being sincere. This external behavior needs to be accompanied by an internal emotional state of friendliness, or the customer will notice the incongruity and perceive the smile as superficial, or as a pretense.

In actual fact, a customer will probably still prefer such enacted friendliness to bearing the brunt of a hostess's, cashier's or colleague's obvious bad mood. The days have long gone when sayings such as: "Better to have a bad temper than to have no temper at all" were acceptable. The excuse a person may have that: "At least, now I'm being sincere!" as a defence of such a bad mood isn't necessarily in and by itself a sign of Emotional Intelligence. Some of your friends will probably make allowances and seek to help you out, or just leave you to wallow in your misery long enough for you to emerge at the other end. However, people who like you less, or know you less well, will not take so kindly to your response. This type of behavior sounds a lot like the person, coming back from a therapist, who decided that, having discovered that they have suppressed their anger for many years, "it is better to be angry." Many traditional therapists will enable their clients to do this and leave them to find out the consequences of their newly-accessed anger, perhaps fueling the emergence of problems further down the line (and further business for the therapist?). Neurolinguists will enable the person to work out the positive intention for the repression of this anger, as well as the positive intention of its expression, and allow these positive intentions and more to be implemented without unnecessary side-effects. As we explained in Lesson 1, the solution for displaying a congruent friendliness comes from learning to manage one's emotions and being in a state of friendliness in the first place.

Application 4:
Leadership and the art of helping to get into rapport with yourself

One of today's freedoms is that one has the right to be assertive and to defend one's rights. In that sense, what you want, what you think and what you feel are facts which can be taken into account. And we can add: as they are facts arising from a First Position perspective, you have the right to listen to and be true to your own needs, provided they do not infringe the rights of others. As we indicated in Lesson 5, this assertiveness, and the ability to pay attention to your own needs, are required conditions for coming to a meaningful, qualitative relationship with others. The better you can pace yourself, the more pleasant you'll find it to pace other people.

These observations can also be applied to leadership. The old definition of leadership was: "Influence people so that they do, think and feel what you want them to do, think and feel." Today's new leadership style finds its inspiration in coaching: "Leadership comes from synchronizing the collaborator and the organization, while ensuring the collaborator is in rapport with themselves." If we think it's important that a good leader should help their employees to be in rapport with themselves, we'll have to explain what this means …

Pacing oneself means being fully aware of the experience you are living right now. An example: a manager has to give a speech before a large audience, without having had much practice in this area. When waking up that morning, the person gets the feeling that their stomach is getting tight, they find it hard to swallow, and their breathing becomes very shallow. They tell their partner: "I think I've got stage-fright." This statement puts a label on the experience they are going through. Maybe someone else would characterize the same experience: "I seem to get a kick out of the idea of having to give this speech in front of 500 people!" In this instance, the person's statement becomes a description of how they feel, maybe without taking the time to be fully aware of the experience they were going through. As an observer, by just hearing the evaluation, you have really no idea of what it is actually like to experience the state the person is in. In this sense, pacing oneself means paying attention to all aspects of one's experience, as suggested by the synchronization categories. It involves asking yourself questions such as: "What is it I am experiencing right now? What do I see? What sounds accompany this feeling? What am I saying to myself?"

Just by doing this exercise, you'll notice that many emotions are negative merely because you decided to label them as such at some point in the past. In the same way that the map is not the territory, the label is not the emotion! In Buddhism, experiences such as pleasure and pain are perceived as occurring on a continuum. Once you begin to observe the details of your experience and your internal state and thoughts, your map of reality becomes more precise. Awareness and detailed description help you to pace yourself better, finding out what's going on at the onset. This kind of process will help you to break through your inner maps and update them to your—and other people's—advantage.

Once you can pace yourself, you can also take the lead in relation to yourself, perhaps choosing to recode this experience by calling it something more appropriate.

Consider a situation when you were stuck in your head, trying to solve a problem. Such stuckness usually involves an internal dialogue. So, become aware of the manner in which this stuckness occurs.

> What are the characteristics of this internal dialogue? What kind of voice is this? Does it sound like someone you recognize? What part of you is responsible for this—where does it come from (which direction?)? How loud does it sound?

> Now externalize this voice by speaking aloud. As a next step, start changing the voice. For instance, make it sound as if it's Donald Duck who is saying it (keeping the content the same). How does this change your experience? What happens to the stuckness?

> Or make it sound loving, caressing, supportive. How does this change your experience? What happens to the stuckness?

> Remember that the meaning of communication is the response that you get. Remind this part of you of this presupposition. Whatever it's been intending, it's not working, though, is it? So ask it to say it differently, perhaps making a constructive comment. How does this change your experience? What happens to the stuckness?

As with the supermarket example we presented at the beginning of this book, pacing oneself early on saves much time, energy and heartache—perhaps even literally—later on.

Conclusion: Observation Skills as Key Elements for Emotional Intelligence

This chapter should have vastly increased your awareness of the amount of information you can gather by interacting with your conversation partner, and that observation is the key to gathering this information. Both the way your internal world is constructed (internal representation and submodalities) and the information you can collect through the other synchronization categories offer you an immense source of data. Emotional Intelligence comes from taking such data into account and, more specifically, in the way we give meaning to that data. As we noticed before, there are several pitfalls in the process of giving meaning. On this subject, Edward T. Hall wrote:[7]

> *The rule of congruence ... in an international debate serious errors are made in interpreting such supposedly simple matters as whether a participant is actually angry or merely bluffing. No wonder there are wars! The sheer frustration of not being able to understand sometimes makes one want to strike out in the feeling that at least the blow will be understood.*

Our aim is to help you to improve your observation skills. The process of ascribing meaning is yet another problem, for which we suggest the following rule of thumb. As John Grinder said, (see Lesson 2), remember that "One observation is just sufficient for an anecdote, two observations are just enough to make a first hypothesis. It takes at least three examples before you really have a pattern." Remember also that the pattern you come up with has two components: first there was your observation, then came the meaning you derived from this observation. Furthermore, remember that the "real" meaning lies with the person who was communicating the data you observed in the first place, so ask that person the necessary questions to make sure your conclusions are on track.

Finally we want to give you a last message concerning your ability to exercise your observation skills. Remember how, as we said at the beginning of this chapter, your conscious mind can attend to only about seven pieces of information at any one time (and this might be even less on a blue Monday). This implies that it is impossible to collect all the possible synchronization information by using just your conscious mind. Indeed, your conscious mind may already be lost just trying to attend to the content of the conversation. So, train your unconscious to help you to keep track

---

[7] Edward T. Hall in *The Silent Language,* Doubleday, 1959—Conclusion to Chapter 8—"The Organizing Pattern."

and to inform you whenever it notices a pattern. You can achieve this by first consciously focusing your observation skills on a certain synchronization category. Once you master it consciously, let it become unconscious again. After all, this is what you have been doing all your life to learn new skills, like driving, reading, etc.

Exercises for this Lesson

Exercise 7.1: Backtracking

Person A talks about something that they have planned for the coming week. Person B listens for the keywords and uses these to give a backtrack. At a certain point in the backtrack, Person B begins to replaces these keywords with their own words. See how Person A responds to this change.

Exercise 7.2: Observation of synchronization categories

Person A talks about a challenge or a personal goal. Person B follows, by pacing the synchronization categories. An observer (Person C) then discusses what synchronization categories Person B has used, and those Person B didn't use.

Exercise 7.3: "Life-observation"

Go to a shop (the counter) or a pub (the bar) and observe how people get into contact with each other. Use only descriptive language to take note.

Exercise 7.4: Rapport with yourself and others during a discussion

Apart from learning what happens during discussions, one of the purposes of this exercise is to learn to pay attention to content and non-verbal information at the same time.

You can do this as a formal exercise with four people or just try it out informally, e.g. while you are participating in a discussion with some friends. If you do it formally with four people, Person C becomes the observer and guardian angel for Person A, and Person D becomes the observer and guardian angel for Person B. For the formal version we recommend you keep a close eye on timing, to avoid getting lost in the content of the discussion. If you do it informally you have to tweak the exercise a bit so that you can have the different steps.

Step 0:   Preparation: Choose a discussion topic on which two parties tend to disagree strongly, so that you are sure to have a "passionate discussion."

Step 1:   Start by letting Person A and Person B have a "free discussion" on the subject, so that both parties know what their respective views are and which are the sticking points (max. 5 minutes).

Step 2:   Person A utters a sentence to clarify one discussion point. Person B backtracks their sentence literally (copying the synchronization categories).
Feedback: if the backtrack is correct, Person A responds positively, otherwise negatively. If the backtrack isn't correct, Person A retakes this step by uttering another sentence to further clarify his point of view. Continue until Person A agrees on the backtrack and feels they are understood.

Step 3:   (As in Step 2) Person B now takes the lead by stating their own point of view. Person A now follows by synchronizing to this. Now Person B gives feedback.

Step 4:   Person A now develops the discussion by seeking to undermine the point of view of the other participant (take it to the extreme, make fun out of it, question critically, etc.). Person B responds by following Person A in the critique which is given (instead of defending their own point of view).

Exercise 7.5: Getting into rapport with a "difficult" customer

Role-play: Person A is the salesperson, Person B the difficult customer. Person B just has to play their role. Person A uses the different synchronization categories in order to get a successful "contact" with the customer.

Note: you can do the same exercise in different contexts: e.g. Person A can be a teacher, a steward at the check-in counter of a plane, … Person B is then a student, a passenger whose luggage is over the weight limit, etc …

Exercise 7.6: Mismatching in order to end a conversation

Step 1:   Person A talks about an experience. Person B listens and builds rapport.

Step 2:   At a given moment (chosen before by Person B, random to Person A) Person B starts to mismatch in an elegant way (not too obvious) so that the conversation dries up.

Step 3:   Once the conversation has stalled, use your rapport-building skills to restart the conversation where it broke off.

(Repeat the steps several times)

Exercise 7.7: Guiding someone to an emotional state

Person A: Decide what good state you would like to guide another person into (e.g. relaxation, alertness, curiosity, etc.). What actions can you put in place to reach this goal (e.g. for relaxation: talking slowly about a peaceful event, while slowing down your movements, etc.)?

Now start a conversation with Person B, e.g. about something that Person B is working on at this moment. Take a few moments to build up rapport with Person B (pacing), before slowly taking the lead in order to reach your goal. Use the different synchronization categories with that purpose in mind.

Exercise 7.8: Calibrating for lies

This exercise is similar to the "mindreading" exercise we presented earlier in this chapter.

Have Person A tell a story that is true, followed by a story that is false. During these stories, Person B calibrates for non-verbal clues that go with telling the truth vs lying.

Now Person A tells a third story (true or false at choice). Based on the non-verbal elements, Person B has to decide whether the story is true or false.

Exercise 7.9: Look for incongruities

Person A talks about a goal they had set for themselves a while ago, but didn't realize, or about a problem that has been present for a while.

Person B looks for incongruities. Where does the non-verbal language contradict the content of what the person is saying?

At the end of the explanation, Person B explains to Person A the incongruities they have noticed. Find out together what these incongruities mean.

Conclusions:
Making Connections, Gaining in Emotional Wisdom

"If you always do what you've always done,
You'll always get what you've always got."
Abraham Maslow

New Emotional Abilities

We are delighted that you have made it to the end of the book, especially considering that 90% of readers don't finish most non-fiction books. We hope that you are already feeling well rewarded by your effort and that you have been enjoying applying the approaches contained in the book in everyday situations, whether at work, at home, or anywhere else for that matter, because they have applications across disciplines and contexts. Tell us of your successes at living, and also of things which could have worked out better, so that we can help you to find out where things went wrong. We also tell our course participants that their success depends on practicing. As with many other things in life, it takes some exercising to achieve mastery in these skills: Rome wasn't built in a day. We added all the exercises to the lessons to give you plenty of ideas as to how to apply your skills. And it doesn't stop here. We invite you to consider what else you might be engaged in to keep honing and developing your Emotional Intelligence.

Over the years, we have noticed how the people who have the highest levels of Emotional Intelligence are also the people who like trying out new things for size, who appreciate making new connections, who enjoy enriching their panoply. In brief, they keep learning. Not only does EQ help you to solve problems that cross your path, but you become better and better at solving these problems. So keep learning. Get in touch with people who have skills you admire and find out how they do it. Ask them questions about how they got to that point of excellence which drew them to your attention in the first place. Keep asking questions until you understand what motivated them to get there, what values drive their competence, etc. Most people, noting that you have a sincere interest in what they are doing, will be only too eager to share this information with you.

Why do we want to stress such a point? Because if you don't learn, how can you expect to move forward? In the fast-evolving world we live in today, you can't even be sure that having the competencies you have will still get you to the things you got before. Whichever way

> ENVIRONMENT
> +
> RESPONSE
> =
> OUTCOME

the environment changes, your response to this environment will determine what outcomes you'll get. Some of you may want to blame the weather, or the economy, or your boss for what's happening, but keep in mind that these elements themselves are not within your control. What is within your control, however, is the way you respond to your environment. You can change your response as and when required, and if you don't know how to change it, look for people around you who can thrive in these chaotic times and ask them how they do it.

Specialized literature[1] will tell you there are at least four ways to learn:

❑ *Learn by modeling:* The models you create come from the interaction between you and the people you observe. As we have explained before, whatever you observe, whatever you recall is filtered. So the model you create may be different from a model someone else created. Modeling is something people do naturally. An infant begins learning about life by mimicking its parents, unquestioningly, warts and all. As adults, we keep finding people who are good at a particular skill, and we want to learn from them, finding out how they do it. What's the difference between the two forms of learning? As adults, the process may involve more conscious reasoning; as we are able to choose our models according to our filters. Babies do not have this option, as they have not yet developed these very filters and their structure. Indeed, in the same way that a child is born with the immune system of their mother to begin with, they unques-

---

1   We recommend the following books in case you want to find out more about ways of learning and learning styles: N.J. Entwistle, *Styles of Learning and Teaching* (Beekman Publishers, 1989) and David A. Kolb, *Experiential Learning: Experience as the Source for Learning and Development* (Prentice Hall, 1983).

tioningly absorb their parents' filters, for the better or the worse, only later (if ever) choosing to retain or reject them. The models we have been introducing you to in this book aim to help you to approach modeling in a more systematic, organized way, thus bypassing some of these filters or updating them. This explains the effectiveness of neurolinguistic training. Because modeling is based on structure rather than content, two different people modeling a person's particular skills by explicitly applying the models we present in this book would actually come to a quite similar model of what they have observed. When such models are used explicitly, we call this analytical modeling. As an example of such an analytical modeling process, we present a recruiting method based on Meta-Programs in an appendix.

❏ *Learn by experimenting*: Observing and modeling aren't enough. Once you think you know how to do something, you have to try out your skill, otherwise it remains abstract, theoretical. You know about a subject from a dissociated perspective. By actively practicing, you embody your experience: associating in the experience, you acquire skills in a sensory-specific fashion and also learn to contextualize your skills. This richer encoding of your learning will considerably speed up your learning. Compare learning a foreign language from books and tapes, with being immersed in the foreign country for a few weeks. Which gives you the quicker results? Of course, you can also experiment without relying on a model, by just trying things out, and finding out where that gets you. Learning by experimenting without a model can be quite slow, though. It took Thomas Edison about 10,000 experiments before he found how to make a good lightbulb which lasted. If you have a model, such as those we have been teaching you in this book, all it takes is finding occasions to try out your new skills. A good way to begin is by asking yourself every evening: "Where do I want to use my EQ competencies tomorrow?"

❏ *Learn from theory*: Books, courses and other sources also give you the knowledge you need to lay the foundation for a new skill. For that purpose we provide you with a list of books, some websites and some pointers on how to learn more about Emotional Intelligence at the end of this book.

❑ *Learn from past experience*: When tackling a new problem, just use your past experience to start from and reason by analogy. Or as we taught you in this book, by remembering a past reference experience, use it as a resourceful state to tackle the new problem.

From what you have just read above, you will notice that these different ways of learning are actually complementary. You may, however, find that you personally use one style more than another. Kolb pointed out that an optimal learning experience contains all four learning styles. You master a skill only if you have a deep knowledge about it, if you have found how to do it (probably by observing people), if you have tried it out and if you have some personal reference experiences of applying it. So if you feel that one of these four learning styles is less developed in what you do to learn, you may want to learn to learn by developing this complementary learning style. The operative expression here is *Learning to Learn*. Identified by Gregory Bateson,[2] (see pp. 108–109) this skill is key to the successful development of your Emotional Intelligence, as it puts you in a position of choice and initiates a lifelong ongoing process of self-optimization.

Making a Full Model of Competence

First we need to define what exactly we mean by "competence" and "competencies" in this context.

Competence = (Cap)Ability, What Makes Someone Able to Obtain a Result

This consists of:

- external behavior (observable steps taken to obtain the process),
- internal processes (including internal representation, conscious and unconscious thinking process, beliefs, …)

and

- internal states that help to obtain this result.

Competencies are skills, demonstrations of competence, aspects of competence.

COMPETENCE				
Skill	*Skill*	*Skill*	*Skill*	*Skill*

---

[2]   Gregory Bateson, in *Steps to an Ecology of Mind,* University of Chicago Press, 1972, calls this ability "deutero-Learning" or Learning II. We referred to it in Lesson 2.

Every result one obtains (whether it is wanted or unwanted) results from sequencing a series of steps. Some of these steps may be observable from the outside, while others consist of mental processing, and often you end up asking what the person is doing to find out what happened exactly. Much of the mental processing involves knowledge, e.g. to sell to a government you might want to know the laws in place for government purchasing. But it also involves your emotional states, the values you adhere to for obtaining that result, etc.

At a competency level, neurolinguistic specialists have been studying a variety of subjects, such as:

- how people take decisions (decision strategy)
- how people motivate themselves (motivation strategy)
- how people learn (learning strategy)
- how people know how to spell words correctly (spelling strategy)

and also:

- how some people heal faster than others
- how people live in remarkably good health, despite their age.

When studying a skill, we do this from a neutral point of view. The competence to feel depressive may be worth studying. If you come across a person who has succeeded in feeling depressed for 10 years, you could call that a pretty effective strategy, even though it's not one you might want to acquire! Studying such competences (whether their effects are positive or negative) will teach you a lot about people's internal processes and how we get ourselves into particular emotional states. Cognitive science, and neurolinguistics in particular, has given us the toolset to study those internal processes, where other branches of psychology have often treated this area as a "black box."

Here is how you might approach making a model of competence for yourself:

Start by finding one or more persons who are competent at what you want to learn. Ask this person questions about several examples where they succeeded at building and maintaining these interpersonal ties. You might want to ask the following questions:

- What was the context (get a concrete example)?
- What was the outcome?
- How do they intend to reach this outcome (method)?
- What was the effect they obtained (did they obtain the outcome, what was the effect upon others)?
- What exactly did they do to obtain that (tasks done, by them and others)?

When you want to model something, you might want to remind yourself of the following advice from John Grinder: "One example is an anecdote, two examples give you a hypothesis, but it takes three or more examples to really call it a pattern." So, we recommend that you do this questioning at least three times. We have given you this anecdote three times in the book. Could this mean there is a pattern? MMMmmm. Once you have the examples, find out what's similar about them, using all the models we have discussed in the seven chapters. For instance: what beliefs are supporting the pattern, what perceptual positions does the person use, what are their dominant Meta-Programs,…? Once you have these patterns, you may want to test with counter-examples to check whether or where it went wrong and then you can try out the pattern for yourself.

How to teach yourself new emotional skills
To end this section, we want to present you with our suggestions in a more structured way. The following six steps describe what you need to include in a process of developing a new competence.

1. Define your goal
Using the model of well-formed outcomes (Lesson 3), find out:
- What exactly you want to learn. (What's your current situation? What's your desired situation?)
- What emotion you want to have when given feedback.

2. Find resources to support your learning process
Let us recommend to you some sources to find resources:
- Where in your life do you have examples of yourself already using this competence? (You might want to anchor the resourceful state that goes with it.)

- Do you know any persons that can demonstrate the competence to you? (You might want to model these people, as described above.)
- Are there any sources such as books, Internet, courses, etc. to help you with the competence?
- Will you have opportunities to experiment with the competence?

3. Supporting values and beliefs

As we saw in Lesson 2, a competency doesn't exist separately from your identity and value system. You have to ask yourself the following questions:

- What beliefs do I need for having this emotion?
- Who do I want to be when I take on this emotion?

4. Make a model of the structure of the competence

Your model should include answers to the following questions:

- What are the different steps included in the emotional competence?
- What are the underlying Meta-Programs that support the competence?
- What perceptual positions are to be used for the different steps of the competence?
- What is the structure of the competence (underlying emotional state(s), sequence of representation systems, etc.)?
- What submodalities are typical for the desired competence?

5. Remove old, unwanted reactions

Start by answering the following questions:

- What would stop you from using this new competence?
- What is different from your current behavior?
- Is there any part of you that has problems with the competence?
- Do you consider yourself worth using the competence, do you allow yourself to do it?
- Have you decided to use it?

Depending on your answers to these questions, decide what techniques to use to solve these problems.

6. Develop a core state and a supporting personal philosophy

Given all that you now know about this competence, how does this relate to who you are? How is this aligned in you to your purpose in life?

After completing these steps allow yourself some time to "rehearse" the emotional competence. Remember that when you learned walking, riding a bike or driving a car, it also took you some time before you were able to run, ride or drive without hesitation or conscious thinking.

Some examples

Let's look at these steps with a couple of examples. A first example could be to be able to handle criticism in a constructive way, without this criticism generating bad feelings. A second example, to deal with memories that used to make you feel bad. We'll present you with some elements of the puzzle of these competencies.

	HANDLING CRITICISM	DEALING WITH MEMORIES
Current Situation	Hurt, internal pressure, guilt.	Sorrow, attached.
Desired Situation	Relaxed, calm feeling while receiving the criticism.	A caring, loving and understanding feeling which comes along with the memory.
Models	Find examples amongst the persons you know or have access to that can handle criticism.	Which person do you know has been good at this skill?
Resourceful State	Think back to a time when you were able to handle criticism.	Was there a time when you had to deal with a loss, or when you really said "goodbye"?

	HANDLING CRITICISM	**DEALING WITH MEMORIES**
Supporting Beliefs	Criticism is just another perspective. I'm allowed to make mistakes. There is no failure, only feedback. Criticism is a gift.	There is still a future for me. Letting go is not the same as forgetting. Life has to go on.
Supporting Identity	I'm not perfect. I'm a learner. I'm self-developing.	I'm connected to everything. As an evolving being I can process the past. I am a Buddhist.
Steps Towards the Competence	While receiving the feedback, take a deep breath and say to yourself: "I can be imperfect." Now look at the other person and repeat the information you got.	If the memory comes up, put the visual image at a distance and in the upper left corner of your visual field and say to yourself: "Thanks for this memory, it helped me be who I am, and now I want to give this memory a resting place so that I can move on." Shift to breathing with your belly.
Representation Channels and Submodalities	$A \Rightarrow K^+ \Rightarrow A_d \Rightarrow V_e \Rightarrow A$ I can put the person giving the criticism at a necessary distance. I can change the submodalities of the voice, so that the criticism sounds like information, instead of "blame."	$V_r \Rightarrow V_c \Rightarrow A_d \Rightarrow K^+$ I put the visual image in the periphery of my mental field, where I put the experiences coming from my past, as opposed to projecting the image in front of myself.
Meta-Programs	Internal reference Goal-oriented Options Other	Difference Options General overview
Perceptual Positions	Meta-Position + Second Position	Third Position

Some Final Exercises

These exercises combine several models in this book into one process, in order to help you integrate these different models.

Exercise 1: The structure of emotions

Take a pair of related emotions, such as {joy and gratitude} or {shame and remorse} or {dislike and hate} or {fear and relief}. Associate (lightly) for yourself in some experiences that are good personal references for you of these emotional states, and answer the following questions:

	EMOTION 1	RELATED EMOTION 2
What is the main logical level involved?		
Time frame (in time/through time; oriented future, past, present)		
Which perceptual position is mainly present? Which one is missing?		
Modal operator (need, must, can, may, want)		
Criteria involved		

Exercise 2: Emotional signal to solution

Choose a context where you frequently experience a recurring negative emotion.

- Why do you have that emotion? What is its purpose? What is its message for you?
- Is the goal well-formed? If not, reformulate.
- Would you be able to reach this goal without the emotional signal?
- What (more successful) ways can you think of to reach that goal?
- What resources do you have to reach that goal? Associate into a resourceful state and improve that state by changing its submodalities.

Exercise 3: Constructing a resource

Write down your current state and desired state. Analyze each of the states according to the models of this book. Find out what's the difference between them according to each model. What resource (or combination of resources) can you think of which has the capacity to bridge the gap? What would be a reference experience for that?

	CURRENT SITUATION	DESIRED SITUATION	RESOURCE
What is the main logical level involved?			
Meta-Model pattern?			
Which perceptual position is mainly present? Which one is missing?			
VAKOG and strategies			
Meta-Programs			

Exercise 4: Pattern detection

What problem are you facing in your work today (or in a relationship or in another context)?

Find three concrete examples of that problem (when, where, what happened, ...).

For each example, analyze it using the models in this book. The following grid may be helpful.

What elements come back in each of the examples? (Is there a common pattern?)

	EXAMPLE 1	EXAMPLE 2	EXAMPLE 3
What's your emotional state?			
What is the main logical level involved?			
Meta-Model pattern?			
Which perceptual position is mainly present? Which one is (perhaps) missing?			
VAKOG and strategies			
Submodalities			
Meta-Programs			

Recapitulation

Moving beyond Emotional Intelligence

As we mentioned in the Introduction, Goleman borrowed Salovey's definition of Emotional Intelligence. He demonstrated the usefulness of this definition by referring to the importance of five specific abilities deemed necessary to the flourishing of Emotional Intelligence:

- Knowledge of your own emotions
- Regulating one's emotions
- Self-motivation
- Recognizing one another's emotions
- The art of human relations

At the beginning of this book, we promised that we were going to give you the tools to develop your own Emotional Intelligence. In a chapter on Best Practices in *Working with Emotional Intelligence,* a follow-up to his first book, Goleman warns against "people [simply] repackaging or slight remodelling of a program they had offered before under another name," and we agree with him. As you have made the effort to get hold of our book, we therefore feel we owe it to you to explain why we think we stand amongst the best practices Goleman was aspiring to.

This book is not mere repackaging, but a comprehensive and structured approach to training on Emotional Intelligence in book form. So, even if you already have a working knowledge of Neuro-Linguistic Programming (NLP), by comparing what traditional NLP books have been covering with the current document, you will notice our book offers a significantly different emphasis, and incorporates much new material.

From the onset, our outcome of giving you the tools to develop your own Emotional Intelligence, which makes use of Salovey's definition, motivated our writing of this book and dictated its very structure. We therefore presented the material you need to achieve Emotional Intelligence in seven steps so that you can:

- **Listen to your emotions** and find out what message they carry for you
- **Ask the right questions** and make use of the different perceptual solutions
- Use a comprehensive creativity strategy to **work out the solutions you want**
- **Plan what you want** so that it is aligned with who you are
- **Manage your emotions** so that this helps to achieve your goals
- **Use your capabilities** cross-contextually and **model excellence you identify in others**
- **Resolve conflicts** and **live in harmony** with yourself and others.

So the remaining question becomes: in what way does our material relate to Salovey's definition, which Goleman used?

Knowledge of one's own emotions, as well as the regulating and management of these, corresponds to the concept of state management (Lesson 1), combined with the principles of the Circle of Excellence. Indeed, you realized the relationship between External Behavior, Internal Processing and Internal State. Using anchoring, association and dissociation processes as building blocks, we explained how you can manage your state and use successful states from the past as resources, successfully **Regulating your emotions**.

Self-motivation is the result of several of the presented models. Using Meta-Programs (Lesson 4) and logical levels (Lesson 2), we can show how people motivate themselves, and how compatible they are with their environment. For instance, an employee whose core beliefs are not shared within their company will experience some friction, which will lead to the development of stress and to de-motivation, even if the person has a strong internal reference. Combined with well-formed outcomes, the TOTE-model (Lesson 3) is another significant building block to achieve self-motivation for the realization of your plans.

Recognizing emotions in another person can be learned by teaching people calibration skills (Lesson 7). Rather than concluding that a certain body posture always has a certain meaning, we have sought to make you find out which non-verbal signals correspond to a certain internal state in the person. A second element Goleman puts under this category is **Empathy**, which we relate to the Second of the perceptual positions (Lesson 5).

Perceptual positions, and the meta-mirror technique in particular (Lesson 5), are useful tools for gaining understanding and developing your own **Art of Human Relations**. The principle of rapport and rapport-building techniques (Lesson 7) help the practitioner in improving his relationship with his environment.

Many of the answers we offered are indeed based on material known as "NLP," the basic building blocks of which were in place by 1980, as we consider this discipline ideal for our purpose. To our knowledge only two persons in the NLP field, namely Leslie Cameron-Bandler and Michael Lebeau, using similar material to some of what we have presented and discussed in this book, attempted to explicitly deal with Emotional Intelligence even before the concept of EQ was defined.

Cameron-Bandler and Lebeau's book *The Emotional Hostage* (1986) seems to be the key reference book Goleman had forgotten to read when he wrote: *"It goes without saying that the most important skills of Emotional Intelligence have a crucial period of time during childhood. Each period represents an opening to teach the child useful emotional habits; but if the opening is missed, it will be much harder to correct this later in life."*[1] Had he read this book, Goleman might have been reached very different conclusions, especially on the difficulty of remedying opportunities missed in childhood, as we have found otherwise.

So, rather than just offering you some topical tips and tricks, as is done by several other books, we have been presenting the very concepts NLP makes available to adults (as well as children) to develop and increase Emotional Intelligence. Hence, applying what you have been learning from this book, and from NLP training in general, will help you to achieve a high score in EQ-tests, such as the one Robert Cooper and Ayman Sawaf present in

---

[1]   See Goleman *Emotional Intelligence*, Chapter 14 (Bantam Books, 1995).

their book *Executive EQ* (1997), in a very short period of time. Indeed, my (Patrick) personal experience is that an adult without any previous knowledge of what we cover in this book can be taught our answers to Goleman's book in about 24 course hours, over a seven-week period. We carry out a pre- and post-assessment during the training and have found that our participants show a 10 to 15% improvement in their Emotional Intelligence.

Conclusion: From Emotional Intelligence to Emotional Wisdom

As we have been suggesting throughout this book, developing your Emotional Intelligence, as commonly defined, is only half the picture. Acknowledging and controlling the emotional content of your intelligence is only the first step. Without this vital step you can't go any further.

However, once this has been achieved there is more to do, and this is where the fun starts. After all, before you sought to do something about it, it was your unconscious which was running your emotional life, leaving you to do other things or not, depending on your emotional state. Now, do you want to spend the rest of your life controlling your emotions? Of course not! Is being in control in and by itself sufficient to fully enjoy life? Perhaps not. Do you need to be a car mechanic to enjoy driving? Remember all the times when you delegated your control to people you trusted explicitly or implicitly, and the fun you had or the freedom you experienced when you did.

Having learnt all that you have about your emotions and those of other people, you have also learnt about the way your own unconscious works and, perhaps for the first time in your life, you are on good terms with yourself, in rapport with your inner being, at one with who you are. You have been going along a road which took you from *unconscious incompetence* about your Emotional Intelligence, when you didn't even realize you might have problems, to one of *conscious incompetence*, when you decided to do something about it, namely getting hold of this book. You may have taken your first steps in acknowledging the role of your emotions and how to change them and have reached a level of *conscious competence* about doing this. Now you are ready for the next steps, which will take you beyond the traditional perspective on Emotional Intelligence. By practicing your skills, you will be, and probably already are, finding that they come to you more and more easily and effortlessly.

What will it be like to just trust your unconscious to give you the best emotion for any given moment? Life will become easier without even trying, as your need to control your emotions reduces. Gradually you will trust your unconscious to operate and apply these new approaches for you, and such improvements in your life will occur without having to consciously work them out. You will begin to operate at a level of *unconscious competence*, where you trust yourself to behave appropriately emotionally, both on your own and with others, because your unconscious will apply its intelligence to be emotional in the right way: you will enjoy being **intelligently emotional**. And this is where the REAL fun begins.

How will it feel to realize that you have come unscathed through situations where once upon a time you might have broken down? What will it be like to notice the manner in which you just glide through such situations now? How will it feel to realize this, to become *consciously aware of your unconscious competence*? That's right.

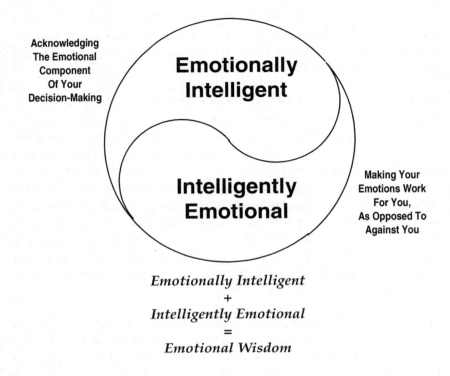

Acknowledging The Emotional Component Of Your Decision-Making

Emotionally Intelligent

Intelligently Emotional

Making Your Emotions Work For You, As Opposed To Against You

Emotionally Intelligent
+
Intelligently Emotional
=
Emotional Wisdom

This is not to say that things will be perfect from now on—what is? However, you will have acquired both tools and methods to pull through, and ways to learn from your experience, so that you may even be able to turn the situation to your advantage. And this is more than Emotional Intelligence, isn't it. This is the beginning of **Emotional Wisdom**.

So, welcome to the rest of your life. Make yourself at home.

And, as they say, and you should know what we mean by now, enjoy.

14 day program:
A "to do" list for the next fortnight

If you want to integrate the tools, competencies and beliefs we have covered over the previous pages we recommend practicing them this regularly, and find out how to use them in your daily life. The following table presents you with a "diet to more EQ" you can live by over the next fortnight and beyond.

Task

Day 1:	Use **"The map is not the territory" as a filter** through which to study the world for the day. **Appreciate other people's opinions** and **find out what there is to learn** when an opinion strikes you as being different from your own.
Day 2:	Whatever happens today, **study what people are saying to you** and what are the boundaries, unspecific nouns and unspecific verbs that you hear. **Question those and examine how you are asking those questions.** Have a **respectful and interested listening attitude** towards the answers.
Day 3:	Today, before asking a question of someone else, first **ask yourself the question "What's my goal, what do I want to know?"**
Day 4:	Check all goals you are working on today for the **well-formedness conditions**.
Day 5:	Start each hour of the day by **accessing a resourceful, optimal state**, and fully associating into a great reference experience for that state.
Day 6:	**Find out what there is to learn** in whatever you come across today. **Put yourself in an optimal learning state** to help you on this path.
Day 7:	**Write down your personal vision and mission statements.** Evaluate the past week in relation to these statements. Where did you miss chances to put your mission into practice? How will you ensure you grab such opportunities in the future?

Task

Day 8: **Today is a day for leaving your watch at home**. Live as time goes by. Okay, if you really need to, you can use external sources to warn you about meetings you might miss.

Day 9: Start the day by **listing all the people you will meet today**. Before meeting those persons, take approximately two minutes for each person to **find out how they will be experiencing this encounter**. Use this information during the meeting. Evaluate at the end of the day to what extent doing this made those meetings different from other occasions you met these persons.

Day 10: List the **people you recently lost touch with**. Think about **how they experienced the last meeting they had with you** (use Second Position). You might want to call some of those people to arrange a new meeting.

Day 11: **What do you notice while listening** to your conversation partner? This is a great day to adapt the representation channel you use based on signs you get about their preferential representation channels (e.g. predicates, eye movements, submodalities, ...).

Day 12: **Observe the body language and especially changes in body posture** of your conversation partners. Do you discover any patterns? What happens if you use some careful matching of body language?

Day 13: Where can you use some more **creativity today**? Handle that specific problem **using the Walt Disney Creativity Strategy**. Is that in a context where you are just by yourself or are there other people involved?

Day 14: **Invent one or two new exercises for each chapter of the book**. This provides you with the "EQ diet" for the next fortnight! If you need some inspiration to invent exercises, put yourself in a creative state or use the Walt Disney Creativity Strategy. If you want to improve the formulation of the exercises, use the well-formed outcomes.

Note: *What about keeping a diary in which you record how those 14 days go by and what you have learned by applying the task we gave you for the day?*

Bibliography and Further Reading

Overview of the Neurolinguistic Literature

Giving you a complete overview of the neurolinguistic literature would take up far too many pages, given we have seen more than 200 books in print! The Internet is a far better medium to provide you with a more complete list. In particular, you might want to check out the alphabetic listing of "Patrick's Library" at:

http://www.7eq.com/books/

With that said, we want to use some space to discuss a few books we like to recommend. Consider it a kind of personal "top 10" by the authors:

❏ **NLP: The New Technology Of Achievement**, Steve Andreas and Charles Faulkner, eds, 1994, NLP Comprehensive.

This book shows you that NLP is full of great things which you can learn for yourself. The book is aimed at a public of readers of business books, self-help books or motivational books. You'll find the traditional NLP material but also a set of new material.

A lot of the material comes from modeling achievers from the academic world, the business world and from other areas. The authors asked the question "What is the same about all these people?," and as a result they came up with a full representation of an achiever. You can read it as a set of results of modeling projects, or use it for your personal development.

This book is a product of several minds and a showcase for the knowledge united in NLP Comprehensive. It is the result of the joint collaboration of the complete team of NLP Comprehensive, maybe one of the biggest NLP institutes in the United States, and certainly the one with the best staff in 1994, when this book was published. After collecting the material,

Charles and Steve spend some six further months in stream-lining it, so that not only does it still contain an enormous wealth of information, but it is also an easy read.

❑ **Introducing NLP: Psychological Skills for Understanding and Influencing People**, revised edition, Joseph O'Connor and John Seymour, 1993, Thorsons.

Introducing NLP is a real bestseller! Almost any library in Europe carrying some NLP books will have this one on the shelves. It is a well-structured book, which contains all the information you'll need up to the NLP practitioner's level (255 pages in a small print). This book can be used as a course book.

❑ **The Emotional Hostage: Rescuing Your Emotional Life**, Leslie Cameron-Bandler and Michael Lebeau, 1986, Real People Press.

Too bad this book preceded Daniel Goleman's *Emotional Intelligence* by about 10 years! *Emotional Hostage* gives the answers to questions Goleman is still asking 10 years later! The book combines NLP as it was known in 1986 with an analysis of emotions. A lot of this material is known nowadays in the NLP field as "state-management." The discussion in the book is based on Time Frames, Modality (Modal Operators), some submodality stuff (intensity, tempo, …), criteria and some Meta-Program stuff (such as chunk-size). You'll find chapters on the structure of emotions, orienting, selecting and accessing your emotions. The book continues with chapters on expressing and employing your emotions. Finally it discusses the abilities of prevention and anticipation.

❑ **Using Your Brain for a Change**, Richard Bandler (C. and S. Andreas, eds), 1985, Real People Press.

At that time I was looking for books about positive thinking, but this book really got my attention. The humorous, provoca-tive examples used throughout the book are typical of

Bandler—whether you like them or not is up to you—and they provide good anchoring when you use this book for self-improvement (don't take it too literally). And, by the way, the topic of the book is in fact submodalities.

❑ **Time for a Change**, Richard Bandler, 1993, Meta Publications.

If you ever go to a seminar that Richard Bandler gives, it would surprise me if you weren't to hear at least one variation on the stories used in this book. In the appendices you'll find some NLP models explained in short (accessing cues, Meta-Model, linguistic presuppositions, submodalities, reframing, etc.).

❑ **Turtles All the Way Down: Prerequisites to Personal Genius**, Judith DeLozier and John Grinder, 1987, Grinder & Associates, distributed by M.A.P.S.

This book is a reworked transcript of a seminar the authors gave in March 1986 in San Francisco. At that time John and Judith were busy inventing the "New Code." The result is a book about consciousness and the unconscious, about double descriptions, dissociation, First and Second Position and changing perceptual filters. In other words, the reader gets a lot of exercise to enlarge the map of the world. Bateson and Carlos Castaneda are the most cited authors in this seminar. Don't try too much to get a conscious map out of this book. As Judy says now, it should have been "Turtles all the way up."

❑ **Skills for the Future, Managing Creativity and Innovation**, Robert Dilts, 1993, Meta Publications.

This book is more than a way to learn about creativity. It also explains a lot of the NLP models when Dilts was involved in their development. You'll find explanations of the TOTE, SCORE and SOAR models (three models related to problem solving). The ROLE and BAGEL models are also integrated in this book, as well as the Walt Disney Creativity Strategy and explanation about well-formedness. This book is applicable for personal creativity, as well as group creativity.

❏ **Therapeutic Metaphors: Helping Others Through the Looking Glass**, David Gordon, 1978, Meta Publications.

David Gordon was around in Santa Cruz when NLP was "invented" by Bandler and Grinder, yet he chose to focus on a different aspect, thus giving us some more material to learn from. This book is about building metaphors, improving upon them using elements that come from early NLP research, and applying them. In short, it is a complete guide to becoming another Milton Erickson or Virginia Satir yourself, or at least as far as storytelling will bring you. You'll learn to use representation systems, submodalities and Satir categories to enhance your story.

❏ **Visionary Leadership Skills: Creating a World to Which People Want to Belong**, Robert B. Dilts, 1996, Meta Publications.

If you want to behave like a leader, without reading a dozen books, this book will help you to get on the road to "creating a world to which people want to belong." You get a combination of material that came to Robert's attention between 1988 and 1991, when he did several modeling projects around Effective Leadership Skills, in Europe as well as in the US, for companies such as Apple, IBM and Fiat. If you have read a lot of NLP material or attended a lot of formal NLP training, some of the material will be familiar, and the same is true if you have read a lot of management literature. Some well-known titles from both areas can be found in the bibliography (many titles that you'll also find in this booklist). But then, how many people have read so many books in these two domains? It proves that Robert did his homework so well before writing this book which is worth having around as a resource. On their own, some of the chapters are already a reason to read the book—unless you have read it elsewhere, of course. But what Robert also adds is a framework. This book goes beyond the typical leadership books when it comes to giving a complete picture. Rather than emphasizing what is effective at a certain moment in time, Robert gives a systemic approach, starting from the principle of requisite variety: if something does not work, try something else!

Topics include: The Parable of the Porpoise (a chapter on giving useful feedback, based upon research in porpoise training), Leadership Styles (with the Leadership Assessment Sheet), Aligning Levels of Change in a System (this chapter is a must if you're involved in change or change management), The Walt Disney Strategy Model, Belief Systems (with the belief Assessment Sheet), etc. As an extra, you'll find a reprint of "Overcoming Resistance to Persuasion with NLP" in the appendix.

In 1998, Robert wrote *Modeling with NLP* as a companion volume to this book. The second part of that book illustrates the application of NLP modeling to the study of effective leadership. Check it out!

❑ **Words That Change Minds: Mastering The Language Of Influence**, Shelle Rose Charvet, 1995, 1997 (revised Second Edition), Kendall/Hunt Publishing Company.

Shelle has been working and training around the LAB profile ever since she "discovered" it at PNL-REPERE, the Paris institute of the *Integral Perspectives Group*, in 1985. The LAB profile is a tool, developed by Rodger Bailey around the Meta-Programs, focusing on how people motivate themselves and how they organize their work. It teaches you how to recognize these categories (e.g. during a recruitment interview) and how to use these distinctions in several business-related contexts (e.g. negotiation) once you have learned them. Among the possible applications are: recruitment, management, culture change in companies, marketing, etc.

Other References for This Workbook

Given the amount of books we have been reading, it became unclear to us which book inspired us and in what way. Rather than trying to "reconstruct" this past, let us point out some books we recommend today for you to read to supplement these seven lessons on Emotional Intelligence. More titles also appear in the footnotes to individual chapters. On our website:

www.7eq.com

you'll find book reviews for several of these titles.

On Emotional Intelligence

- Cooper, Robert K. and Sawaf, Ayman (1998). *Executive EQ— Emotional Intelligence in Leadership and Organization,* Perigee.
- Frank, Robert H. (1988). *Passions within Reason—The Strategic Role of the Emotions,* London, W.W. Norton & Company.
- Goleman, Daniel (1995). **Emotional Intelligence**, New York, Bantam Books.
- Goleman, Daniel (1998). **Emotional Intelligence at Work**, New York, Bantam Books.
- Ortony, Andres; Clore, Gerald L. and Collins, Allan (1998). *The Cognitive Structure of Emotions,* Cambridge, Cambridge University Press.
- Segal, Jeanne (1997). *Raising your Emotional Intelligence— A Practical Guide,* New York, Owl Books.

Related to Emotional Intelligence

- Bolton, Ph.D., Robert (1979). **People Skills: How to Assert Yourself, Listen to Others and Resolve Conflicts,** New York, Touchstone, Simon & Schuster.
- Carnegie, Dale (1935, 1998). *How to Win Friends & Influence People,* Pocket Books.
- Covey, Stephen R. (1989). *The 7 Habits of Highly Effective People,* New York, FireSide, Simon & Schuster.
- Covey, Stephen R. (1994). *First Things First,* New York, FireSide, Simon & Schuster.

- Day, Laura (1997). *Practical Intuition for Success*, HarperCollins.
- Keeney, Bradford P. (1983). *Aesthetics of Change*, New York, The Guildford Press.
- Kelly, Robert E. (1998). *How to Be a Star at Work*, New York, Times Books.
- Zelinski, Ernie J. (1997). *The Joy of Not Working: Book for the Retired, Unemployed and Overworked*, Ten Speed Press.

Related business reading
- de Geus, Arie (1997). *The Living Company: Growth, Learning and Longevity in Business*, London, Nicholas Brearley Publishing.
- Senge, Peter M. (1990). *The Fifth Discipline—The Art and Practice of the Learning Organization*, London, Century Business, Random House.
- Senge, Peter M., et al., (1994). *The Fifth Discipline Fieldbook—Strategies and Tools for Building a Learning Organization*, London, Nicholas Brealey Publishing.

Written communication for the 21st century
- Angell, David and Heslop, Brent (1994). *The Elements of E-Mail Style*, Addison-Wesley.
- William Horton, *Designing and Writing Online Documentation*, John Wiley & Sons.

On Systems Thinking
- O'Connor, Joseph and McDermott, Ian (1997). *The Art of Systems Thinking: Essential Skills for Creativity and Problem-Solving*, London, Thorsons.

On Language
- Pinker, Steven (1994).*The Language Instinct: How the Mind Creates Language*, Harmondsworth, Penguin.

With a philosophical flavor

- Pirsig, Robert M. (1974). *Zen and the Art of Motorcycle Maintenance: An Inquiry into Values,* London, Arrow Books Limited, Random House.
- Capra, Fritjof (1996). *The Web of Life,* London, HarperCollins.

Psychology and Cognitive Sciences

- Gardner, Howard (1985). *The Mind's New Science: A History of the Cognitive Revolution,* New York, Basic Books.
- Kellogg, Ronald T. (1997). **Cognitive Psychology**, London, Sage Publications.
- Mithen, Steven (1996). *The Archeology of the Mind,* London, Thames & Hudson.

The Internet

In 1994, when "Merl's World on Neurologistics" launched, it was one of the few and very first sites on NLP and Emotional Intelligence. At that time the Internet was still virtually unknown, and the growth of the web also brought us an enormous increase in websites, to a point where it no longer makes sense to try to give you an overview of the places to visit on the web. Therefore, we limit ourselves to some addresses which can serve as "portals" on your quest into the area of NLP and Emotional Intelligence.

"Merl"s World" still exists, and provides you with the major links within the world of NLP. You'll also find a global list of more than 250 NLP institutes, reviews of more than 100 NLP books and a FAQ on the domain of Neurologistics.

http://www.7eq.com/nlp/

7 Steps To Emotional Intelligence now has its own website, which was first launched in 1998, when the first version of this book came out. This website will also provide you with the monthly 7EQ newsletter (FREE), which provides you with a steady flow of new EQ stories, bloopers, links and new developments.

http://www.7eq.com

Solutions to the exercises in this book

We want to keep in touch with you. Tell us what you learned from this book, ask us extra questions. To motivate you to give us some feedback, we offer you the following service.

If you ask us for the solutions to the exercises mentioned below, we will send them in exchange for feedback. If you send your feedback and the request by e-mail, this service is free. If you want us to send it by post, we'd like you to add 2 USD (banknotes: for outside Europe) or 2 EURO (stamps: inside the EU) to cover our replying costs.

Exercise 2.2.   Find the neurological level
Exercise 3.1.   Making goals well-formed
Exercise 4.1.   Representation channels: "Sensory-specific observation"
Exercise 4.11. Recognize the Meta-Programs
Exercise 5.1.   Code the perceptual positions
Exercise 6.3.   Inventing questions
Exercise 6.7.   Presupposition identification
Exercise 6.10. Facts versus opinions

Appendix 1: Neuro-Linguistic Programming

About half of the material of this book is explicitly inspired by Neuro-Linguistic Programming (NLP), a discipline co-created by Richard Bandler and John Grinder in the 1970s. This appendix is meant for those of you who want to learn more about this discipline or who want to know where it comes from.

An often used definition for "Neuro-Linguistic Programming" is

> **"The Study of the Structure of Subjective Experience,"**
> which some people complete by adding:
> "and anything that can be derived from it."

To put it less formally: NLP offers you a user-manual to your brain.

Another workable definition is

> **The Structure of Excellence**

This is because NLP is fascinated by what works, and seeks to model it. This explains why the model has been expanding so rapidly.

NLP is a philosophy, a frame of mind, an attitude, supported by a rigorous methodology and a series of techniques/processes which outsiders to the field may be most familiar with. To quote Richard Bandler:

# NLP Represents:	
An Attitude:	a mindset, characterized by a voracious, omnivorously insatiable sense of curiosity and adventure, motivated by a tenacious resolve to succeed, a commitment to seize any opportunity to learn and make the most of life, and a wanton willingness and drive to experiment with the necessary flexibility to achieve and influence.
A Methodology:	the structure of subjective experience can be studied, modeled, learned, taught, replicated and altered to our requirements. Our tools are our perceptual and language skills.
A Technology:	the processes developed by NLP enable those who practice it to organize and reorganize information, sharpening our perceptual and language skills to achieve desired results.

Bandler and Grinder may have borrowed the term "neuro-linguistic" from General Semantics. General Semantics was developed in the early 1930s as "a discipline which explains and trains how to use our nervous systems most efficiently" (Alfred Korzybski in *Science and Sanity*). Korzybski also pointed out the importance of epistemology (the study of how we know what we say we know).

NLP evolved out of cognitive science research (linguistics, psychology, computer science [cybernetics], anthropology) at the University of California (in Santa Cruz) between 1972 and 1981. In fact, John Grinder was an assistant professor of linguistics there at the time. He had studied with Noam Chomsky. NLP seems to have given up its scientific aims since then to become a set of tools that will enhance your communication skills, your Emotional Intelligence, etc. Of course cognitive science hasn't stopped since then, and modern NLP has also known its extensions. So look for cross-fertilization between the two fields.

Bandler and Grinder, prompted by Bateson, began to study outstanding communicators, more especially those who excelled in the field of psychotherapy, including:

- *Fritz Perls*, then foremost light of **Gestalt Therapy**,
- *Virginia Satir*, matriarch of **Family Therapy**,

and

- *Milton Erickson*, who revolutionized the field of **Hypnosis**.

Seeking to find out how each of them did what they did which made them excel in their field, Bandler and Grinder carefully analyzed their verbal and body language patterns. This led them to identify key commonalities between these, which enabled them to formulate an explicit model of what produced such excellence in these famous therapists.

NLP then moved on to study and analyze many other activities requiring skilled performance and outstandingly successful operating strategies, such as those of *Carl Rogers* and *Moshe Feldenkrais.* This enabled early NLP developers to refine their understanding of the nature of excellence in performance and to identify the key patterns and processes which produce this excellence, enabling the successful communication of these patterns and processes in order to successfully replicate them through a process known as *modeling.* Furthermore, teaching these specific skills to people not involved achieved results similar to those of the experts they had studied and, in many cases, even improved on them.

Neuro-Linguistic Programming, as its name implies, relates to:

The way our brain and the whole of our nervous system actually operates and runs our body via our senses: ❖ Visual V ❖ Auditory A ❖ Kinesthetic K ❖ Olfactory O ❖ Gustatory G	**NEURO**
The way our language, in the widest sense ❖ Verbal ❖ Tonal ❖ Body Language shapes, fashions and structures our behavior and that of others around us.	**LINGUISTIC**
Our own mental "software," the processes which underlie how we behave and what we believe about ourselves, other people and the world about us.	**PROGRAMMING**

**OPERATIONAL STRUCTURE OF OUR
INTERNAL MAPS AS IDENTIFIED IN NLP**

OUR LINGUISTIC RE-PRESENTATION OF REALITY A_D	**META-PROGRAMS** **ATTITUDES** **PRESUPPOSITIONS** **BELIEFS** **VALUES** **CRITERIA**	**PROGRAMMING**
	INTERPRETATIVE/ EVALUATIVE LANGUAGE / **ABSTRACT LANGUAGE**	**LINGUISTIC**
	DESCRIPTIVE LANGUAGE / **SENSORY-SPECIFIC LANGUAGE**	
OUR SENSORY RE-PRESENTATION OF REALITY $V_I\,A_I\,K_I\,O_I\,G_I$	**SUBMODALITIES** *(INDIVIDUAL COMPONENTS WITHIN A MODALITY)* **SENSORY FILTERS**	**NEURO**
	OUR SENSES: **MODALITIES OF PERCEPTION** *(ALSO CALLED REPRESENTATIONAL SYSTEMS)*	

V_e VISUAL (*SIGHT*)
A_e AUDITORY (*SOUND*)
K_e KINESTHETIC (*TOUCH, FEELINGS, ETC.*)
O_e OLFACTORY (*SMELL*)
G_e GUSTATORY (*TASTE*)

OUR EXPERIENCE OF REALITY

REALITY (*WHATEVER THIS IS*)

© Denis Bridoux, from Michael Hall

Appendix 2:
Meta-Programs in Recruiting and Management[1]

In job interviews we look for the best candidate for a specific function. Apart from whether they are capable enough or whether they have potential, we also want to predict how they will respond while doing their job. However, by focusing on a person's professional skills, this forecast does not seem to work very well in practice. When a company hires the person who was the best in the job interviews, they often turn out later on not to have been the best choice, from an emotional perspective, as the skills they professed or displayed during the selection process are undermined by their emotional make-up. Neurolinguistics provides you with the means to look for the best candidate from a psychological and emotional perspective. In this example we will use only the above-mentioned Meta-Programs. We will distinguish between three steps in the recruiting process: the preparation before the visit of the candidates, the job interview and the support (managing) of the hired person.

Step 1: Establishing the Desired Profile

To establish this profile, we need to take a look at the person who is currently doing the job that the newly hired person will have to do as well. Naturally we pick the best employee in the post. We ask questions in order to discover this person's Meta-Programs (note: these are the questions that you found on previous pages). Our profile will be based on the answers to these questions.

- Pick two additional, good employees with a comparable function and write down their Meta-Programs. The Meta-

---

[1] Additional Reading: in September 1997 an International Colloquium was held in Belgium about "Learning and the Support of Employment." During this event Patrick Merlevede gave a lecture on "Analyzing Language and Behavior in Top Performers and its Uses in the Employment Area." You will find the text of his presentation on the Acknowledge website:

http://www.acknowledge.net/analyzin.htm

Programs which are the same in the three people are the most important ones for the post.

- Choose one of the worst employees with a comparable function. The Meta-Programs which differ the most from the Meta-Programs of your best employees are the most important ones.

Note: The dominant Meta-Programs within the company determine which Meta-Programs are the best ones for the company. You cannot just say: a good bookkeeper is a *Specific* person or fast-food restaurants need *External* people because they need to serve the clients. When you ask the question you need to make sure that the questions are about the professional context, since we often notice that the Meta-Programs differ according to the context (personal vs leisure vs professional) you are talking about.

An example: profile of a distribution truck driver

The truck driver has a fixed distribution round and needs to deliver small amounts of goods to the same retail customers. It is extremely important to fill out the receipts correctly. The driver needs to get on with people, especially since they meet the same people several times a month.

We interrogate our best drivers and we arrive at the conclusion that the following Meta-Programs are the most important ones:

1. *Away from*: the drivers pay a lot of attention to the filling out of the documents and they drive carefully in order to avoid "accidents."
2. *Procedure*: the driver has a fixed round, elaborated by the company's planner. The deliveries occur according to strict rules.
3. *External reference*: the drivers aim for a good understanding between the customer and themselves.
4. *Similarity*: fixed rounds, the job is not changing.

We check this with our worst driver, who recently resigned because he wanted a job as an international driver. Apparently he needed variation, he has been whining about the procedures for a long time, and his style of driving seems to attract accidents, although he is never to blame.

Step 2: The Selection Interview

Now we have established the desired profile and candidates are reviewed. We will inquire into their Meta-Programs. Again we make sure the answers come out of a professional context. We ask the Meta-Program questions for more Meta-Programs than just those Meta-Programs which came out of the preparation phase as being the most relevant, because these Meta-Programs might be useful in the final selection, when two candidates have an equal score on other selection criteria, or to balance out the job experience of one candidate with other, more emotional criteria.

The example: our candidate truck drivers

After a first selection, based on resumés, we have a selection of motivated candidates.

- John is 22. He has been a licensed truck driver for four years and has been driving ever since to France, Spain and Italy. He transported all kinds of goods. Because his wife is pregnant he prefers a more quiet distribution job.
- Leo is 49. He used to work in the railway parcel service, but got fired in a reorganization. This was probably because, in a period of fifteen years, he had asked for another round twice. Since then he has been doing international transport for the company between the retailing outlets. However, he misses contact with clients and sometimes finds it hard to be so far away from home.
- Mark is 32. He previously worked for a company for seven years and he had an ice cream round. After that he wanted some more freedom and, in his latest job, has had the opportunity to travel everywhere in the country delivering furniture. However, the company went bankrupt and since then he has been driving tank containers. He loves contact with people and that is why this job appeals to him.

META-PROGRAM	JOHN	LEO	MARK
Motivation direction	Towards	Away from	Away from
Motivation reason	Options	Procedures	Options
Motivation source	Internal reference	External reference	External reference
Decision factors	Similarity	Difference	Difference
Attention direction	Extrovert	Extrovert	Extrovert
Stress response	Choices	Choices	Choices
Scope	General	Specific	Specific

None of them meet the four most important criteria. Now we see whether the Meta-Programs are important and whether they can compensate for the missing ones. We also consider adapting the job in order to compensate for the weak points of the drivers. Eventually Leo is hired, although the company initially objected to his age.

Step 3: Managing the New Co-operator

Based on the person's Meta-Programs we also know the factors we will have to take into account when managing this person in order to make them operate optimally. For this we also use the less critical Meta-Programs. As a manager we adapt our language to the Meta-Programs of this co-operator. By doing this in an honest way, you increase the likelihood that you will be able to motivate the person.

An example: Leo, our new driver

When hiring Leo, we provide him with clear procedures and explain that he will be questioned about this on his first working day. We explain to Leo that in his first week he will be able to drive together with a driver who is leaving, so that he will get to know the route and his clients. We do not mind him trying to find out the differences between individual clients, so that he is able to adapt himself to each of them. On the other hand he should know that routes are fixed: we do not expect him to try and find out whether there is another route. If he gets tired of the round in a few years we will be able to give him another one. We explain to Leo that his evaluation will be based on mistakes in the procedure and his understanding with the clients. We promise him that we will have regular evaluation talks and that, if something is wrong, he can always drop in for a talk.

What Can We Use in Recruiting?

In the first two steps of the example our emphasis was on discovering the Meta-Programs and using the model as a criterion for selection. Indeed, the Meta-Program model is already used internationally in a number of important companies. For more information, we'd like to refer you to the **www.jobEQ.com** website. From experience in France we know that it is a suitable instrument to hire assistant managers for a chain of shops. By rewriting an advertisement in Belgium we managed to double the reaction to a job vacancy of a company (who hired 26 salespeople) because it met the Meta-Programs of the candidates we were looking for. The manager and the HRM, who were responsible for the recruitment, noticed that they needed less time for job interviews and, in the end, they agreed about the suitable candidates.

In the third step we are fully in the domain of this book, Emotional Intelligence. We adapt our communication style in order to meet the Meta-Programs of our subordinates, but of course the same principle applies for colleagues and boss.

Appendix 3:
Integral Perspectives Group

Training Programs

At this moment, our training centers in the UK and in France (Paris) offer Open English Language Programs based on this book, or building on it. Get in touch with them to find out about subjects and dates. Next to that, members of the group give training in the United States, Russia, Germany, Italy, Belgium, Hong Kong, and elsewhere.

We also carry out a lot of in-house training. Our customer base includes several well-known companies. Next to Emotional Intelligence programs, training subjects include recruiting, sales, cultural change, coaching, leadership, communication skills, etc.

Consulting

What is the secret of your excellence? Modeling will help you to find this out. This type of project falls into the core-competence of the *Integral Perspectives Group*.

- *Model-Based Recruiting*: Take the three best employees for a function. Compare them to three lesser gods. What's the difference? From this kind of study, we help you to identify what attitude factors and which skills are critical for the function, how to design a job advert which focuses on this profile, and how to structure the recruiting process and interviews to select the best candidate. Once the candidate is hired, we suggest what coaching may be needed to bridge the gaps between the profile of excellence and the candidate.
- *Model-Based Marketing*: Who are your good customers? How do they make the decision to buy and use your product? Use the answers to these questions to design your marketing campaigns.
- *Knowledge Management*: Since the 1980s the problem with knowledge has been "How can we distribute our core

knowledge throughout the company?" This has been coined the "knowledge acquisition bottleneck." We have developed training programs and CD-ROMs introducing people to companies' values and culture. We have also helped companies to make this knowledge explicit and find better ways to manage it (including expert systems for planning, financial decision-making, etc.).

Coaching

- *Action-Oriented Coaching*: Based on an analysis of on-the-job performance, we identify the patterns which explain the weak points in a person's area of performance. We help the person to define the actions which will tackle and remedy their weak areas.
- *Competence Development*: Based on an analysis of their competences, we help a person to overcome their blockages and to find the necessary resources for the areas which they want to improve.

Integral Perspectives Contact Addresses

France and International:
PNL-REPERE
78, Av. Général Michel Bizot
     F-75012 Paris
e-mail: formation@repere-pnl.com
website: www.repere-pnl.com

UK:
PGPE (Denis Bridoux)
Post-Graduate Managerial and
     Professional Education
P.O. Box 506, Halifax,
     W. Yorks., HX1 5UF
Tel: +44 (0)1422 343165
Fax: +44 (0)1422 251296
e-mail:
     PGPE@outcome.demon.co.uk

Acknowledge (Patrick Merlevede)
Bardelare 18
B-9971 Lembeke
Tel +32 (75) 87.08.52
Fax: +32 (9) 378.48.88
e-mail: PatrickM@acknowledge.net
website: www.acknowledge.net

Belgium:
School voor NLP
     (Rudy Vandamme)
St. Reneldisplein 3
B-3001 Leuven
Tel: +32 (75) 61.45.23
Fax: +32 (16) 60.15.23
e-mail: goforconnection@pi.be
website: www.ping.be/connection

Glossary

In this section we group short definitions of the most important terms in the neurolinguistic vocabulary. All these terms have been extensively covered in the seven lessons.

Alignment: a way of ensuring congruence between all the components of communication and personality so that all converge and mutually support each other. (see: *congruence, ecology, rapport, synergy*)

Anchor: in general, any stimulus which causes a response (as defined in behaviorism). More specifically, a way to activate or recall an emotional *state*. Although most anchors come into existence in an unconscious, "spontaneous" way, one can deliberately create one's own anchors.

Anchoring: the process of linking a stimulus to a response, so that if the stimulus gets activated, the response (often an emotional state) follows immediately.

Associating: to experience a situation or memory from within one's body, accessing all the sensory information available at the time. A type of digital submodality. (see: *dissociating, submodalities*)

Calibration: the way we have of utilizing our sensory perceptions to educate our guesswork about what happens inside a person's head by learning to associate repeated behavioral patterns with specific internal states and ways of thinking.

Congruence: when our behavior matches our beliefs in a resourceful fashion. When no internal conflict is observed and internal rapport is achieved. (see: *alignment, ecology, rapport, synergy*)

Content: the information contained in an experience, usually expressed in a narrative fashion.

Criteria: a type of value which is necessary to the satisfaction of an outcome.

Disney Creativity Strategy: a particular model aimed at generating creativity based on a type of Meta-Program which sorts people into Dreamers, Realists, and Critics, validating all three.

Dissociating: to experience a situation as if from outside one's body and seeing oneself from the outside. A type of digital submodality. (see: *associating, submodalities*)

Ecology: an awareness of the consequences of a given behavior, checking that it will benefit all parties and harm none, both internally and externally. An authentic "win/win."

Eye-accessing cues: the directions our eyes flick to in order to enable us to access an internal sensory representation as a memory or construct. (see: *lead system*)

First Position: the way the person perceives the world from within their body: observing a system (the world) from your own point of view (your map of the world). (see: *associating, perceptual positions*)

Fourth Position: the system as observed by the system itself, as a whole. (see: *perceptual positions*)

General Semantics: a discipline evolved in the 1930s which investigates the way we map out reality around us. A forerunner discipline to NLP.

Language: in its broadest sense, this incorporates biochemical information, body language, tonality, words and the way all these interact and interrelate.

Leading: having paced and synchronized oneself with another person or group, purposefully introducing a new component in the communication or behavior so that the other follows. (see: *pacing, rapport, synchronization*)

Lead System: the sensory system one preferentially uses to access an internal representation as a memory/construct. Identified through the eye-accessing cues. (see: *eye-accessing cues*)

Logical Levels: in general, logical levels are a series of levels in logical thinking where a higher level encompasses a lower level, indicating the limits of the lower level and the rules to which that level has to comply (for more information, read the works of Gregory Bateson and L. Michael Hall). The field of neurolinguistics often mentions *neurological levels*, which is a model developed by Robert Dilts. (see: *neurological levels*)

Matching: the way one modifies one's behavior consciously or unconsciously by developing behavior patterns similar to the person one seeks to achieve rapport with. (see: *pacing, synchronization*)

Meta-Model: a language model consisting of a series of language patterns one can observe during communication. These language patterns are linked to the filtering process (deletion, generalization and distortion) which occurs between the facts as the person observed them and the story the person tells based on these facts. The Meta-Model also indicates what questions to ask when one comes across these patterns, and what results to anticipate having asked the question. The Meta-Model was based on Noam Chomsky's linguistic theories as they existed around 1970.

Meta-Position: a dissociated observer position, linked to one of the four perceptual positions: one takes a higher level or Meta-Level in relation to that position. For instance, if you take a Meta-Position in relation to First Position, you (yourself) are looking at the system which includes yourself (e.g. as if you were watching a movie in which you play a role). (see: *dissociating, perceptual positions*)

Meta-Programs: a series of mental filters which determine how one behaves and what one pays attention to during observation (e.g. do you focus on the information or on people? Are you thinking about what might go wrong or do you stress the goal that has to be achieved?). The Meta-Programs that one uses are not absolute or fixed in time, space or context: in different contexts a person may have other Meta-Program preferences. Among other things, Meta-Programs can be used to predict whether a person will be motivated by a certain job and thus can serve as an instrument during recruiting, coaching and training people.

Mindreading: the way one imagines what goes on inside someone else's head by guesswork. A type of distortion. (see: *calibration, Meta-Model*)

Modeling: used by an individual, modeling can serve as a way to learn. Used by a larger entity, modeling becomes a tool for knowledge management. Modeling is the core of NLP. In the

NLP sense of the word, one models by analyzing a competence using the range of approaches which are presented throughout this book. (see: *Meta-Model, Meta-Programs, (neuro)logical levels, perceptual positions, representation channels, TOTE*)

Neurological Levels: developed by Robert Dilts, this model helps to structure into levels the information you collect during communication. The model distinguishes subjective experience into the following levels: environment, behavior, capabilities, beliefs, identity and spirituality. (see: *logical levels*)

Pacing: the way in which we adapt our behavior to that of another person to achieve rapport with them. (see: *leading, rapport, synchronization*)

Perceptual Positions: a model describing the different positions one can assume to observe the world or a system. (see: *First Position, Second Position, Third Position, Fourth Position, Meta-Position*)

Predicates: an expression from the field of linguistics which refers to terms such as verbs, adjectives and adverbs, which denote a processing in action. (see: *Primary System*)

Presuppositions: a series of ideas and beliefs one consciously or unconsciously accepts to be true and which, as such, are used as basic building blocks for a theory (as axioms in mathematics)—the resulting theory is built on top of these presuppositions. The "givens" in any communication/ behavior. A theoretical system may fail if its presuppositions are proven to be false or erroneous.

Primary System: the representational channel one mainly uses to process information. Identified by listening to the sensory-specific language used by a person and especially the predicates used. (see: *predicates*)

Rapport: the result of processes called *pacing* and *leading* which two or more people have consciously or unconsciously applied to achieve a better understanding and to get enough synchronization in order to have a successful communication. A synonym for *synergy* in the context of communication.

Reframing: literally: "to put in another frame." To give another interpretation to an event or to something one has observed.

Representation Channels: our sensory modalities. Our senses are used not only to observe the world, but also to construct our internal representations of the outside world and to structure our own thinking. Also known as representational systems. (see: *VAK/OG*)

Resourceful State: a state of mind/body which enables us to think, feel and behave appropriately to attain an outcome. Several NLP applications you'll find in this book rely upon anchors and emotional states as resources to better obtain the desired outcome. (see: *anchoring, state*)

Second Position: the system (or world) as observed by the other party (associated: using that person's beliefs, state, etc.). As if you were standing in the other person's shoes, observing yourself—but thinking like that person. Having empathy requires going into Second Position. (see: *perceptual positions*)

SMART goal: a mnemonic to remember the key criteria to achieve a goal: simple/specific, measurable/meaningful to you, achievable/as if now/all areas of your life, realistic/responsible, timed/towards what you want. (see: *well-formed outcome*)

State: synonym for "emotional state" or "mood." A state consists of a series of thinking patterns, beliefs, feelings (emotions) and behaviors one uses at a certain moment in time.

Strategy: one could compare a strategy to a computer program. In general it is a sequence of steps (in thinking and/or behavior) which lead to a predictable and reproducible result. In a more narrow sense the term is often used in NLP to describe a series of steps in representation channels (micro-strategy): e.g. I see a book which makes me say to myself that "I still have to finish this task" and suddenly I feel energized to start doing it (Visual ⇨ Auditory ⇨ Kinesthetic).

Submodalities: filters one applies to sensory-specific external or internal information, which affect the format of this sensory information. The parameters of sensory information. The way that submodalities are formatted affects the quality of an experience and therefore its meaning. Also known as Representational Distinctions.

Synchronization: the way we consciously or unconsciously adapt our behavior to become more like that of another person to achieve rapport. (see: *pacing, rapport*)

Synergy: when all parts of a system work harmoniously together, the total of the energy available is greater than the sum of the energies provided by each part. New properties emerge from a system in synergy. (see: *alignment, congruence, ecology, rapport*)

Third Position: the viewpoint from which an outsider can observe the complete system (meaning one can see both the *First Position* and the *Second Position* at the same time). (see: *perceptual positions*)

TOTE-model: TOTE is an abbreviation for "Test-Operate-Test-Exit." The TOTE-model is a planning model that can be used to define a goal plan and decide how to reach this goal and how you will use feedback to correct the actions you take while working towards the goal. The model was first described in the book *Plans and the Structure of Behavior* (Miller, Galanter & Pribram, 1957). (see: *Well-formed Outcome*)

Unconscious: any aspect of you, external or internal, behavioral or cognitive, that you're not aware of at any moment in time. That aspect of you which does things for you so that you can attend to more important things, like reading this book.

VAK/OG: abbreviation to indicate the five senses: *V*isual, *A*uditory, *K*inesthetic (feelings and tactile), *O*lfactory (smell) and *G*ustatory (taste). (see: *representation channels*)

Well-formed Outcome: a goal which satisfies the following criteria: it is formulated using positive wording, it is specific, it lies within one's own control, it is ecological and the results and the progress can be measured.

Index

Alignment, 385, 390
Alzheimer's Disease, 27
Analog, 174–176
Analysis,
    Contrastive, 155, 179–180, 220
Anchoring, 35, 43, 51, 59, 61, 143, 354, 363, 385, 389
Anger, 11, 16, 26, 32, 35–36, 40, 55, 68, 95, 98, 108, 138, 158, 304, 331
Aggressiveness, 32, 95, 103–104, 133, 317
Aristotle, 11, 228, 257
Assertiveness, 79, 107, 135, 205, 233, 252, 331
Association, 5, 46–47, 49–50, 68, 87, 148, 202, 242–243, 354
Asking Questions, 3, 66, 69, 242, 257–258, 260, 262, 264, 285, 288, 309, 323, 341
    • Meta-Model, 270–271, 281–282, 284–285, 289, 297–298, 363, 387–388
    • Transformational grammar, 285
Assumptions, 1, 12, 31, 75, 104, 117, 157, 223, 255, 299
Auditory, 161–168, 170, 174–176, 179, 216, 287, 308, 328, 374–375, 389–390
Away-from, 185–186, 190–191, 213, 310, 378, 380

Backtracking, 316, 318, 336
Bailey, Roger, 205, 365
Bandler, Richard, 4, 35, 135, 172, 180, 266, 270, 311, 323–324, 362–364, 371–373
Bateson, Gregory, 14, 77, 105, 107–108, 246, 302, 304, 344, 363, 373, 386

Behavior, 8, 16, 18–19, 34–42, 44, 46, 48–49, 52, 55, 64, 75–76, 78–79, 82–89, 91, 93, 96–101, 103, 106, 108, 112–114, 117, 121, 123, 131, 138, 142, 144, 157–158, 185, 200, 212, 223–224, 228–229, 231–232, 235, 237–238, 240, 243, 252–253, 266–267, 276, 279, 293, 299, 302–306, 311–317, 319, 324–325, 330–331, 347, 354, 374, 377, 385–390–392
Beliefs, 2, 8, 13, 35, 37, 41, 75, 78–80, 82–85, 88–89, 92, 99–104, 106, 110, 113, 115, 139, 141, 173, 180–181, 194, 238, 252, 276–277, 295, 300, 302, 306, 309, 346–347, 349, 354, 359, 375, 385, 388–389
Bell Curve, 8–9
Big Picture, 10, 184
Bodenhamer, Bobby, 4, 98, 172, 186
Body Language, 45, 66, 82, 90, 139, 170–171, 173, 300–301, 303–305, 307, 311–314, 316, 319–320, 360, 373–374, 386
Boundaries, 26, 255, 263, 266, 268, 359
Brecht, Bertolt, 134
Breathing, 29, 37, 40, 45, 47, 56, 72, 101, 114, 170, 256, 307–308, 314–315, 332, 349
Briggs-Myers, Isobel, 184
Buddhism, 16, 32, 55, 332
Billings, Josh, 210

Calibration, 3, 177–178, 299, 303, 306–307, 312, 314, 318, 354, 385, 387
Cameron-Bandler, Leslie, 159, 184, 355, 362
Capabilities, 8, 78, 83–84, 86, 141, 212, 354, 388
Carnegie, Dale, 258, 366
Carroll, Lewis, 263, 272, 285
Charvet, Shelle Rose, 186, 365

Choice, 8, 18, 40, 56, 58, 81, 88, 113, 117, 120–121, 130, 143, 151, 163, 172, 186, 193, 204–205, 212–213, 223, 244, 267, 279, 338, 344, 377

Chomsky, Noam, 285–286, 373, 387 (also see Transformational Grammar)

Cicero, 17, 143, 268

Coaching, 3, 5, 207, 233, 239, 247, 284, 332, 383–384, 387

Cognitive Science, 3, 345, 372–373

Communication, 2–3, 14, 19, 34, 40, 75, 77–79, 81–83, 85, 87, 89–91, 93, 95, 97, 99, 101, 103, 105, 107, 109, 111, 113, 115, 127, 133, 141, 152, 161, 169, 178, 184, 187, 198, 207, 215, 223, 225–226, 233, 245–249, 255, 270, 293, 299–303, 306, 308, 311, 313, 323, 326, 330, 333, 367, 373, 381, 383, 385–388

Competence, 1, 32–33, 39, 49, 82, 185, 197, 304, 341, 344–349, 357, 384, 388

Competencies, 8, 78, 157, 184, 342–344, 348, 359

Confidence, 41–44, 52, 212

Conflict, 26–27, 81, 85, 201, 224, 228, 232–233, 235, 242, 256, 307, 313, 385

Congruence, 90, 318, 334, 385, 390

Connectedness, 78, 81, 84, 103

Connections, 3, 10, 81, 158, 225, 262, 275, 277–278, 311, 341, 343, 345, 347, 349, 351

Content, 5, 18, 23, 157, 160, 173, 181–184, 191, 200, 224, 246, 301, 308–309, 317, 320, 326, 333–334, 336, 339, 343, 356, 385

Conditioning, 28, 33, 139, 142

Context, 1, 8, 14, 16, 18–19, 25–26, 31–32, 37, 40–41, 52–53, 58, 64, 68–71, 76, 78, 80, 84, 102, 108, 110, 126, 142–143, 158, 163, 187, 194, 199, 203, 205–206, 212, 220–221, 235, 246–247, 253, 264, 274, 293, 310, 320–321, 344, 346, 350, 352, 360, 378–379, 387–388

Control, 11, 27, 31, 33–35, 41, 44, 53, 56, 88, 95, 99, 124–126, 134–135, 138–139, 143, 145, 153, 174, 185–186, 188, 224, 228, 232, 235, 239, 246, 262, 264, 279, 342, 356–357, 390

Conditioned Reflexes, 138

Convictions, 13, 78–80, 103, 276

Cooper, Cary, 134

Cooper, Robert, 355, 366

Core
- Identity, 80–81
- State, 348
- Values, 63, 85, 89–90, 101–102, 112

Co-operative, 206, 209, 213

Copying, 314–316, 322, 337

Creativity, 2, 24, 61, 63–65, 80, 146, 149–150, 194, 197–198, 202, 245, 319–320, 354, 360, 363, 367, 385

Criteria, 62, 64, 114–115, 123–126, 152, 187, 191–192, 195, 200, 309, 320, 362, 375, 379–380, 385, 389–390

Critic, 62–66, 250

Csikszentmihalyi, Mihaly, 58

Darwin, Charles, 303–305

Deadlines, 127, 190, 202, 209, 269

Deconditioning, 139

Deductions, 89

Deletions, 247, 271, 282

DeLozier, Judith, 225, 363

Depression, 21, 26, 50, 93, 105, 134

Details, 10, 16, 63, 67, 184, 210–211, 235–236, 263, 295, 332

Devlin, B., 9

Dialogue,
- Internal, 42, 165–167, 238–239, 333

Digital, 39, 89, 166–167, 174, 176, 216, 228, 322, 385–386

Difference, 3, 14, 17–18, 22, 48, 52, 102, 115, 117–118, 123, 131–132, 143, 147, 155, 158–159, 172, 174, 178–180, 183, 193, 196–198, 209, 213, 224, 232–233, 238, 259, 261, 279, 281, 286, 292, 302, 312, 317, 321, 328, 342, 349, 351, 380, 383

Dilts, Robert, 4, 10, 61, 77–78, 107, 170, 225, 327, 363–364, 386, 388

Disgust, 27, 234, 304

Disney, Walt, 5, 12, 61–63, 65, 146, 149, 186, 360, 363, 365, 385

Disraeli, Benjamin, 7

Dissociation, 46, 48–51, 87, 99, 354, 363

Distortions, 245, 255, 282

Drivers, 178–179, 378–380

Dominance, 95

Doubt, 94, 136, 143, 145, 171, 271, 317

Dreamer, 61–66

Echoing, 25, 315

Ecology, 19, 80, 105, 115, 128, 131, 182, 302, 344, 385–386, 390

Effectiveness, 85, 118, 187, 247, 249, 343

Einstein, Albert, 5, 106, 245

Eisenhower, Dwight, 120

Ekman, Paul, 304

Ellis, Albert, 267

Emotional,
- Emotional Intelligence, 1–8, 10–14, 16–18, 21–22, 24–26, 28, 32, 34, 36–38, 40–42, 44, 46, 48, 50, 52, 54–56, 58, 60–62, 64, 66, 68, 70–71, 76–78, 80, 82, 84, 86, 88, 90, 92, 94, 96, 98, 100–102, 104, 106, 108, 110, 112, 114, 117–118, 120, 122, 124, 126, 128, 130, 132, 134, 136, 138, 140, 142–144, 146, 148, 150, 152, 154, 156–162, 164, 166, 168, 170, 172, 174, 176–178, 180, 182–184, 186, 188, 190, 192, 194, 196, 198, 200, 202, 204, 206, 208, 210, 212, 214, 216, 223–253, 255–258, 260, 262, 264, 266, 268, 270, 272, 274, 276, 278, 280, 282, 284, 286, 288, 290, 292, 294, 296, 300, 302, 304, 306, 308, 310, 312, 314, 316, 318, 320–322, 324, 326, 328, 330–334, 336, 338, 341–344, 346, 348, 350, 352–358, 360, 362, 364, 366, 368, 372–374, 378, 380–381, 383–384, 386, 388, 390, 392, 394, 396, 398
- books, 366–367
- definition, 8
- Emotional Wisdom, 341, 356, 368

- Emotional State, 1, 11–12, 31, 35, 40, 42–43, 76, 135, 158, 176–177, 245, 299, 323, 330, 338, 347, 356, 385, 389

Empathy, 11, 26, 223–224, 233, 244, 252, 355, 389

Emptiness, 94

Energy, 2, 13, 21–24, 26, 37, 40, 56, 66, 95, 149, 188, 205, 208, 243, 318, 333, 390

Entwistle, N.J., 342

Environment, 9, 11, 18, 32–34, 39, 58, 69, 72, 78, 82, 84, 95, 101–103, 106, 110, 114, 117, 119, 148, 191, 199, 207, 212, 229, 238, 262, 284, 288, 306, 310, 342, 354–355, 388

Epstein, Tod, 170, 172

EQ, 1, 5, 7, 12, 128, 177, 341, 343, 355–356, 359–360, 366, 368

Erickson, Milton, 46, 364, 373

Exaggerations, 273, 282

Excellence, 19, 22, 38, 70–71, 172, 341, 354, 371, 373, 383

Exhaustion, 94

Exit, 121–123, 159 (also see TOTE)

Expectations, 2, 146–149, 212, 225, 237

Experience, 2–3, 5, 12, 14, 18, 23–24, 33–42, 45–47, 49–55, 58–60, 63, 66, 68, 70, 72, 75, 77–83, 85, 87–91, 93, 95–101, 103, 105, 107, 109, 111, 113–115, 129, 131–132, 134, 136, 140–143, 147–148, 150, 157–161, 168–169, 171–174, 177, 179, 183–184, 187, 195, 202, 208, 211, 215, 221, 223, 226, 234–236, 239, 242, 248, 252, 255, 258, 260, 263, 270–273, 275, 281–284, 286–287, 297–299, 313, 318, 325–326, 329, 332–333, 338, 342–344, 350–351, 354, 356, 358–359, 371–372, 375, 379, 381, 385–386, 388, 390

External,
- Attention, 68
- Behavior, 18, 35, 37–41, 44, 231, 306, 330, 354
- Reference, 195–196, 218, 378, 380

Eye-accessing cues, 164–165, 307, 386

Filters,
- Neurological, 261
- Socio-cultural, 261
- Personal, 232, 262

First Position, 226–227, 231, 234, 236–237, 241–243, 245, 250–252, 331, 386–388, 390

Fear, 26–27, 36, 50, 57–58, 94–95, 98, 138, 143, 158, 191, 208, 215, 237, 304, 350
- Fear of Failure, 36, 94

Feedback, 4, 14, 19, 45, 86, 117, 121–123, 129, 133, 145, 195, 239, 251, 253, 260, 288, 337, 346, 349, 365, 369, 390

Feelings, 8, 11, 26, 33–34, 36–38, 48, 50–51, 55–57, 63, 69, 72, 90, 94, 105–106, 141, 160–162, 166, 176–177, 179, 204, 208–209, 238, 240, 242–243, 245, 247, 282, 301, 316, 320, 324, 329, 348, 375, 389–390

Flow, 24–25, 58, 243, 258, 318, 368

Flynn, J.R., 9
- Flynn Effect, 9

Format, 171–173, 301, 389

Formatting, 171, 183

Fourth Position, 225, 230, 241, 243–244, 250, 386, 388

Freedom Restrictions, 274, 276

Fun, 4, 13, 19, 31, 35, 46, 55, 143, 146, 150, 173, 181, 183, 191, 291, 314, 319, 337, 356–357

Gains,
- Secondary, 114, 154

Galanter, 121, 390

Galbraith, J.K., 17

Gateways, 41, 43

General, 4–5, 14, 61–62, 66, 68, 77, 123, 134, 141, 147, 152, 210–211, 213, 218, 224, 264, 274, 279, 349, 355, 372, 380, 385–386, 389

Generalizations, 82, 89, 209, 247, 211, 273, 282

General Semantics, 4, 14, 141, 147, 372, 386

Goals, 2, 4, 11, 31, 75, 117, 126, 132, 136, 143–144, 146, 148, 152, 156–157, 173, 186, 190–191, 206, 209, 218, 223, 255, 299, 312, 354, 359, 369

Goleman, Daniel, 5, 11, 34, 159, 353–356, 362, 366

Gordon, Thomas, 247, 249, 364

Grammar,
- Transformational Grammar, 285

Grief, 95

Grinder, John, 83, 225, 263, 270, 311, 323–324, 334, 346, 363–364, 371–373

Grof, Stanislav, 139–140

Guilt, 27, 95, 139, 348

Gustatory, 161–163, 166, 168, 174–175, 374–375, 390

Hall, Edward T., 203, 275, 334

Hall, L. Michael, 4, 32, 40, 43, 46, 98, 108, 136, 140–141, 147, 172, 186, 342, 375, 386

Hamer, M.D., Ryke Geerd, 27

Happiness, 39, 56, 58, 75, 102, 139, 146, 149–150, 304, 326

Hearst, Patricia, 295

Hierarchy, 100, 114–115, 191–192

Hitler, Adolf, 197

Hofstadter, 127

Hormones, 88

Identity,
- Core-Identity, 80–81, 89–90
- Role-Identity, 80–81

Independent, 4, 15, 188, 206, 209, 213

Induction, 89

Intelligence,
- Classic Intelligence, 1–2, 7–10
- Emotional Intelligence, (see Emotional Intelligence above)

Intention,
- Positive, 75, 93–94, 96–98, 114, 140–141, 149, 182, 185, 244, 252–253, 293, 331

Internal,
- Dialogue, 42, 165–167, 238–239, 333
- Reference, 195, 201, 212, 349, 354, 380
- Processes, 37–38, 40, 240, 345
- States, 36, 385

Interpreting, 311, 334
Interview, 38, 57, 189, 288, 312, 365, 377, 379
IQ, 1, 6–10

Jealousy, 36, 95, 210
Johnson, Mark, 170
Jung, Carl, 25, 184

Kennedy, John Fitzgerald, 5, 12
King, Martin Luther, 12, 120
Kinesthetic, 160–163, 165–170, 172, 175, 179, 215–216, 287, 308, 328–329, 374–375, 389–390
Knagg, 131
Kolb, David A., 342, 344
Korzybski, Alfred, 14–15, 147, 223, 372

Labels, 35, 272
Lakoff, Robert, 170
Language,
- Descriptive, 239, 307, 336, 375
- Evaluative, 183, 239, 307, 375
- Interpretative, 239, 375

Lazarus, Richard, 134
Leadership, 143, 205, 327, 331–332, 364–366, 383
Leading, 3, 65, 233, 319–320, 327, 386, 388
Lead System, 163–165, 216, 386
Learning, 10, 24, 31–32, 46, 60, 88, 107–109, 117, 129, 132, 146, 161, 177–178, 187, 192, 208, 223, 238, 258, 274, 276, 304, 326, 331, 336, 341–346, 355, 359, 367, 377, 385
Lebeau, Michel, 159, 355, 362
Linguistics, 3–4, 163, 278, 372, 388
Listening, 27, 82, 150, 169, 215, 226–227, 239, 249, 312, 314, 329, 359–360, 388
Logical Levels, 77–78, 82, 85–88, 91, 101, 103, 105, 107, 141, 309, 354, 386, 388

Loneliness, 36, 95, 215
Love, 5, 32–33, 76, 89, 92–93, 95, 97, 111, 141, 146, 149, 166, 169, 171, 178–179, 193, 196, 210, 214, 236, 238, 261–262, 272, 295, 320, 322, 329–330
Louis XV, 120

Machiavelli, Niccolo, 119
Management, 3, 23, 65, 96, 104–105, 115, 126, 131, 134–135, 177, 192, 195, 231, 238, 309, 354, 364–365, 379, 381, 383, 387
Matching, 41, 72, 234, 312–315, 317, 320, 322, 360, 387
Magritte, René, 16
Maslow, Abraham, 96, 104, 130, 341
Maturana, Umberto, 15
MBTI, 184 (also see Myers-Briggs)
McClintock, Martha, 313
McGregor, Douglas, 104
McWhirter, John, 277
Mead, Margaret, 304
Meaning, 2, 19, 26–28, 49, 77, 88–91, 96, 99–100, 139–142, 147, 158, 165, 171–172, 174, 183, 223, 246, 253, 255–256, 258, 262, 272, 280, 283, 285, 299–301, 307, 311, 326, 333–334, 355, 390
Meta-Model, 270–271, 281–282, 284–285, 289, 297–298, 351–352, 363, 387–388
Meta-Position, 223, 225–226, 231, 238–240, 242–243, 245, 320, 349, 387–388
Meta-Programs, 158, 184–187, 191, 194, 199, 201, 204–205, 207, 211–212, 218, 220–221, 310, 320–321, 343, 346–347, 349, 352, 354, 365, 369, 375, 377–381, 387–388
Meta-States, 4, 108, 140–141
Modality, 172, 362, 375 (also see VAKOG, Representational Channels)
Miller, George, 121, 301, 390
Mind Reading, 324
Mirroring, 314–315
- Crossover, 315
Mismatching, 312, 317, 319, 322, 338

Mission, 2, 8, 10, 76, 78, 81, 89,
    101–104, 110, 114, 359
Model of the World, 13, 18–19,
    147–148, 185, 281, 299, 302–303
Modeling, 19,22, 61, 342–343, 361,
    364–365, 373, 383, 387
Morris, Desmond, 50
Motivation, 23, 78, 145, 149, 187–188,
    190, 192, 194, 201, 207, 213, 220,
    345, 380
Murphy's Law, 131
Myers-Briggs, 184

Neuro-Linguistics (neurolinguistics),
    5–6, 10, 12–13, 17, 35, 39, 61, 80,
    126, 132, 141–142, 173, 179, 225,
    228, 302, 304, 306, 312, 320, 345,
    377, 386
    ● Neurolinguistics books, 361–365
Neuro-Linguistic Programming, 353,
    371–375
Neuro-Semantics, 4, 141
Neurological Levels, 75–77, 85,
    101–102, 105, 141, 184, 211, 386,
    388
Neurotransmitters, 88

Observer, 15, 136, 179, 194, 221, 225,
    244–245, 250, 287, 332, 336, 387
Olfactory, 161–163, 166, 168, 174–175,
    374–375, 390
Operate, 13–15, 19, 31, 76, 142–143,
    157, 160, 163–164, 168, 173, 176,
    186, 205, 261, 300, 302, 311, 357,
    380 (also see TOTE)
Ostrander, Sheil, 32
Opportunities, 52, 78–79, 84, 129, 132,
    141, 146, 191–192, 236, 326, 347,
    355, 359 (also see SWOT)
Options, 70, 97, 186, 192–194, 213, 216,
    228, 245, 259, 287, 320–321, 349,
    380
Orr, Leonard, 13
Other, 3–6, 8–10, 17–19, 21, 23–26, 29,
    31–32, 34–35, 37, 39, 41, 44, 47–49,
    51–52, 56, 60–61, 63, 65–66, 68, 72,
    76–77, 80–87, 89–91, 95–97, 99–101,
    106–108, 112–113, 118–119,
    124–126, 128, 131, 133, 136, 139,
    141–142, 145–150, 156, 159, 161,
    163–164, 166, 168–170, 172–175,
    180, 184–185, 187–191, 193,
    195–196, 198–202, 204–206,
    208–217, 224–225, 227–238, 240,
    242–246, 248–249, 251–253,
    255–258, 260–262, 264, 266, 268,
    270, 273, 275–277, 280–281, 283,
    285, 288, 290, 294–295, 299–303,
    305–306, 310–320, 322, 324, 326,
    329–332, 334, 336–337, 341, 343,
    345, 349, 355–356, 359–361, 363,
    366, 373–374, 379–380, 385–387,
    389

Pacing and Leading, 3, 319–320, 327,
    386, 388
Parkinson's Disease, 27
Patton, 126
People, 1, 4–6, 8–9, 11, 13–15, 17, 19,
    21–25, 27–29, 32–35, 37, 39, 41, 44,
    46, 48–50, 52, 55, 57, 64–66, 68–69,
    71, 76–83, 85, 89–90, 93–96, 99–103,
    105–108, 112, 115, 118, 120, 125,
    127, 129, 131, 133–139, 143–144,
    146, 148–149, 159–165, 168,
    172–173, 176–177, 179–180,
    182–190, 193–198, 200–213,
    215–216, 218, 221, 223–229, 231,
    234–241, 243, 250, 252, 255,
    257–258, 267, 270–271, 273–277,
    280–283, 285, 288, 299–300,
    303–308, 310–314, 317–320,
    322–323, 325, 329–332, 336,
    341–345, 347, 353–354, 356,
    359–362, 364–366, 371, 373–374,
    378–379, 384, 386–388
Perls, Fritz, 373
Permanent, 28, 115, 126, 136, 197 (also
    see Three Ps)
Pert, Candace, 25
Perceptual Positions, 3, 142, 223–225,
    227, 229, 233–234, 236–237,
    241–242, 244–245, 250, 252,
    346–347, 349, 355, 369, 386–390

Personal, 13–14, 22–23, 26, 35, 46, 66, 71, 76, 97, 99, 103, 110, 112–113, 115, 118–119, 125, 131, 136, 139, 142, 144, 160, 184, 186, 194, 212, 221, 232, 236, 240, 262, 267, 272, 275, 297, 307, 336, 344, 348, 350, 356, 359, 361, 363, 378 (also see Three Ps)

Perspective, 12, 15, 17, 21, 35, 62, 75, 100, 142–143, 148–149, 160, 168, 175, 179, 223, 225–228, 230, 232, 237, 241, 244, 257, 260, 279, 321, 331, 343, 349, 357, 377

Pervasive, 136 (also see Three Ps)

Pirsig, Robert M., 17, 368

Planning, 2, 109–110, 117–121, 123, 125–129, 131–133, 135, 137, 139, 141, 143, 145, 147, 149, 151, 153, 155, 186, 202, 384, 390

Plomin, Roger, 8

Polarity Responders, 317

Popper, Karl, 12

Positive, 5, 18, 23–24, 27, 37, 51, 56, 60, 64, 68, 75, 84, 92–100, 114, 122–124, 126, 140–141, 145, 148, 152, 182, 185, 190, 228–229, 238, 240, 244, 251–253, 280, 293, 301, 330–331, 337, 345, 362, 390
- Intention, 75, 93–94, 96–98, 114, 140–141, 149, 182, 185, 244, 252–253, 293, 331

Position,
- First Position, 226–227, 231, 234, 236–237, 241–243, 245, 250–252, 331, 386–388, 390
- Fourth Position, 225, 230, 241, 243–244, 250, 386, 388
- Meta-Position, 223, 225–226, 231, 238–240, 242–243, 245, 320, 349, 387–388
- Observer Position, 387
- Other Position, 231
- Second Position, 98, 225, 227, 238, 240–245, 249–253, 316, 322, 349, 360, 363, 388–390
- Self Position, (see Self)
- System Position, 225
- Third Position, 229, 241, 243–245, 250–251, 253, 349, 388, 390

Preconceptions, 82, 194

Prejudices, 82

Predicates, 163, 167, 169, 183, 214, 217, 328, 360, 388

Presuppositions, 1–2, 12–14, 18–19, 75, 85, 138, 145, 158, 215, 224, 258, 277–278, 280, 292–296, 309, 363, 375, 388

Pribram, Karl, 121, 390

Primary Systems, 163

Prigogine, Ilya, 286

Priorities, 28, 128–129, 210, 236, 284

Proactive, 158, 187–189, 212–213

Procedures, 19, 149, 186, 193–194, 213, 320–321, 378, 380

Projection, 234–235, 252

Proximity, 206, 209, 213

Psychosomatic, 25, 28–29, 35

Purpose, 6, 71, 75–77, 81, 96, 100, 227, 242, 246–247, 253, 257, 268, 280, 284, 300, 307, 314, 324, 338, 343, 348, 350, 355

QFD, 105 (also see Quality Function Development)

Quality, 65, 80, 105, 126–127, 159, 176, 178, 236, 259, 265, 300, 302–303, 389

Quality Function Development, 105

Rapport, 3, 19, 76, 90, 96, 163, 178, 185, 245, 257, 260, 270, 299–300, 306–307, 311–315, 317–322, 326, 331–332, 336–338, 355–356, 385–388, 390

Reactive, 188–189, 213

Realist, 62–66

Recruitment, 3, 144, 365, 381

Reference Experience, 45–46, 52, 96, 143, 252, 344, 351, 359

Reflex,
- Conditioned, 58

Reframing, 363, 389

Regret, 27

Relevance, 128, 133

Representation,
- Channels, 158, 161, 166–167, 169–170, 177, 214–215, 328–329, 349, 360, 369, 388–390
- Systems, 159, 172, 177, 215, 217, 347, 364

Resourceful States, 35, 44, 63
Restrictions, 266–267, 270, 274, 276, 288, 290
Robbins, Anthony, 327
Role, 9, 66, 76, 78, 80–81, 86, 90, 110, 133, 142, 164, 193, 196, 206, 231, 279, 283–284, 320, 337, 356, 363, 366, 387
Russell, Bertrand, 107

Sadness, 26, 36, 56, 93–95
Sales, 5, 57, 76, 79, 103, 125, 192–194, 203–204, 211, 231, 251, 320, 383
Salovey, Peter, 8, 11, 353–354
Satir, Virginia, 311, 323, 364, 373
Sawaf, Ayman, 355, 366
Schroeder, Lynn, 32
Secondary Gain, 93
Second Position, 98, 225, 227, 238, 240–245, 249–253, 316, 322, 349, 360, 363, 388–390
Segal, Jeanne, 71, 366
Self, 22, 26, 57, 139, 195, 200–201, 213, 225, 233, 306–6
● Self-Awareness, 11
● Self-Confidence, 11, 50–51, 53, 55, 129–130, 238
● Self-Esteem, 36, 57, 86–87, 95
● Self-Realization, 96
● Self-Respect, 238
Seneca, 117
Senge, Peter, 35, 258, 367
Senses, 18, 150, 157–159, 161–162, 166, 217, 261, 286, 299, 306, 374–375, 389–390
● Representation Systems, 158, 172, 177, 215, 217, 347, 364
● Submodalities, 115, 142, 171–182, 215, 217, 252, 334, 347, 349–350, 360, 363–364, 375, 385–386, 389
Sensory Specific, 61, 156, 176, 194, 197, 228, 261, 300, 322, 357, 383, 402–403
Service, 4, 133, 209, 260, 328, 369, 379
Shame, 27, 95, 139, 350
Similarity, 158, 196–199, 213, 317, 328, 378, 380

Skills, 1, 3–4, 7, 11, 38–39, 50, 64, 75, 78–79, 83–84, 86, 103, 106, 135, 142, 145–146, 152, 178, 181, 184, 186, 205, 224, 227, 229, 232–233, 252, 257, 270, 299–300, 306, 309, 318, 321, 325, 327, 330, 333–335, 338, 341, 343, 346, 354–355, 357, 362–364, 366–367, 372–373, 377, 383
SMART goal, 389
Space, 26, 48, 72, 78, 95, 106, 127, 136, 141, 160, 170, 176, 181, 191, 238, 245, 308, 361, 387
Specific, 12, 26, 31, 35–36, 44–45, 64, 75, 83, 88, 90, 92, 98, 106, 124–126, 131, 135, 142, 153, 163–164, 167, 172, 185, 188–189, 193–194, 202, 204, 207, 210–211, 213, 248, 261, 263–266, 269, 271, 275, 280, 288, 307, 320–321, 353, 360, 373, 377–378, 380, 385, 389–390
Spence, Gerry, 244–245
Spirituality, 78, 81, 84, 103, 106, 388
State, 1, 9, 11–12, 24–25, 31–46, 51–54, 57–61, 65, 68–71, 76, 84, 100, 117, 120, 123, 126, 130, 135, 142–143, 148, 150, 158, 162, 164, 176–178, 209, 234, 238–239, 243, 245, 279, 299, 306–308, 311, 316, 318, 322–323, 325, 330–332, 338, 344, 346–348, 350–351, 354–356, 359–360, 385, 389
Stern, William, 8
Stockholm Syndrome, 295
Strategies, 3, 9–10, 35, 37, 61, 109, 194, 367, 373
Strengths, 84 (also see SWOT)
Stress, 22, 26, 44, 81, 92, 94, 118, 127, 134–136, 144, 174, 204, 213, 220, 278, 322, 342, 354, 380, 387
Structure, 1, 3, 5, 10–11, 14, 17, 37, 76, 118, 120–121, 146, 157–161, 172–173, 175, 177, 183–185, 187, 191, 196, 199, 223–224, 226, 234, 266, 269, 282, 286–287, 299, 305–306, 322, 342–343, 347, 350, 353, 362, 366, 371–372, 375, 383, 388–390
Stuckness, 333

Submodalities, 115, 142, 171–182, 215, 217, 252, 334, 347, 349–350, 360, 363–364, 375, 385–386, 389

Success, 2, 5–7, 9, 13, 33, 38, 50, 56–58, 71, 75, 80, 83, 91–92, 104, 117, 119, 121, 123, 125–127, 129–131, 133, 135, 137, 139, 141, 143, 145, 147, 149, 151, 153, 155, 188, 207, 245, 341, 367

Symbionese Liberation Army, 295

Synchronization, 306–307, 310, 313–315, 317, 320–322, 324, 326, 329, 332, 334–338, 386–388, 390

Synergy, 24, 319, 385, 388, 390

System, 2, 18, 24–25, 31–32, 66, 84, 109, 118, 138, 163–165, 168–169, 172, 176, 178, 180, 183, 194, 215–216, 223, 225, 229–230, 233, 241, 243–244, 295, 302, 319, 347, 365, 374, 386–390

Systemic, 14, 38, 121, 142–143, 170, 223, 230, 364

Tactile, 160, 162, 166, 176, 390

Talleyrand, 122

Test, 1, 8, 114–115, 121–123, 153, 205, 259, 278, 293, 318, 323–324, 346 (also see TOTE)

Things, 3, 17, 21, 27, 35, 38, 60, 62, 65, 68, 77–79, 83, 93, 102, 112, 125, 128, 130, 132, 143, 150, 156, 162, 167, 169, 173, 188, 190, 193, 196–197, 202, 206, 208–209, 213, 218, 220, 227, 240, 243, 264, 267–268, 285, 310, 326, 341–343, 356, 358, 361, 366, 387, 390

Thinking, 7, 10, 15, 35–36, 39–40, 44, 70, 75, 82, 92, 99–101, 106, 133, 137, 158, 161–162, 179, 181, 183, 185, 190, 202, 204–205, 210, 213, 228, 230, 232, 236, 256–258, 264–267, 269, 282–283, 285, 304, 307, 320, 324, 329, 348, 362, 367, 385–387, 389

Third Position, 229, 241, 243–245, 250–251, 253, 349, 388, 390

Threats, 84 (also see SWOT)

Threshold, 121, 228, 261, 300, 302

Time, 4, 11, 13, 15–17, 24–25, 28, 31–32, 34–36, 42–43, 45–48, 50–51, 54, 56, 59–61, 63, 68–72, 76–78, 80, 86–87, 93, 96, 98, 100, 109, 117, 120–121, 126–129, 131–133, 136–137, 139–145, 148–151, 159–160, 162–163, 165, 168, 171, 173, 176–177, 182, 184–186, 196, 198, 201–203, 206, 208–209, 211, 217–218, 220–221, 223, 228, 230, 233–234, 237, 240, 243–245, 250, 253, 261–263, 268, 271, 275–276, 280–281, 290–291, 295, 297, 301–303, 312–313, 315–316, 318, 320, 323–326, 330, 332–334, 336, 348, 355–357, 360, 362–364, 368, 373, 378, 381, 385, 387, 389–390

• In Time—Through Time, 202–204

• Time Management, 131

Tolstoy, Leo, 325

Tonality, 43, 174, 176, 181, 308–309, 312, 325, 386

TOTE-Model Questionnaire, 64, 153–154

Towards, 3, 6, 76, 90, 96–97, 107, 117, 145–146, 149–150, 159, 161, 173, 186–187, 190–191, 213, 229, 231, 237–240, 242–243, 245, 259–260, 268, 295, 309, 349, 359, 380, 389–390

Transformational Grammar, 285

Transference, 322

Truman, Harry, 143

Twain, Mark, 131

Unconscious, 10, 14, 18, 25, 27–29, 41, 70, 132, 185, 299–302, 304, 316, 323, 334–335, 356–357, 363, 385, 390

VAKOG, 161–163, 172, 214–215, 286

Values, 2, 8, 37, 40–41, 63, 75–85, 88–89, 91, 95, 101–103, 106, 112–113, 115, 141, 184–185, 192, 212, 225–226, 228, 256, 276–277, 281, 302, 306–307, 309, 341, 345, 347, 368, 375, 384, 392

Varela, Francisco, 15

Visual, 51, 63, 67, 161–170, 172–173, 175, 181, 216–217, 287, 308, 328–329, 349, 374–375, 389–390

V-K dissociation, 51
Voltaire, 144

Watzlawick, Paul, 246
Weaknesses, 84 (also see SWOT)
Well-formed outcome, 389–390
Wilson, Robert Anton, 12, 295
Win-win, 229, 233, 242, 260
Wisdom, 3, 17, 42, 93, 158, 199, 256,
    341, 343, 345, 347, 349, 351, 356,
    358
Wittgenstein, Ludwig, 255
Whitehead, 75, 107

Zheng Ho, 130

TEST YOUR EMOTIONAL INTELLIGENCE

You can now test your current level of emotional intelligence at the jobEQ.com website for free.

The jobEQ website has been developed by Patrick Merlevede with the help of Denis Bridoux and many others.

It is designed for use by recruiters, mentors and coaches following on from the principles of the book. As our reader, you can now access the jobEQ tools for free at the site for your own personal use.

Being emotionally intelligent means having the right attitude and pre-requisite competencies or skills; jobEQ allows you to test your attitude and to carry out a stocktake of your inner resources at a given moment in time.

Based on objective measurements, the tests will enable you to become aware of your strengths in order to build on them and of your limitations so you can find ways of resolving them with the book's help.

- **ATTITUDE:** The iWAM test allows you to test your own Meta-Programs *(covered in Chapter 4)* in a work context.

- **COMPETENCE**: COMET technology has been used to develop the COMET/EQ questionnaire. Enabling you to test your competence in the 9 areas related to emotional intelligence, the feedback you receive upon completion of this questionnaire will indicate which section of the book to go to in order to work on enhancing this competence.

For more information, go to:
http://www.jobEQ.com/7steps

Use this password to log on to the JobEQ website:

1702159967

USA & Canada *orders to:*

Crown House Publishing
P.O. Box 2223, Williston, VT 05495-2223, USA
Tel: 877-925-1213, Fax: 802-864-7626
E-mail: info@chpus.com
www.CHPUS.com

Australasia *orders to:*

Footprint Books Pty Ltd,
4/92A Mona Vale Road, Mona Vale, NSW 2103, Australia
Tel: +61 (0)2 9997 3973, Fax: +61 (0)2 9997 3185
E-mail: sales@footprint.com.au
www.footprint.com.au

UK & Rest of World *orders to:*

The Anglo American Book Company Ltd.
Crown Buildings, Bancyfelin, Carmarthen,
Wales, SA33 5ND, UK
Tel: +44 (0)1267 211880/211886, Fax: +44 (0)1267 211882
E-mail: books@anglo-american.co.uk
www.anglo-american.co.uk